# TEXAS WOMEN IN WORLD WAR II

# TEXAS WOMEN IN WORLD WAR II

CINDY WEIGAND

REPUBLIC OF TEXAS PRESS
*Lanham • Boulder • New York • Toronto • Oxford*

Published by Republic of Texas Press
An imprint of The Rowman & Littlefield Publishing Group, Inc.
4501 Forbes Boulevard, Suite 200
Lanham, MD 20706

Distributed by NATIONAL BOOK NETWORK

**Library of Congress Cataloging-in-Publication Data**

Weigand, Cindy J.
    Texas women in World War II / Cindy J. Weigand.
        p.   cm.
    ISBN 1-55622-948-8 (alk. paper)
    1. World War, 1939–1945—Women—Texas—Biography.   2. World War, 1939–1945—Veterans—Texas—Biography.   3. Women veterans—Texas—Biography.   4. Texas—Biography.   I. Title: Texas women in World War Two.   II. Title: Texas women in World War 2.   III. Title.
    D736 .W45   2003
    940.54'082'09764—dc21                                      2002151735

∞ ™ The paper used in this publication meets the minimum requirements of American National Standard for Information Sciences—Permanence of Paper for Printed Library Materials, ANSI/NISO Z39.48-1992.

Manufactured in the United States of America.

*For Candace*
*and future generations*
*. . . that they will realize their debt to democracy*

# CONTENTS

# ACKNOWLEDGMENTS

Several people have thanked me for compiling these stories of women World War II veterans. I tell them that I could only write the book if I had a publisher to print such a book, so I thank Ginny Bivona, acquisitions editor at the Republic of Texas Press, for this opportunity. I also thank Heather Armstrong, Alden Perkins, and Jane McGarry, editors at Rowman and Littlefield, and Elizabeth Weiss, publicist for the title, for their hard work in getting the book published.

Special thanks to Terri Slone-Baker, Texas field representative for the Women in Military Service for America Women's Memorial, WIMSA. Not only did she share her story with me, her assistance in locating veterans and her support of the project were invaluable. I owe her much. Also, thank you to the Women's Overseas Service League of San Antonio for their support.

Others who assisted in finding veterans as well as sharing their stories are Mary Ellen Guay and Patsy Palmquist with the American Legion. Elizabeth Enright, former marine of the Vietnam era and member of the AL in Weatherford, aided in finding a "few good women" for my project. Doris Cobb set up several interviews for me at the Army Residence Community in San Antonio. This saved many miles and much time traveling. Thanks also to American Legion posts across the state of Texas in helping me get the word out.

Dorothy Davis Thompson was an invaluable source concerning the war in the Pacific, the geography of the area, and in providing documents of information as well as sharing her remarkable story.

Thanks to Willis, my wonderful husband, who has played so many roles in helping me write this book, including automobile mechanic, technology consultant, business conferee, proofreader, and ardent supporter of my efforts. Thanks to Candace, my ten-year-old daughter, for her mature understanding of why I wanted to write this book and why I needed to be away from home to conduct interviews. She thinks it's cool. I think she is.

Special thanks to Phyllis Moses and Mary Ellen Guay for lending their expertise by reading parts of the manuscript and offering suggestions. Other people who reviewed parts of the manuscripts are Janet Kilgore, Austin, and Joan Hall, Georgetown. Sara McBryde, also of Georgetown, took a couple of photographs for me.

Thanks to Lee Precht and Philip Montgomery at the Woodson Research Center, Fondren Library, Rice University in Houston. Also of assistance were William P. Hobby, Jr., Delores Chambers, Peggy Buchanan, Mattie E. "Patty" Treadwell, Alfred Shire of Houston, and Betty Bandel of Vermont.

Most of all, I thank God for the talents he has given me and the blessings he has bestowed upon me and our nation.

## World War II
## December 8, 1941–September 2, 1945

"Between these dates, there lies a saga of women determined to pay their debt to freedom, determined to mortgage their future and their lives if need be, for the future freedom of all the men and women of good will. In days and years to come, this saga will be of increasing strength to the nation in service."

—Oveta Culp Hobby,
first WAAC Director

# INTRODUCTION

Since America's beginnings, women have wanted to do their part for our country in times of armed conflict. Records exist as early as the Revolutionary War of women serving in some capacity. In 1778, Mary Hays McCauley, better known as Molly Pitcher, took her husband's place firing a cannon at the Battle of Monmouth when he was unable to continue. A year earlier, Margaret Corbin did the same thing at the Battle of Fort Washington. Wounded during the battle, Corbin was taken prisoner by the British and sent home.

During the Mexican-American War in 1847, Elizabeth Newcom, disguised as Bill Newcom, marched over six hundred miles with her unit, Company D, to their winter quarters. While there, she was discovered to be female but continued to serve in some capacity until mustered out a year later. Who knows how many more women served disguised as males?

The most consistent and accepted use of women in war was to care for the men wounded in battle or those taken ill. During the Civil War, women such as Clara Barton, Dorothea Dix, Dr. Mary Walker, and Mary Ann Bickerdyke, as well as contract nurses, provided medical care for soldiers. Later, nurses were also used in the Spanish American War and World War I. Nurse Rose Heavren served in both of those wars.

Women served in other capacities during World War I. By the time the United States entered that war, the Allies were experiencing a severe shortage of men. Americans mobilized rapidly, leaving shortages stateside. When it was discovered that there was no regulation that a yeoman *had* to be male, the navy and marine corps used women. Known as yeomen (F), about twelve thousand women served during WWI and were paid the same as men. Three hundred other women served in the marine corps.

The U.S. Army Signal Corps recruited and trained 230 bilingual telephone operators and sent them to France. These women routed messages between headquarters and the front lines. In addition, approximately fifty skilled stenographers worked in supply offices in France with the Army Quartermaster Corps.

When the United States entered World War II, it's no surprise that women wanted to serve their country in the military. In an address to the first WAAC officer candidate class, Director Oveta Culp Hobby told them that they "had a debt and a date. A debt to democracy and date with destiny." Wanting to repay a debt to America for the freedoms they enjoyed: this sums up why the women profiled in this book, and four hundred thousand others, joined the military during this time.

On the following pages, twenty-five women now living in Texas share their experiences in the military during World War II as they remember that time. When necessary, I've confirmed dates or provided additional information. Born on the heels of World War I and having grown up during the Great Depression, life hadn't been easy for these women, yet they wanted to serve their country to preserve the ideals they held dear. Each individual intended to pay her debt, even if it meant at the cost of her life.

On a trip to Washington, D.C., I was looking at the Vietnam Women's Memorial, near tears, wondering what that war must have been like for the women who served. The next moment, a young woman sat on the monument, crossed her legs, and smiled pertly while someone took her picture. I was taken aback at such flippancy and then gave the girl the benefit of the doubt; probably she didn't know what these women veterans had experienced. It was then that I decided to make it my mission to let people know the experiences of our female veterans, especially those in World War II.

It's for this reason, to let people know, that I believe these wonderful ladies agreed to share their experiences. They went about their jobs efficiently and quietly, always with a sense of humor. After the war, most returned to civilian life without fanfare to raise families or to resume careers.

We owe much to the men who fought on the front lines of combat in World War II. Yet, I feel victory would not have been possible or would have been delayed and with a greater loss of American lives, if each woman in uniform hadn't answered America's call to do her part and thus release a man for combat duty. In another address, Oveta Culp Hobby said, "It's not just the combat forces we need. . . . Total war means everybody is involved in the struggle." Certainly, this was the case in World War II. Women served in the army, navy, coast guard, and marine corps. The American Red Cross worked closely with all branches of the military.

One of the veterans, grateful that she had not been placed in harm's way, told me that our veterans deserve the support of a thankful nation. Indeed, America needs not only to express gratitude to all our veterans but to realize our debt to democracy and consider how we as individuals might pay that debt.

From the bottom of my heart, I thank these extraordinary ladies for trusting me with their stories. They are my heroes and they are role models for young people today. I have made a personal connection with many and been inspired by all. My life is richer for having known them.

# 1

## OVETA CULP HOBBY

*Director, Women's Army Auxiliary Corps,*
*Women's Army Corps, Washington, D.C.*

"WAACs will be neither Amazons rushing to battle nor
butterflies fluttering about."

—Oveta Culp Hobby

Oveta Culp Hobby strode into the office of Gen. George Marshall, army
chief of staff. He looked at her expectantly when she handed him the
list he had requested. On the roster were candidates to head the proposed
new women's army, a radical concept in 1941. General Marshall glanced at
the list, then turned the paper face down on his desk. He looked intently at
Mrs. Hobby. "I would rather you take the job," he said.

"Thank you for your confidence, general," she replied, "but I cannot.
I have a husband and two children at home in Houston."

When Mrs. Hobby told her husband, former Texas governor William
"Bill" Hobby, what the general had said, Gov. Hobby told her she *could* take
the job. "Any thoughtful person knows," he said, "that we are in this war,
and that every one of us is going to have to do whatever we are called upon
to do."[1] Convinced that this was how she should serve her country, Mrs.
Hobby accepted the position General Marshall offered. At thirty-seven years
of age, Oveta Culp Hobby became the director of the first official women's
military branch in the United States except for the army and navy nurse
corps. The group was known as the Women's Army Auxiliary Corps,
WAAC.

Speaking of this experience later, she said, "It never would have
occurred to me to command an army of women. I never did learn to salute
properly or master the 30-inch stride."[2] Some say leaders are born with the

4

*As WAC Director. Photograph courtesy of the Woodson Research Center, Fondren Library, Rice University*

ability to lead; others say a crisis propels one into a leadership position. Most, however, say leaders are a result of mentoring. Surely, all of these applied to Oveta Culp Hobby. By virtue of her life experiences and accomplishments, she seemed destined for this important role in history.

Oveta Culp was born in Killeen, Texas, on January 19, 1905, the second of seven children, to Isaac "Ike" and Emma Hoover Culp. Mrs. Hobby's sister, Lynn, who was nine years younger than Oveta, once asked their mother, "What was Oveta like when she was young?" to which their mother replied, "Oh, Oveta was never young."[3] Indeed, Oveta exhibited forethought and a sense of her abilities early on.

A temperance movement swept through Texas when she was about six and all children were invited to sign a pledge not to drink, but Oveta refused. Asked why afterward, she said that she wasn't sure what temperance meant and couldn't promise something she wasn't sure she could do.[4] From that time on, Oveta must have been confident of every task she undertook, for she accomplished much in a short period of time.

Oveta learned about caring for others from her mother. Emma Culp enlisted her daughter's assistance in collecting food, clothing, and money for the poor. Mrs. Culp then assembled baskets of goods and sent her daughter to deliver them to neighbors going through difficult times. In high school, Oveta formed a group of teenage musicians and actors who gave benefit performances to raise money to buy church organs.[5] Later, this sense of caring for the needs of others would be extended to the troops under her command.

Oveta attended public schools and often went to her father's law office after school dismissed. She listened to the men talk and she read her father's books. By age ten, she was reading the *Congressional Record;* by thirteen, she'd read the Bible three times. Also, Oveta started collecting books of her own. In 1919, when Mr. Culp was elected a state legislator, his daughter regularly accompanied him to Austin. There she astutely observed legislative sessions and learned how the government operated. She also studied elocution at this time.[6] Although she missed many days of school, she graduated easily from Temple High School.

Oveta attended Mary Hardin-Baylor College in Belton, Texas, for two years. While there, she taught elocution, put on plays, and worked as a cub reporter for Austin's newspaper, the *Statesman.* By age nineteen, her private library totaled 750 volumes, including *Cases of Common Law Reading, Revised Civil Statutes, Jefferson and Hamilton, The Private Papers of Colonel House,* and the poetry of Edna St. Vincent Millay.[7]

In 1925, the speaker of the Texas House of Representatives asked Oveta to be legislative parliamentarian. Only twenty years of age at the time, she held the position for six years. At this time, she also audited law classes at the University of Texas. She clerked in the legislature's judiciary committee and on the State Banking Commission, codifying the banking laws of the state of Texas.[8]

In 1931, Oveta moved to Houston to work for the city attorney. Earlier, the new president of the *Post-Dispatch,* former Texas governor William Pettus Hobby, had moved to Houston from Beaumont.[9] Oveta knew Mr. Hobby previously as a friend of her parents; Isaac Culp knew him through the legislature. As a leader in the suffrage movement, Emma Culp had campaigned for Hobby when he ran for governor.[10] However, Mr. Hobby and Oveta established their own relationship. On February 23, 1931, Oveta Culp married Mr. Hobby, a man more than twice her age.

Over the next ten years, Mrs. Hobby learned the communications business from her husband by working in various positions up to executive vice president. During this time Mrs. Hobby also wrote a book on parliamentary procedure, *Mr. Chairman*, that was adopted by the public schools in Texas as a handbook on the subject. A member of several civic organizations, Mrs. Hobby served as president of the Texas League of Women Voters.[11] Eventually, the Hobbys bought the *Post* and a radio station.

Mrs. Hobby was in Washington, D.C., in June 1941 on business with the Federal Communications Commission when Gen. David Searles, with the War Department, asked her to organize and head a section on women's activities. At the urging of her husband, she first accepted the position of director of the Women's Interest Section of the War Department of Public Relations.

As head of this department, she traveled to England to study ways the French and English utilized women in the war effort, and she prepared a plan for the United States. The Japanese bombing of Pearl Harbor prompted General Marshall and Secretary of War General Henry L. Stimson to ask her to draft a plan for a women's army and present the plan to Congress. General Marshall then asked her for recommendations of women to head the proposed new branch of the military.[12] On Mrs. Hobby's list were the names of successful career women including an advertising executive, a business manager, a bank president, and several educators.

Congresswoman Edith Nourse Rogers, author of the bill creating the WAAC, submitted only one name to head the corps—Mrs. Hobby's. The assistant chief of staff for personnel, G-1, submitted three names. Mrs. Hobby's was first on the list.[13]

Associates of Mrs. Hobby knew her for her energy, magnetism, sincerity, and idealism. They also observed that she could be diplomatic, yet stubborn, when pursuing major issues. Officers of G-1 wrote, "She has ability, vision, and is broad-minded enough to assemble a staff of capable assistants around her. [She is] already known to most of the key people in government and War Department circles."

In his recommendation, General Marshall, who had not known Mrs. Hobby before her work with the War Department, based his decision on her brilliant work with the Bureau of Public Relations. He wrote:

> In all these duties she displayed sound judgment and carried out her mission in a manner to be expected of a highly trained staff officer. She has won the complete confidence of the members of the War Department

Staff with whom she has come into contact, and she made a most favorable impression before the Committees of Congress.

. . . This Corps can be of great assistance to our military effort, and it can easily be a great embarrassment to the War Department. I therefore urge the appointment of Mrs. Hobby.[14]

Mrs. Hobby began her work with the rank of major before the bill was officially approved. Two days after approval by the House and Senate on May 14, 1942, Mrs. Hobby was sworn in at the rank of colonel. Her staff had procured Fort Des Moines, Iowa, a former mounted cavalry post, as a training center and announced that the first Officer Candidate School would begin July 20. Mrs. Hobby demanded that she be allowed to attend the school to experience firsthand military training, but General Marshall told her that it wasn't possible under the army's system of rank.[15]

Thirty thousand women applied for the first OCS. Of particular interest to Colonel Hobby were the responses to the essay question "Why I Desired Service." She personally read every response of the 4,500 to reach the final board during what she called "four days of careful, almost prayerful, work of making the final selections." The numbers were whittled down to 1,300. Finally, 360 women were selected for the first class.[16]

Mattie E. "Patty" Treadwell of Houston, Texas, was in that first class of officer candidates. She remembers the trauma of military life. "I'd had something of a shock," she says, "from the chaotic barracks, the heavy army food, the ill-fitting clothes, the untrained instructors, the heat—the gnats. There was a certain sinking feeling that I might have made a terrible mistake . . . that I could have given better support to the war effort in some other way."[17] Then, on the fourth day, Colonel Hobby spoke to the class. In her address, she said:

May fourteenth is a date already written into the history books of tomorrow. . . . You are the first women to serve, never forget it. . . .

You have just made the change from peacetime pursuits to wartime tasks—from the individualism of civilian life to the anonymity of mass military life. You have given up comfortable homes, highly paid positions, leisure. You have taken off silk and put on khaki. And all for essentially the same reason—you have a debt and a date. A debt to democracy, a date with destiny.[18]

"Her words wiped out my potential guilt-trip," Ms. Treadwell says. "I would be working with great people like Colonel Hobby; she was not afraid; there was no other place where I could serve as well as here. She was brave, so I was brave. I guess that's leadership just as in combat."

Ms. Treadwell graduated from the first Officer Candidate School as third officer, the equivalent of second lieutenant, in August 1942. She was still living on the post in September when a cold front swept through Iowa. Temperatures plummeted to seventeen degrees and it snowed. The WAACs had not yet received their winter clothing. "Colonel Hobby showed up from Washington to personally expedite the shipment of winter clothing to the training center," Treadwell says. "The word spread . . . that she was wearing an overcoat when she arrived and immediately discarded it since her troops had none." She then arranged to have men's overcoats delivered to the women in the event the shipment for the women was delayed.

Later, Ms. Treadwell served as assistant to Colonel Hobby in addition to other assignments. "Colonel Hobby was always very thoughtful of others," she says. "She was considerate, kind and gentle toward those who worked with her. She fought hard for her troops, combining diplomacy with a stubborn refusal to give up on major issues."[19]

Betty Bandel of South Burlington, Vermont, was another officer in that first class. "I looked upon Colonel Hobby then, as I do now," she says, "as a person of exceptional gifts and powers. Like many others, I gladly followed her lead."[20] Bandel was promoted to first officer and acting deputy director. Later, she was appointed air WAC officer with the rank of major. As the second-ranking officer to Colonel Hobby, Bandel was the first lieutenant colonel in the WAC.[21]

Bandel remembers another of Mrs. Hobby's characteristics. "In my judgment," she says, "humor and courage go hand in hand; they certainly did in Oveta's life and work." Lieutenant Bandel and Colonel Hobby would exchange jokes, then privately share them in meetings to alleviate boredom or pointless discussion.

On a tour of England to further observe the women's services, Colonel Hobby and Lieutenant Bandel stayed in a London hotel. Preparing a speech one night, Colonel Hobby noticed that Lieutenant Bandel had a loose button on her jacket. "Take off that jacket," she ordered. Lieutenant Bandel complied and Colonel Hobby proceeded to sew the button on. When she realized it was a subordinate's uniform, she pointed at Lieutanant Bandel and jokingly said, "You're fired."[22]

Certainly, Colonel Hobby and her staff needed every resource possible to make the new women's army work. Colonel Hobby's task was daunting.

Initially, she traveled continuously around the country to address various groups about the proposed Women's Army Auxiliary Corps. Even with a staff after the corps was officially established, she often worked all day and into the night, going home only for a few hours to shower and change, then return to work.[23]

Original WAAC plans were to increase the numbers from 12,000 in 1942 to 25,000 the next year. Officials anticipated enlistment to reach 63,000 by 1944. However, recruitment proved so successful that this number was reached by June 1943.[24] At one time, projections of need were as high as 1,500,000. Initial analysis indicated that women could perform fifty-four positions. By war's end, they were assigned to 239.[25]

Tasks to be accomplished were legion. Officers needed training to instruct enlistees, command squadrons, and recruit more women. Recruits required transportation to bases for training and barracks to live in while there. Mess halls and supply chains had to be established. The troops had to have uniforms and other clothing appropriate for the jobs they would perform and suitable for the weather. Jobs had to be assigned for graduates. Time was of the essence.

America was fighting a war on three fronts; casualties were mounting. According to estimates, the army ground forces were short 160,000 men by the summer of 1942.[26] Women weren't allowed in armed conflict, but their placement in other positions could free men for combat duty.

Despite efforts to make the WAAC full members of the army, Congress approved them only as an auxiliary. This presented problems getting things done. For instance, when Colonel Hobby requested army engineers to draw plans for women's barracks, the engineers refused because they didn't consider the WAAC army. The army also refused to pay women physicians that Colonel Hobby had recruited until General Stimson called for a special act of Congress.[27]

The fact that they were auxiliary presented problems with discipline and the chain of command. Also, if assigned overseas, they weren't eligible for benefits should they be killed in the line of duty. This fact would soon test Colonel Hobby's leadership regarding her troops.

In December 1942, Gen. Dwight D. Eisenhower urgently requested WAACs to serve as typists and telephone operators after the invasion of North Africa. Three hundred women assembled in Daytona Beach, Florida, for shipment overseas. A few days later, five WAACs already deployed for the European theater boarded a ship for North Africa. Near the coast, their ship was attacked and sunk and they were rescued by a British destroyer. As auxiliaries, had they been killed, captured, or injured, they would not have been eligible for any benefits afforded men in the same position.

Upon hearing of the attack and rescue, Colonel Hobby traveled to Daytona Beach to talk to the troops preparing to leave. After telling her soldiers about the incident, she reminded them they lacked military status and its protection; therefore, she would not order anyone to go against her will. Then in a speech spectators said was reminiscent of William B. Travis's at the Alamo, Colonel Hobby asked for volunteers. Of the 300 women in the room, 298 stepped forward instantly. Moved by the action of her troops, Colonel Hobby was unable to continue and retreated to a broom closet for a few moments of privacy. Later, she learned the other two did not step forward only because they had invalid parents.

Of the three hundred, about half were selected to go overseas.[28] According to WAAC Lois C. Jones, who shipped to England, Colonel Hobby had a letter written, and personally signed, ready for each girl to send home. The letter informed the parents of the assignment and gave their daughter's address.[29]

By the end of 1942, Colonel Hobby and her staff had accomplished much. They had recruited and trained 12,767 WAACs, exceeding their goal of 12,000. Two training centers were ready with a third soon to be on line. Twenty-seven Aircraft Warning Service Units and nine service command companies had shipped or were ready to ship. There were three secret units with the antiaircraft artillery; one on its way overseas. Four hundred WAACs were chosen to work on the top-secret Manhattan Project. Graduates, including two black units, had been assigned work as clerks, drivers, telephone operators, cooks, and bakers. Officers were assigned as administrators or training officers at the WAAC training centers and schools, as WAAC recruiters, or as officers leading WAAC units.[30]

Colonel Hobby telegraphed her staff that first Christmas to thank them and remind them how much more they needed to accomplish. The telegraph read, "May God bless you and give you strength for the task ahead."[31] They would indeed need emotional strength as well as physical stamina.

Late in 1942, there appeared an organized slanderous campaign meant to discredit the WAAC. There were unsubstantiated rumors of numerous pregnancies, immoral behavior, and drunkenness. So rampant were the rumors that army military intelligence, with the assistance of the FBI, investigated and found them to be groundless. Despite the publication of these findings, the rumors persisted for a year.[32] Recruitment declined and the troops became demoralized. Investigators discovered the rumors were started by military personnel and other Americans who had had no contact with the WAAC.

The campaign and its effect on her troops disturbed Colonel Hobby to the extent that she could not continue talking when she assembled her staff to tell them of the rumors. She reassured her troops and family members through public denials. President and Mrs. Roosevelt, General Stimson, Lt. Gen. Brehon B. Somervell of the army service forces, other WAAC officers, and members of Congress also publicly denied the rumors.[33] Eventually, they ran their course and stopped.

Under Colonel Hobby's leadership, the WAAC moved forward. By the spring of 1943, their strength had increased to 60,000. The problems of administration became so great, Congress approved a bill on July 1, 1943, giving the corps full military status and a new name, the Women's Army Corps, WAC. The WAAC went out of existence in September, but 41,777 enlisted women joined the new corps, and 4,600 WAAC officers accepted commissions in the WAC.[34] The number increased to 57,500 by January 1, 1944, with 260 units in the field in the United States and overseas including England, France, Germany, the Middle East, the China-Burma-India theater, Africa, and the southwest Pacific area.

Colonel Hobby visited her troops in the different theaters whenever possible. Reports reached her that conditions under which her troops lived in the Southwest Pacific Theater of Operations were particularly difficult. The women's health and well-being concerned Colonel Hobby, so she made plans to visit the area. However, repeated hospitalizations due to her own deteriorating health prevented her from doing so.[35] The stress of her position and long hours required in performing her duties took their toll on Colonel Hobby. She was hospitalized several times in 1944 at Walter Reed General Hospital for anemia, exhaustion, and a throat ailment. Army doctors even ordered her to Brooke General Hospital in San Antonio for six weeks followed by rest at an address known only to her family.

Colonel Hobby had thoughts of resigning at this time but was persuaded not to because the war was still going strong. Officials feared the effect her resignation would have on her troops. With a reduced staff, in equally poor health, she returned to limited activity. She told one reporter, "Until everybody can get out of the army—I won't. . . . No matter what you've heard, I'm staying in until the Pacific war is over."[36]

However, the distress of not being able to visit her troops in the Pacific and her husband's ill health that demanded her attention, in addition to her own health concerns, proved unbearable even for Colonel Hobby. She believed that her resignation would hasten a visit to the Pacific by the new director. Victory in Europe (V-E) Day was proclaimed on May 8, 1945. Soon afterward, Colonel Hobby submitted her resignation, which was announced on July 12, 1945.[37]

Under Colonel Hobby's leadership, the WAC numbered 100,000 by the end of the war and performed 239 different jobs. In some instances, one WAC performed the duties of two men.[38] In recognition of her leadership, the army awarded Colonel Hobby the Distinguished Service Medal, the army's highest noncombat award. The citation read:

> Without the guidance of precedents in United States military history to assist her, Colonel Hobby established sound initial policies, planned and supervised the selection of officers and the preparation of regulations. The soundness of basic plans and policies promulgated is evidenced by the outstanding success of the Women's Army Corps, composed of nearly 100,000 women and comprising an essential and integral part of the Army.[39]

Following her resignation, Mr. Hobby met his wife with a stretcher and took her by train to a New York hospital for complete rest. She then returned to Houston and resumed the positions of director of KPRC radio and KPRC-TV and executive vice president of the Houston *Post.* Mrs. Hobby served on the boards of various organizations and remained active in politics.

In 1953, newly elected President Dwight D. Eisenhower appointed her chairman of the Federal Security Agency, which was a noncabinet position, but invited her to sit in on meetings. In the spring of 1953, he nominated Mrs. Hobby for the position of secretary of the new Department of Health, Education, and Welfare, a position she held for two years. Afterward, she returned to the *Post* as president and editor. During her lifetime, she was awarded many honorary degrees and served on the boards of several corporations.[40]

A few years before she died, Oveta Culp Hobby withdrew from society but kept in close contact with family. She died peacefully in her home on August 16, 1995, at the age of ninety. Her memorial service was attended

*In later years. Photograph courtesy of the Woodson Research Center, Fondren Library, Rice University*

by former directors and officers of the Women's Army Corps, as well as former directors of the Women Accepted for Volunteer Emergency Service for America (WAVES), Women's Marine Corps Reserve, and by women in the U.S. Air Force. Former chiefs and the current chief of the Army Nurse Corps also attended, as well as other military dignitaries.

Our nation faced the crisis of war when Oveta Culp Hobby became director of the Women's Army Auxiliary Corps. Although she often said, "Everything that ever happened to me fell in my lap. And nothing in my life would have been possible without Governor,"[41] Mrs. Hobby seemed poised to step into a position of leadership in her own right. Mentored by Governor Hobby, military leaders, and her parents, and possessing the necessary traits, Oveta Culp Hobby became one of the greatest leaders in the history of the United States.

Perhaps friend and former comrade Betty Bandel best describes her leadership. "To me, Colonel Hobby was 'un chevalier sans peur et sans reprôche,' to quote a very old statement about another leader."[42] Upon hearing of Mrs. Hobby's death, Bandel said, "Oveta Culp Hobby was a great lady. We shall not see the like of her again."[43]

## REFERENCES

Crawford, Ann Fears, and Crystal Sasse Ragsdale. *Women in Texas*. Austin: State House Press, 1992.

Hobby, William P., Jr. "Oveta Culp Hobby." In *Handbook of Texas*. Austin: Texas State Historical Association, 1952–1976, 637–40.

Holme, Jeanne M. *In Defense of a Nation: Servicewomen in World War II*. Washington, D.C.: Military Women's Press, 1998.

Shea, Nancy. *The WAACs*. New York and London: Harper & Brothers Publishers, 1943.

Shire, Alfred, ed. *Oveta Culp Hobby*. Houston: Western Lithograph, c. 1997 (privately published with limited distribution).

Treadwell, Mattie E. *The Women's Army Corps: The U.S. Army in World War II*. Washington, D.C.: Office of the Chief Military History, 1954.

## ENDNOTES

1. William P. Hobby, Jr., "Oveta Culp Hobby," in *Handbook of Texas* (Austin: Texas State Historical Association, 1952–1976), 637.

2. Hobby, "Oveta Culp Hobby," 638.

3. Alfred Shire, ed., *Oveta Culp Hobby* (Houston: Western Lithograph, c. 1997), 1.

4. Hobby, "Oveta Culp Hobby," 637.

5. Hobby, "Oveta Culp Hobby," 637.

6. Hobby, "Oveta Culp Hobby," 637.

7. Hobby, "Oveta Culp Hobby," 637.

8. Hobby, "Oveta Culp Hobby," 638.

9. Hobby, "Oveta Culp Hobby," 638.

10. Hobby, "Oveta Culp Hobby," 638.

11. Hobby, "Oveta Culp Hobby," 638.

12. Hobby, "Oveta Culp Hobby," 638.

13. Mattie E. Treadwell, *The Women's Army Corps: The U.S. Army in World War II* (Washington, D.C.: Office of the Chief Military History, 1954), 28.

14. Treadwell, *The Women's Army Corps*, 29.

15. Shire, *Oveta Culp Hobby*, 46.

16. Treadwell, *The Women's Army Corps*, 58.

17. Shire, *Oveta Culp Hobby*, 46.

18. Treadwell, *The Women's Army Corps*, 66.

19. Shire, *Oveta Culp Hobby*, 46.

20. Betty Bandel, correspondence dated August 22, 2002.

21. Shire, *Oveta Culp Hobby*, 1.

22. Shire, *Oveta Culp Hobby*, 3.

23. Hobby, "Oveta Culp Hobby," 638.

24. Treadwell, *The Women's Army Corps*, 41.

25. Hobby, "Oveta Culp Hobby," 639.

26. Treadwell, *The Women's Army Corps,* 62.

27. Hobby, "Oveta Culp Hobby," 638–39.

28. Treadwell, *The Women's Army Corps,* 106.

29. Lois C. Jones, conversation with, July 5, 2002.

30. Holme, Jeanne M., *In Defense of a Nation: Servicewomen in World War II* (Washington, D.C.: Military Women's Press, 1998), 43–44.

31. Treadwell, *The Women's Army Corps,* 110.

32. Holme, *In Defense of a Nation,* 48.

33. Treadwell, *The Women's Army Corps,* 206.

34. Holme, *In Defense of a Nation,* 48–49.

35. Treadwell, *The Women's Army Corps,* 456.

36. Treadwell, *The Women's Army Corps,* 719–20.

37. Treadwell, *The Women's Army Corps,* 722.

38. Hobby, "Oveta Culp Hobby," 639.

39. Treadwell, *The Women's Army Corps,* 721

40. Hobby, "Oveta Culp Hobby," 639–40.

41. Hobby, "Oveta Culp Hobby," 638.

42. Bandel, correspondence dated August 22, 2002.

43. Shire, *Oveta Culp Hobby,* 3.

# 2

# MAC McWILLIAMS BARRY

*Women's Army Corps, Continental United States*

"During inspection, the officer said, 'Private, your slip is showing.' It was my panties."

Mac's heart pounded with excitement as the theater audience quieted. Slowly the curtain began to rise. Beside her on stage, standing stiffly at attention, was a representative from each branch of the women's military service—WAVES, SPARS, Women Marines, and WASP. Suddenly, a spotlight shone on them and flags waved. The entire audience stood and applauded. At the sound of their applause, Mac and the other young women stood even straighter and prouder.

"What a thrill that was," Mac says. "We were at the Roxy Theater to see the Roxyettes, a farm team of the Rockettes. Five of us in the different women's services stood at attention with flags and spotlights on us." Mac McWilliams was the representative for the Women's Army Auxiliary Corps, or WAAC.

Not caring much for her given name, Verna Leene, Mac has always insisted that her friends call her "Mac," while her family calls her "Sissy." Mac and I have not personally met but have spoken over the phone and communicated via e-mail. You can tell a lot about a person by tone of voice and carefully worded anecdotes. She possesses a quick wit and fun sense of humor. We developed an immediate rapport.

As one of the first women to enlist in the Women's Army Auxiliary Corps, it's apparent that Mac enjoyed her time in the service. Her story illustrates the naiveté, and enthusiasm, of the early enlistees, as well as the skepticism and initial disapproval of the military and public. In addition, despite the best-laid plans, the military still was not entirely ready for women.

WAC Mac McWilliams.
Photograph courtesy of Mac Barry

"There were ten children in my family—five boys and five girls," Mac says. "All five brothers were in the service during WW II. The oldest, Dalton, was in the air force; Elwood was in the army and was killed in the invasion at Salerno, Italy; Ronnie was in the navy and received the Silver Star; Garrett was in the marines and served in Okinawa; Billy was also a marine but did not serve overseas. My father was a Texas Ranger. Mom had a service flag in the window of our home with six service stars, one for each of us.

"I was the youngest girl, born between the two older brothers and three younger brothers," she continues, "and certainly a tomboy. Guess that's one reason I joined the service—if my brothers could do it, so could I!"

Mac was living in Ozona, Texas, when she joined the Women's Army Auxiliary Corps in October 1942. The branch had been in existence less than six months. She traveled alone by bus to Randolph Field in San Antonio to be sworn in. "I had a physical there and was put on a train for Fort Des Moines, Iowa," she says. "This was no troop train, dearie, but a first-class sleeper. I made friends right away with two other WAACs, one from Texas and one from Arkansas. We were in the same outfit and had lasting friendships until their deaths.

"As some of the earliest enlistees," Mac continues, "we had no uniforms. It was cold, wet, and muddy, so we were issued enlisted men's overcoats and wore our civvies underneath. Some of the women had come in high heels and rather dressy clothes. Thank goodness I decided my cowboy boots and jodhpurs had to go with me."

Having coats so large did little to protect the women against the cold. "The overcoats were heavy and clumsy," Mac explains, "and didn't do much to keep the cold wind out since the top button came almost to my waist. We were an eager bunch, though, and practiced our 'about face' in the day room until we had it down pat, never taking into consideration we would be wearing the overcoats. When the officer shouted the command, most of us got caught in the folds of the coats and fell flat on our face.

"At first the guys were jealous," she continues, "but we woke up early for reveille and went through rigorous training. We did pushups and had to learn to wear a gas mask and stay in the gas chamber a certain length of time. Some panicked but had to go through it until they made it. There was also a class in reading maps. We got strenuous exercise going through an obstacle course, not to mention the great exercise we got cleaning the latrines."

Mac remembers the excitement, and amusement, of finally getting their uniforms and official army clothing. "We got a hat (called a Hobby hat) that looked like a conductor's cap, a jacket and skirt, two shirts, a tie, shoes, and hose like my grandmother wore. Then we were handed underwear—a bra that Mae West could have worn, a slip and panties made from olive drab iron, and a girdle.

"I personally had never owned a girdle," Mac laughs, "and didn't know if you put it on over the head or stepped through it. I tried the head-first approach and almost suffocated before a bedmate pulled it off. I remember the first time I got dressed and fell out for inspection. Being rather short, with the skirt, shirt, girdle, and the long-legged panties, it was hard to tell where one began and the other ended, but I stood there straight and stiff. The inspecting officer stopped at me and stared, then said, 'Soldier, your slip is showing.' It was my panties! I knew then that I was in it for the long haul."

*Publicity photograph; Mac is on the left. Photograph courtesy of Mac Barry*

The only time she was ever put on KP, Kitchen Police, was the first week in basic training. "I was awakened at 4:30 a.m. and told to report to the mess hall," she says. "I went out into the cold and dark and started looking for the hall. Since we always marched everywhere we went, I had no idea where I was going. After stumbling around for an hour, I gave up and went back to the barracks and back to bed. I guess there were enough on KP that I wasn't missed, because nobody ever said a word to me."

Being from a big family, Christmas was always special in the McWilliams household. Mac remembers how difficult being away from home was that first Christmas. "All we heard on the radio was the song 'I'll Be Home for Christmas,'" she says. "I said to myself that if I heard that song one more time, I was going home. Sure enough, I heard the song again and packed my bag and went to tell my CO that I was going home. She tried to tell me I couldn't go because no one got furloughs, but I stood my ground. I told her that I'd called my dad, and he'd wired me money for train fare. Finally, bless her heart, she said that if I was set on going, she'd write me out a five-day pass because she didn't want me to be AWOL. She wrote me a pass and I went home for Christmas."

After basic training, Mac was assigned to the WAAC Recruiting Office in Washington, D.C., with the rank of first sergeant. She remembers meeting Colonel Hobby. "She came to the recruiting office and inspected us," Mac says. "She was very friendly and easy to talk to. Because we were both from Texas, we had an especially friendly conversation. She was such a handsome woman, too."

Her adventures proceeded similarly to the way they started. "We were told that 'the eyes of the world' would be on us," Mac says, "so we should set an example by our military demeanor. There were no barracks, so we were billeted in the YWCA. Walking to the office every morning, we passed the Willard Hotel and a big 'uniformed officer' who stood outside the door of the hotel. We snapped to attention and saluted every morning for a week. Finally, the 'officer' told us he was the doorman and didn't expect a salute.

"Then there was the time a week or so later," she continues, "when three of us stood in line for tickets to the theater. Along came this elderly gentleman with braid covering half his body. Although we didn't recognize him as American, we knew there were umpteen foreign military in D.C. Assuming he was one of them, we snapped to attention and saluted. Then we heard laughter and an American officer say, 'Since when does a member of the armed forces salute a Western Union man?' That's how I met my future husband, John Barry. This was mid-January 1943."

On January 31, Mac and Johnny attended President Roosevelt's Birthday Ball on their first date. The event raised money for infantile paralysis. Johnny was stationed at Valley Forge General Hospital in Phoenixville,

Pennsylvania, so they were able to get together only on weekends in the ensuing months. "Our dates were almost always chaotic," she says, "because at least some of the time during the weekend, I would have to appear for some function or another." Johnny was with Mac the evening she appeared with the other service women at the Roxyette show, and he attended all three performances. "He said he'd never had such a hard time keeping track of his date!" Mac says.

While most of Mac's experiences in the army were pleasurable, others were not. She recalls the time the WAAC were slandered in the media. "We were harassed by some of the men who resented us," she says, "and by an uprising of black dissidents who dressed up in women's clothes pretending they were one of us. We were forbidden to go out on the streets alone, and never at night, for days until it was stopped."

Being a new service branch, the army actively recruited women to join. "When selling anything, publicity is it," Mac says. "We were selling the WACs. The ads ran in the Sunday paper. On Monday, the women came to enlist."

Mac remembers frequent visits to the Pentagon. After the girls signed up, she accompanied them there to take physicals. She worked as a clerk in the lab when the regular clerk couldn't and accompanied her captain to the Pentagon for meetings. Two interviews for Officer Candidate School were at the Pentagon. "It had everything. I never got over that fact," she says. "One could be born, grow up, work, have all the amenities one needed, and die in the Pentagon. When it was attacked [in 2001], I really felt it."

While in Washington, Mac was selected to do what a lot of girls probably dreamed of doing. "Somebody thought I was cute," she says, "so they chose me to pose for recruiting posters, ads, and things like that." If you've seen World War II recruiting posters, you may have been looking at Mac. Her image appeared in newspapers and magazines including *The American Federalist*. Mac also pitched the Women's Army Corps over the radio. In September 1943, the Women's Army Auxiliary Corps had converted to the Women's Army Corps.

As part of this job, Mac was required to make appearances, such as the time she attended the Roxyette performance. She also attended dances and balls and escorted celebrities and dignitaries to certain functions. "This made my dates with Johnny rather chaotic," she says. Nevertheless, Johnny and Mac were married on October 6, 1943, at Fort Meyer Chapel. Attendees included officials from the Pentagon and other military officials as well as

*All-services photograph. Photograph courtesy of Mac Barry*

Mac's officers and other enlistees, and Johnny's officer buddies. They rented a small one-room apartment in nearby Cheverly, Maryland. "We did this so we could really play house and have friends over," she says.

Often, Mac escorted new recruits to Union Station to catch the train for basic training at Fort Des Moines, Iowa; Fort Oglethorpe, Georgia; or Daytona Beach, Florida. "All the gatemen knew me," she says. "When I went with Johnny to catch his train back to Pennsylvania after a weekend together, one of them would yell to the other, 'Here comes the sergeant's husband, let him in!' He was grateful, but being a first lieutenant, he was a little embarrassed."

Mac and Johnny had been married only a few months when Johnny received orders to ship overseas. He left in May 1944. "When Johnny got his orders to ship out, we gave up our apartment," Mac says, "and came back to my barracks to say goodbye. We'd promised each other that we would kiss, and hug, then turn and walk away. Neither of us could keep our promise. Through our tears, we hugged one last time and walked away. I

*Mac and Johnny Barry in 1943.*
*Photograph courtesy of Mac Barry*

didn't know if I would see him again. I cried myself to sleep that night. During all the years we were married, almost fifty-nine, that last hug meant so much to us that every morning of our lives together we gave each other a hug."

Mac had applied and been accepted for Officer Candidate School but turned down the offer so she could be with Johnny longer. "There was a quota for each OCS class," Mac says, "and they were filled far in advance. When I turned down the chance to go, I had to wait a certain length of time before I could reapply, so I remained in Washington until I was accepted. I didn't mind because our office personnel were our best friends and like family. We worked together, played together, and laughed and cried together."

In April 1945, Mac left for Fort Des Moines, Iowa, for Officer Candidate School and graduated in July 1945. "They called us ninety-day wonders," Mac says. "The day I graduated, Johnny landed in New York and had a thirty-day leave before he was to go to Japan. Regulations stated that spouses received leave at the same time, so we met in New York and hitchhiked on planes to get back to Texas to see my family.

"All went well until we were returning to my assignment at Fort Benning, Georgia," she continues, "and got stuck in Memphis. We were getting desperate until a kind air force pilot let us on his plane with the stipulation that we had to use names of GIs who couldn't make the trip. If we went down, their names would be on the manifest, not ours. I couldn't remember my name, but thank goodness I didn't have to. While we were on this flight, the first atom bomb was dropped.

"We couldn't believe it," she says. "This changed everything for Johnny. He had enough points to get discharged, but I didn't, so he went to Fort Benning with me until I had enough points." While at Fort Benning, Mac was personnel officer for the paratroop school. She kept records on students coming in for training, their progress, and eventual graduation and assignments. By November 1945, Mac earned enough points to be discharged from the army and was mustered out at Fort Bragg, North Carolina, as master sergeant.

As a hospital administrator in the United States Public Health Service, Hospital Division, Johnny's job required that they live in New York City; Savannah, Georgia; Boston, Massachusetts; and Norfolk, Virginia. When he retired at the rank of colonel, they returned to San Angelo, Texas, to be near Mac's family. In San Angelo, Mac worked at various secretary jobs and Johnny taught in the nursing department at San Angelo State University.

In retirement, Mac continues to stay busy. An avid bridge player, she plays twice a month in a club she calls a "Bloody Mary, lunch, and wine" club; and plays once a month with her partner, Frankie, in the Day Time Marathon Bridge group. On Tuesdays and Wednesdays, she takes Tai Chi before she goes line dancing. She also attends the symphony and local theater performances, sings in the church choir, and belongs to the Holy Angels women's organization.

In more leisurely times, Mac enjoys listening to music of all kinds and loves to read. Recently, she wrote a "meller drammer" for her church choir. Besides communicating with me via e-mail, she also keeps in close touch with family and friends the same way. Mac has one daughter, Shelly Suksta; a granddaughter, Joelle Barry Dowe; and two grandsons, Jamie Barry Linderman and John Barry Suksta. Her son, Michael, was tragically killed three years ago.

Active in community service, Mac serves her community in the same

*Mac and Johnny Barry in 2002.*
*Photograph courtesy of Mac Barry*

spirit she served her country. She has delivered meals for the elderly and has taught adult reading courses. Through her church, she is a member of Helping Hands, a group that buys and prepares a dinner for the family of deceased members on the day of the funeral. Her line dance group gives performances at local nursing homes. She also gives one hour on the first Friday of the month to the altar of the Sacred Heart in her church.

# 3

# THERESE SLONE-BAKER

*Women's Army Corps, Continental United States*

"There I was . . . the only WAC who knew the president had
died."

There and the other enlistees stepped off the truck at Fort Des Moines,
Iowa, talking excitedly. She was finally getting the opportunity to serve
her country in the military. A tiny, feisty young woman in a uniform greeted
the group. Therese counted two stripes on her shoulder. *Must be a general.*
At that moment, the officer called out in a voice befitting such a rank: "Fall
in!"

*What'll I do?* Therese and the others wandered about, bumping into
one enlistee after another, trying to figure out what the order meant. *I can't
believe this is happening. This is like a comedy routine.* The "general" watched
the women swarm about before yelling an order more easily understood:
"Just line up in front of me!"

"After that first day, there was no misunderstanding what 'fall in'
meant," Therese says. "That was my introduction into military life."

A native of New York City, Therese is a first-generation American
born of a Polish father and Ukrainian mother. Her story is one of knowing
what she wanted in life and confidence in her abilities to achieve her goals.
Therese still exudes confidence and self-assuredness.

Therese's mother was a widow by the time she graduated from high
school, so Therese immediately took a job in a department store to help
support her. Wanting more security for herself, she sought a position with
the civil service. Accepted, she was appointed the secretary to the actuarial
consultant of the Social Security Administration. "After Pearl Harbor Day
and as the war progressed," she says, "I felt that I needed to do something

27

*WAC Therese Slone.*
*Photograph courtesy of Therese Slone-Baker*

more than work for Social Security. I went through the personnel files and found out the U.S. Maritime Commission was looking for women with a secretarial background. I applied, was accepted, and transferred to Long Beach, California."

Long Beach was the location of Consolidated Steel, a company that assembled Liberty ships. Nicknamed "ugly ducklings" by President Roosevelt, Liberty ships were designed for emergency construction. Standardized for mass production, 250,000 parts were prefabricated throughout the United States in 250-ton sections. These sections could be welded together into a completed ship in 70 days. In one instance, a ship was built in four and a half days. Costing about two million dollars each, Liberty ships were 441 feet long and 56 feet wide. The holds of the vessel could carry over 9,000 tons of cargo plus airplanes, tanks, and locomotives fastened to the deck. In all, it could carry 2,840 jeeps, 440 tanks, or 230 million rounds of rifle ammunition.

"I had an excellent position as secretary for all the inspectors of the Maritime Commission," she laughs. "I was the only woman in an office of ninety-five men, so that's a pretty good deal." Despite her position, Therese was still restless. "I have always been of the type that felt she could do better. I still felt I wasn't doing enough." Even though she worked in an industry that supported the war effort, Therese wanted to join the military.

While she kept telling her boss she was going to resign, she had good reasons for not doing so. Therese explains, "My boss wouldn't release me without ramifications because I was working in a defense industry. It would have shown up on my records that I'd resigned from such a position." By resigning, Therese risked not being hired back in civil service after the war and losing the security she had worked so hard to achieve.

Early in 1945, with the war winding down, Therese's boss finally told her that he would sign her off in good standing. "My mother and I lived right around the corner from the army recruiting office," she says, "so I joined the army. I enlisted for the duration plus which meant the duration plus six months. I knew that if I came back, I could go back to the civil service." She could serve her country and attain the security she so desired.

Therese boarded a train with about thirty other girls from southern California. "The trip took about three days," she says. "We didn't have sleeping accommodations, therefore we had to sit up all night and all day. I was glad when the seat ahead of me was empty so I could turn it around to put my feet on it. It was a rough trip, but we were all sharing the misery. We all became friends within an hour and survived very well, I think."

At Ottumwa, Iowa, a small town outside of Des Moines, the train stopped to refuel. "The women of that town, having heard that young women were going to Fort Des Moines for basic training, came to the train with box lunches for us. I thought that was one of the nicest things to do. I'll always remember that."

At the railway station in Des Moines, the girls stepped off the train onto a truck bound for Fort Des Moines where the little "general" awaited. "The first two weeks of our training we lived in what was called 'Stable Row.' Fort Des Moines had been a cavalry post before it was converted to a WAC training center. I must tell you that even in 1945 when I arrived, the place still smelled of horses. It was something. I finally got used to the smell."

The first two weeks in "Stable Row" was an indoctrination period. "They wanted us to really feel like we were in the army. They issued us uniforms, but after three years or so of servicewomen, they still didn't have enough overcoats and we were issued men's. Mine came to my ankles and the sleeves were so long that you couldn't see my hands," she laughs. "If I tried to salute, all I had was a flopping cuff in front of my face."

Basic training was eight weeks long. "The army is big on two things—marching and inspection," she says. "Marching was fine. I enjoyed that because I loved military band music." Inspections were another matter. For one, Therese pulled the duty of washing the insides of the windows on the second story of the barracks. "I didn't know how. My mother would not allow her little girl to dirty her hands," she laughs. "I was handed a bucket and a cloth. Then I was handed a box of Kotex. I was told to use them to dry the windows."

In April of 1945, Therese was selected to appear for inspection for the honor of being awarded guard duty. "You had to be dressed just right. Your shoes had to be sharp and shiny. The inspecting officer would then select the best-prepared enlistee. He selected me," Therese says. "I was honored with being the commander's orderly for a day instead of guard duty." Excitedly, Therese ran back to the barracks. Girls were hanging out the windows yelling, "What happened? What happened?" to which Therese replied, "I'm going to be an orderly. I'm going to be an orderly."

The day she reported for duty proved to be a somber occasion. "I was given a little crop, you know, because that's what the colonel did," she says. "That was my authority." The day Therese had orderly duty coincided with the day President Roosevelt died. "I was in the reviewing stand sitting next to the commander ready to watch the WAC parade in review. A lieutenant ran up to the commander and said, 'the president just died,' then asked the commander if the parade should be canceled. The commander would not think of it. Instead, he said, 'let the parade begin,'" Therese says. "There I was, the only WAC who knew at the time that the president had died. There were all my friends marching in front of me. That was a memorable time."

Following basic training, Therese was assigned to Camp Davis, North Carolina. A separation center for men returning from the war, the camp was also a rehabilitation center for the men with stress disorders. "I was a stenographer to the officer in charge of Special Services. That was kind of nice because we set up entertainment for the troops and things of that nature." However, her duties quickly changed. "The general called my boss, who was a major, and the next thing I knew, I was transferred to be the general's secretary. A buck private as the general's secretary. Most of my assignments there on in were good assignments because first, I had been an experienced secretary when I went in; second, I wasn't a kid. I had the prestige of the base. I liked my position."

By then, it was June. Germany had surrendered, but the war was still going on in the Pacific, so Therese requested an overseas assignment. "I was sent back to Fort Des Moines, the ORD, Overseas Replacement Depot, to be trained to go overseas. You had to wear combat stuff and a helmet and climb Jacob's ladder up the side of a ship and down again. I went up the side of the ship and was afraid to go down." Just as Therese completed training, V-J Day, Victory in Japan Day, was announced.

From Fort Des Moines, Therese went to Indiantown Gap, Pennsylvania, also a separation center. Located near a wealthy residential area, the presence of WACs presented some problems on laundry day when they hung their lingerie out to dry. "The women of the town called the commander because they did not like to see *khaki* underwear flapping in the breeze. The CO asked us not to hang our khaki underwear outdoors," laughs Therese, "so we hung it indoors." One day, another WAC accidentally found a solution. "She spilled bleach on her underwear and it came out orange, whereupon, we all bleached our underwear and hung our *orange* underwear on the line because they weren't khaki anymore."

When Indiantown Gap was closed, Therese's boss didn't want her to leave with the others so he arranged for reassignment to Baltimore, Maryland, at the Second Army Command Headquarters recruiting center. "To me, that was the prime assignment. I had my first experience of being a boss, on my own. I was given a department for which I was responsible."

Even though the war was over, the army had lost so many men that there was a great recruiting effort to enlist replacements. Therese was responsible for making plans for recruitment and ensuring that they were carried out. While there, she devised a successful plan in conjunction with the American Legion. "I called it VALAR," Therese says, "for Voluntary American Legion Army Recruiting. For that, I was given the Army Commendation Medal. The recruiting commander was Gen. Manton Eddy, a nice old gentleman. He called me into his office along with two men to present my medal to me, and then didn't know how to pin it on. Finally, I said, 'Sir, if you like, I'll pin it on myself.'" The general obliged.

With her mother getting older and living alone, Therese decided to resign from the army even though she loved the military. Superiors encouraged her to stay on because "she could do big things." However, she was discharged from the army as a tech/sgt. "In less than two years, I made it from buck private to tech sergeant. Pretty good," she says.

Returning to California, Therese couldn't find a job that suited her. "I really loved the army and I didn't want to go back to some nondescript job. The only work that interested me was at an Air Force Reserve Training Center." At that point, she decided to join one of the Air Force Reserve Units at the center. She applied and qualified for a direct commission as a second lieutenant. Shortly thereafter, she was called to active duty with the air force.

Assignments with the air force included tours in Germany, Bermuda, Kansas, Ohio, and Texas. She remembers fondly two sobriquets she earned in her career. The first was at Lackland Air Force Base in San Antonio where she was assigned as WAF (Women of the Air Force, a post–World War II organization) squadron commander. "I always wanted my girls to look neat, to be ladies. Whenever I made an inspection, I wouldn't put their name on a 'gig' list if their rooms were not in order. Instead, I left them a note that said: *Your room is not tidy, T. S.* I found out later they called me 'Tidy Terri' behind my back."

As a recruiter at Wright-Patterson Air Force Base in Ohio, Therese was known for her tough recruiting standards. "I had the responsibility of

*Therese Slone-Baker in May 2002.*
*Photograph by Cindy Weigand*

selecting the women coming into the air force. I had to review all applications," she says. "All who applied were qualified, but I had to choose the *best* qualified. I thought my standards were pretty good." Often the field recruiters couldn't meet their quotas. Laughing, Therese says, "I found out the field recruiters called me 'Old Iron Girdle.'"

Therese retired in 1972 with the rank of lieutenant colonel, eventually settling in San Antonio. "I was able to accomplish what I wanted. I became independent. I had my own source of income. I didn't marry until after I retired because my goal was set on furnishing myself security and not relying on anyone else. I'm stubborn that way."

Therese Slone-Baker is active in the Women's Overseas Service League. In addition, she is a field director for the Women in Military Service for America (WIMSA) Memorial Foundation, Inc., located in Washington, D.C. Due to Therese's efforts and guidance, and those of field representatives throughout the state, Texas contributed $79,800 to the memorial, a dollar for every woman veteran. Texas is listed on the Honor Roll of States in the Women's Memorial as the second largest contributor.

# 4

## PATSY BRUNER PALMQUIST

*Women's Army Corps, Camp Fannin, Tyler, Texas;*
*Headquarters, 8th Command, Dallas, Texas; War*
*Department Personnel Center, San Antonio, Texas*

"There's just something about women. We can do anything, I
guess."

Patsy Bruner and three friends walked to the recreation building at Camp
Fannin in Tyler, Texas. Having just finished basic training, they chatted
excitedly about their first assignment. They giggled over the fact that they
were the only four women on base. Rumor had it that 17,000 young men
there were finishing boot camp. At the door, they paused to straighten their
uniforms and then stepped inside the building. Men looked up from the
games they were playing—cards dropped to the table, Ping-Pong balls
bounced to the floor, conversation ceased, and silence fell on the room. The
next instant, the girls were surrounded by GIs.

"What's your name?" asked one with brown hair and brown eyes.

"Where are you from?" the handsome blond wanted to know.

"How do you like being in the service?" someone from the back called
out.

From somewhere behind them, another asked, "What's it like to be a
woman in the army?"

The girls looked warily around them as the men continued to gather.
"Okay guys, move back." A man with *MP* on his armband made his way
through the crowd. "Give the ladies some room," he said. Three military
police followed him, and they forced the GIs back to a more comfortable
distance.

"They'd never seen a woman in uniform," Patsy laughs. "Actually,

*WAC Patsy Bruner.*
*Photograph courtesy of Patsy Palmquist*

they just wanted to talk to us. It was really strange because they *all* wanted to talk to us. They nearly smothered us to death. By the way, I met my future husband that night. Later, he and others would come to our day room, and we'd play the piano and sing. We had a lot of fun doing that."

Patsy Palmquist talks pleasantly and laughs easily. It's not the type of laugh that makes you chuckle but rather a laugh of warmth so that you smile and feel completely at ease in her presence. We met at the Texas State Convention of the American Legion. On Saturday, Patsy and friends were going to celebrate a special occasion. Ten years earlier, she was elected the department (state) commander of the American Legion, the first, and only, woman to hold the position.

Born in Houston, Patsy was the adopted daughter of Beecher Henry and Frances Hunter Bruner. "No one could have had greater parents," she says. "I owe them such a wonderful life." While her mother was patriotic, she preferred traditional roles for women. Her father, on the other hand, had a different mindset and encouraged Patsy to consider all options available.

When the United States entered the war, Patsy wanted to join the military, but she was too young. "My daddy had taught me to love this country so much," she says. "I wanted to go in so badly, and I did a lot of community things for the service people at the YW and YMCA until my birthday. When I turned twenty on May 29, 1944, there was no stopping me joining the service. My Dad thought it was a nice thing to do and went along with me. He was never able to get into the service because he was flat-footed. I think he lived through me by me being in the military. He was proud I chose that route."

After she celebrated her twentieth birthday, Patsy and her father traveled to Ashburn Hospital in McKinney, Texas, where she took her physical examinations. On the train, they got acquainted with a famous pianist who was in the army. "I really wanted to be in the navy, but they didn't have a chaplain's assistant which is what I wanted to do. I'd always wanted to be a missionary. This woman really opened some doors for me to do what I wanted. I wasn't dying to be in the army, I just wanted to be in the service."

Patsy boarded a train in Dallas to travel to Fort Oglethorpe, Georgia, for basic training. "That was experience enough," she laughs. "They put me on the train with a whole bunch of men. I was the only woman." Even though women had been in uniform since late 1942, a woman in the military was still an oddity to a lot of people. "I told them I'd just joined the Women's Army Corps," she says. "They just couldn't believe I would do a thing like that. It was real strange at first how the men accepted the women in the service.

"I had a great time at basic training," she continues. "There were about 360 of us. We were trained in the routine of army life. I loved getting up at 5 o'clock a.m. and doing exercises. We marched and did that gas thing, too. There was an obstacle course with live ammunition fire. Talk about being scared." Patsy laughs aloud remembering that aspect of basic training. "But we were brave. We just went through it like you're supposed to. There's just something about women. We can do anything, I guess. I remember Colonel Hobby coming to inspect us. She was a very nice person, a genuine person, a leader. We had great officers in basic training."

At Camp Fannin, she and the chaplain saw the ravages of war. "I got to see firsthand the men in the hospital. They came back from Italy. Some had been prisoners of war. We would go through the ward and talk to them and hold their hand if need be. There was a Sergeant Bob." Patsy stops speaking momentarily when she remembers this officer. "Oh, my. He'll live in my memory forever," she says.

Her next assignment was in Dallas, in the office of the commandant at the headquarters of the Eighth Service Command. "We lived right in the heart of Dallas in a protected area with fencing around us. My job was to know everyone who came in and out of the building. I met Audie Murphy. He'd just been awarded the most decorated soldier in the war." Patsy laughs when she thinks about the irony of what he told her after watching her work. "He watched me type and couldn't understand how I could type so fast."

On April 12, 1945, Patsy received the news by Teletype that President Roosevelt had died. "That was a very sad moment for all of us. We had a big parade in his memory." From Dallas, Patsy reported to War Department Personnel Center, WDPC, in Fort Sam Houston in San Antonio, Texas. There, she saw the POWs from the Pacific theater unloaded from planes and taken to the hospital. "These were the last ones brought in," she says. "Quite a few of our girls had husbands who were prisoners of war. There was one from Jacksonville, Texas, and we went through that with her. We cried together; we laughed together. I also heard about a nurse who had her tongue cut off by the Japanese.

*WAC Patsy Bruner in funeral parade for President Roosevelt, Dallas, Texas. Photograph courtesy of Patsy Palmquist*

"When I first went home, after I was discharged," she says, "I didn't want a phone in my house. I didn't! That's really strange, isn't it? I had taken so many calls about sad things that I had to tell the girls, I just didn't want a phone." Patsy pauses to reflect on that time so long ago. "I didn't want a phone," she says softly.

"I remember when the atomic bomb was dropped," she says. "We brought in sandwiches and Cokes and sat in a great big circle in the barracks to listen to the only radio we had. We wanted to hear to what was going on in Japan and other news. My mother arrived, so she joined us, but Dad had to stay in the recreation room."

At WDPC, Patsy was in charge of the records of the women leaving the military. WACs were some of the first troops discharged from the army. "I stayed day and night, night and day, getting the women through the process," she says.

Meanwhile, Patsy had married Roger Palmquist, that GI she met while at Camp Fannin, before he shipped out to the south Pacific with the Eleventh Airborne. From Japan, Roger wrote her that he would be home in January 1946, so Patsy decided to leave the service to make a home for them. "When I got that letter," she smiles, amused, "I walked in and told the colonel that I was going home that day. He said I wasn't because he'd put in for another stripe for me, but I told him I was going home. I typed up my discharge papers myself and went over and got my money. Then I went back and told him what I'd done. I did the whole thing myself because that was my job. Did you ever hear of anyone getting out that easy?"

Reflecting on her time in the army, Patsy says, "I had a great time while I was in the service, even though it was a sad time for our country. I was fortunate because it was like an adventure, really. I'm so proud of this country for letting women in the service. We worked wonderfully together with men. I've encouraged several young women to go in and they have. I think it's a wonderful way for a young women to get training, but there is a place for the women and there is a place for the men."

By staying active in the American Legion, Patsy feels as if she's still in the military. "That first night when I got home, I paid my dues and now I'm a lifetime member—fifty-eight years. When I first started going to the American Legion, I was the only woman. I wanted to join the auxiliary, but my husband encouraged me to come to the regular meetings. He said, 'You are a veteran. You're entitled to come to the meetings.' Those old WWI fellas were just precious to me.

"The American Legion is important to me," she explains, "because I'm still able to do things for this country. Our programs are dedicated to everything about America. We have children and youth programs and National Security programs. There's also VAR, Veteran's Affairs Rehabilitation." Patsy was elected the first female department commander for the state of Texas and served the 1991–1992 term. During her tenure, membership was the highest since 1947. "It's hysterical," she laughs, "first, I'm the only woman at the post, then later I'm elected department commander."

Patsy was appointed by then-Governor Ann Richards to the Texas Veterans Commission and served as commissioner from 1994 to 2000, the first woman to serve in that capacity. While in this position, Therese Slone-Baker organized the fundraising effort to benefit the Women in Military Service for America in Washington, D.C. Patsy presented the check in the amount of $79,800 from Texas.

When we talked, nearly a year had passed since the tragedy America experienced on September 11, 2001. On that day, terrorists simultaneously attacked the World Trade Towers in New York and the Pentagon in Washington, D.C., and a hijacked jetliner crashed in Pennsylvania, destination unknown. Patsy's reflections on that day are encouraging. "It touched everyone's life. It touched my life," she says. "I have always loved the Lord and thought he was always on our side. Even today, I think if we just pray a lot and hang in there, that we're all going to make it regardless of this terrible thing that happened to us."

*Patsy Palmquist in July 2002.*
*Photograph by Cindy Weigand*

# 5

## LOIS C. JONES

*Women's Army Auxiliary Corps, Women's Army Corps,*
*Eighth Air Force, Stone, England;*
*continental United States*

"Before we sailed, they showed us a film about American ships being attacked."

Flashlight in hand, the CQ, charge of quarters, tiptoed across the room and tapped Lois on the shoulder. "Time to get up, private," she said, and walked silently away.

Lois jerked out of her slumber, rubbed the sleep out of eyes, and looked at the clock. *Five forty-five.* After a quick trip to the latrine, she hurriedly put on her uniform, then clicked open the case that held the bugle. Blowing softly into the mouthpiece to warm it, Lois walked outside. After placing the mouthpiece on the horn, she put it to her lips promptly at 6:00 a.m. and played reveille to awaken the other trainees.

"While we were in Daytona Beach, someone found out I played the trumpet and French horn," Lois says, "so my commander, Sue Cornick, got me a bugle. I wanted to go overseas, but thought I'd have to stay in the United States and play in the band if they knew. Sue liked to hear the bugle and was going to England, so I got to go overseas with the group." Lois's battalion was the first large group of WAACs in the European Theater of Operations.

Lois C. Jones was born in San Antonio, Texas. She attended and graduated from parochial schools. She was working as a clerk and office manager at a tile company before enlisting in the Women's Army Auxiliary Corps in November 1942. "I didn't go into the navy because I wanted to go overseas. My aunt had been in Europe during World War I."

*1st Sgt. Lois C. Jones, 1943.*
*Photograph courtesy of Lois C. Jones*

Called to active duty in January 1943, she traveled to Daytona Beach, Florida, for basic training, staying there an additional two months to attend administrative school. She then joined the First Separate Battalion at Camp Polk, Louisiana. In training for about five weeks, the troops were housed in what had been a prisoner of war camp. "It was pretty desolate," Lois says, "because the latrines, wash areas, and lavatories were just a trough. The commodes were side by side with about 15–20 of them in a row, back to back. Of course, we were walled off from the rest of the post."

The battalion then traveled by troop train to Fort Devens, Massachusetts, by way of Canada. "We were in Southern Railway cars, and they were about as dirty as anything I'd ever seen." She says, "I think it was a three-day trip, so we were pretty messy by the time we got there. We slept two of us to a berth. At Fort Devens, we found the barracks had been closed for quite some time, so we had to clean them up. Then we had to learn how to fire the furnaces. It was May by then, but it could still get cold in Massachusetts."

While training at Fort Devens, the army made five companies out of two companies training there. Lois was put in the 169th Company with 1st

Bugler Lois C. Jones.
Photograph courtesy of Lois C. Jones

Officer/1st Lt. Vera E. Von Stein as commander. Here, they received training for shipment overseas. After long road marches, they had chemical warfare training and heard lectures on military sanitation. They practiced
infantry drill and were instructed in first aid, military customs and courtesies,
and the identification of insignias, and they learned French. The day ended
with retreat, parade, and review. "We didn't know when we were going
overseas," Lois says. "They kept going back and forth on that, but we did
know we were going."

Finally, her group left Fort Devens for Camp Shanks in New York for
shipment overseas. While there, the group received more training. Every
morning, they marched in full gear to a nearby lake where they received
swimming instruction. In the afternoon, they were lectured on safeguarding

military information and participated in gas mask drills. Other classes were in stenography and telephone switchboard operation for technicians.

At this time, their mail was censored. Abruptly, they found out they were to leave on July 8, 1943, but the destination was still unknown. "The night before we left," Lois says, "they showed us a film about a convoy of American ships attacked by submarines. They did this because we would be traveling across the Atlantic unaccompanied. That was quite a picture to see before getting on board a ship to sail across the Atlantic."

A band played as Lois and her comrades marched down the pier to the British transport ship the *Aquitania*. She carried with her an "A" barracks bag, a mussette bag (a type of bag carried across the shoulders), and a helmet. For lifeboat drills, they were considered "women" rather than "troops."

Along with the 560 women, including some Red Cross workers, boarding the ship that day were 15,000-plus male troops. "The men were on the lower decks and the women would pass notes to them on strings from the windows above," she says. "It was quite warm when we reached the Gulf Stream, so we took off our winter uniforms and put on our green seersucker exercise suits that included bloomers. They told us to not go where the men were because they didn't want them exposed to females." Also aboard the ship was Doris Freesen, World War II journalist and frequent contributor to *The Ladies Home Companion*.

About dusk on July 15, the *Aquitania* docked at Gourock, Scotland. The next morning, they went ashore. American and British officials greeted the first large group of WAACs to England. While a Scottish band played, they boarded a train bound for Stone, England. "In Stone," Lois says, "we were processed and selected for assignments by company. Some had individual assignments. I was sent to Marks Hall about sixty-five miles northeast of London, approximately fifteen miles inland from the channel. That's where B-26 Bombers of the 8th Air Force were. It was later changed to the 9th Air Force. We replaced the WAAF, the British equivalent of the WAAC, as teletype and telephone operators, stenographers, secretaries, and plotters for aircraft." Colonel (later General) Samuel E. Anderson was the commander.

"We had mess with the men and stayed in Nissen huts in England and were issued bicycles to use for transportation," she says. "They had brakes on the handlebars. Nobody knew how to ride them. We were also close to the airdrome where they took off and landed on their missions over to Germany, so got well acquainted with the men. Some of the women were quite good artists and painted on the nose or tail of the planes, whichever the men wanted. The men loved us and were so happy to have us there. They entertained us quite well. We had dances and ice cream parties."

At first, commanders tried to follow WAAC housing regulations to the letter. One rule was that the women's barracks had to be at least 150 feet from the men's. Wanting to protect the women, the commander suggested putting barbed wire around their barracks and posting MPs at the entrance. WAC Staff Advisor Mary E. Hallaran didn't think such measures were necessary but agreed *if* the necessity presented itself. She soon had proof that the wire fence wouldn't be needed. One night, some GIs got drunk in town. They wandered into the women's barracks because they were the closest to the front gate. They came out feet first. Several even landed in the clinic with bruises. Finally, the commander was convinced.

In August 1943, the WAAC ceased to exist and the new women's branch, known as the Women's Army Corps, became an official part of the army. Eighty-three enlisted women and three officers were inducted into the WAC. "We took the oath, then Colonel Lewis gave us the green and gold ribbon. He was the chief of staff. That's all there was to it."

So pleased was General Anderson with the work of the WACs that he sent Colonel Hobby a letter in January 1944 following her visit. The letter read:

> I often have wanted to place on record in an informal manner the high esteem which members of this Headquarters hold for personnel of the Women's Army Corps working with them.
>
> The Wacs have made a unique and valuable contribution to our work here. They have won our respect by showing great interest and conscientiousness in their work. They are well trained, capable, and handle both routine and highly important assignments smoothly and efficiently. In spite of rain, mud, cold, and an occasional night bombing attack, they remain cheerful and determined to see the jobs through. I am as proud of them as I am of any unit in the IX Bomber Command. If these are typical Wacs, and I believe they are, the United States has reason to be proud of its women soldiers.

As an enlistee, Lois was accepted into Officer Candidate School, so she left England in late August 1944 for training in Fort Oglethorpe, Georgia. Later, the battalion in England followed the army into Normandy after the D-Day invasion, the first WACs to do so. Lois graduated from OCS in

November 1944 and was assigned to extended field service at Fort Ogle-thorpe for two months. "Two companies of us stayed behind to train the postal unit that was commanded by Capt. Charity Adams, the all-black woman postal group that went over," she says. "There were three or four companies. We did all the training for their overseas duty." Lois was promoted to first lieutenant while in the EFS.

Lois was at Fort Oglethorpe when President Roosevelt died. "There was a parade and memorial service in his honor. I remember the drums were muted. Everyone wore a black armband and the troops passed in review."

Lois went to Fort Des Moines for six months before reporting to Bolling Air Force Base in Washington, D.C. On September 2, 1945, the Japanese officially surrendered to the Allies. However, by spring of 1946, the army was trying to get women to stay in the service. "They were running short of help," Lois says. "The men were all getting out, so they had a group of WAC officers go out and visit the army and air force bases along the East Coast. I was picked to go to some of these as far north as New Hampshire and south into South Carolina. After a few months, I decided to leave the military for a while or get out for good. I went back to San Antonio and got a job working for Braniff Airways."

*Lois C. Jones in July 2002.*
*Photograph by Cindy Weigand*

Lois considered becoming a hostess but decided to work as a reservation clerk instead. "I didn't like the way the supervisors treated the employees, so I decided to do some traveling. When I got back, I had a letter from the 4th Army Headquarters asking me to go back into the service." She was assigned to recruiting headquarters in Louisiana, then to Fort Sam Houston. "There, I took the examination for regular appointment and passed. I transferred from the army reserves to the air force reserves as a first lieutenant." Lois did recruiting in Texas, New Mexico, Oklahoma, Louisiana, and Arkansas. After tours at the Pentagon in Washington, D.C., and in Iceland, California, Colorado, and Texas, Lois retired from the military in December 1966 after twenty-four years of service.

In retirement, she has raised poodles, managed a trout ranch in the Ozarks, sold recreational vehicles, and worked in the sporting goods department of Sears.

# 6

# RUTH HAMILTON PRENGLE

*Army Nurse Corps, 193rd General Hospital, Malvern, England; 117th General Hospital, Bristol, England*

"We saved arms and legs that would have been amputated in World War I."

Ruth Hamilton Prengle looked at the soldier who had just made a fresh remark to her. Staring at the soldier in disgust, she turned up her lapel. On the underside she'd pinned a picture of Bill, her husband. "I'm a married woman," she said simply. The young man said no more.

Ruth's husband initially disapproved of her joining the military but quickly warmed to the fact, realizing she would want to do her part in the war effort just as he did. Bill Prengle then sent instructions to her that sounded more like that of a superior officer than a spouse. He reminded Ruth of her duty to God and country, to herself, and to her subordinates. Above all else, he said, she was to remember that she was an officer and a lady. Indeed, Ruth remained a lady while in the service, a trait that endures today.

When she was five years old, Ruth Hamilton dreamed of being a nurse. "My mother had a friend named Binty who was a nurse and she told me such interesting stories," she says. "Binty took care of Ann Harding, a famous movie star of that era. I thought that sounded pretty exciting." Ruth didn't get to care for a movie star but served her country in the oldest, and perhaps noblest, branch of the women's military, the Army Nurse Corps. At a general hospital in England, she assisted plastic surgeon Dr. Clifford L. Kiehn. Through special techniques that Dr. Kiehn developed combined with Ruth's nursing skills, arms and legs were saved that would have been amputated in WWI. Ruth tells her story with modesty and pride.

*Army Nurse Ruth Hamilton Prengle, 1943.*
*Photograph courtesy of Ruth Hamilton Prengle*

Born in Greensburg, Pennsylvania, Ruth graduated from the University of Michigan School of Nursing in 1941. She worked in Grand Rapids until she heard that she had passed the licensing exams. Afterward, she moved back to her hometown and started to work at the local hospital. In the meantime, her future husband had graduated from Carnegie Mellon University in Pittsburgh and had accepted a position in Buffalo, New York.

"The plan was that I would go to Buffalo and work at Millard Fillmore Hospital," Ruth says. "Toward the end of the year we would be situated so that we could get married. We set December 27, 1941, as the date to get married in Pennsylvania." Her fiancé, William "Bill" Prengle was an officer in the U.S. Army Reserve. Thanksgiving week, he received orders to report on December 8, 1941, for one year of active duty. Efforts to get him deferred failed.

Hurriedly, Ruth and Bill married on December 6, 1941, so Ruth could go with him. "Well, Sunday the seventh of December was our famous Pearl Harbor Day," she says. "Bill reported for active duty Monday

*Bill and Ruth Prengle, Colwyn Bay, Wales, 1944.*
*Photograph courtesy of Ruth Hamilton Prengle*

morning. The army told to him forget that one year because the United States was revving up for big things." Bill was stationed at Langley Field, Virginia, before going overseas in July 1942.

Although Ruth considered enlisting at the time, the Army Nurse Corps policy was to not accept married nurses. "Nurses were marrying like mad because they had boyfriends going overseas," Ruth says, "then they were discharged with no replacements. I thought how foolish! There were a lot of nurses like myself who had no children. There was no reason we couldn't be army nurses."

In late 1943, the army announced that it would enlist married nurses. "I didn't tell anybody I was going to do this," Ruth says. "I enlisted, signed the papers, got my orders notarized, and was sworn in, then I told my family. No one objected or they kept their objections to themselves. They couldn't object, but they didn't faint either." Ruth reported for duty in January 1944.

Basic training at Fort Mead, Maryland, was a rigorous six weeks. "We had to learn all about hospital regulations and the paperwork that we would have to do," Ruth recalls. "This was when you just sat down and did your paperwork with a pencil and made five copies of everything." The nurses also learned how to be a soldier. "We marched and drilled. They taught us how to put on a gas mask and we went through the gas chamber. This was real. We climbed up the webbing they have on the sides of ships. There was a whole course like that."

At the end of the six weeks, the nurses were allowed to choose their assignments. "I found out there were several General Hospitals getting complements to go overseas," Ruth says. "I checked the uniforms they were taking. Bill had taken only winter uniforms and ended up in England, so that's what I checked for. I could've ended up in Newfoundland or Greenland but fortunately I ended up in England, too."

Ruth signed with the 193rd General Hospital established at the University of Michigan and set sail late in February 1944. For nine days, the ship journeyed across the north Atlantic unaccompanied. They ate two meals a day. A few days into the voyage, she assisted a surgeon to perform emergency surgery. Passengers that worked in the hospital got three meals a day, so Ruth worked her way across the Atlantic. "Not that I was a chow hound," she says, "but I would eat a bit at every meal."

The ship landed in north Scotland where they boarded trains headed south. "Nobody ever told you anything, you just did as you were told," Ruth says. Night had fallen by the time the one hundred nurses reached their destination for the day. "I found out we were in Colwyn Bay in North Wales. My roommate and I were billeted in a private home. It was bitter cold."

Next morning, Ruth traveled into England. Once they were settled, a staff nurse already serving in the United Kingdom called on the new recruits. She told them what to expect and announced that the chief nurse of the United Kingdom, a Colonel Schaefer, would visit them. "The nurse warned us," Ruth laughs. "She told us to polish our shoes that night and not forget the heels because Colonel Schaefer was very particular. We were scared to death of this Colonel Schaefer." She turned out to be a pleasant surprise for Ruth.

"The next morning, we were spit and polished and called to attention," Ruth says, "and here came Colonel Schaefer. I was sitting in the front row and Colonel Schaefer looked at me and smiled. I smiled back. My gosh, it was my operating room supervisor at the University of Michigan when I was a student. I hadn't seen her since I left." Col. Margaret Schaefer's assistant returned to inform Ruth that the colonel wanted to see her. "We had a real good time catching up on one another. I thought it was really nice that I ran into her. I always liked her. She was my favorite instructor."

During her tour of duty, Ruth considered Colonel Schaefer her guardian angel. She felt the colonel was responsible for her assignment on the plastic surgery ward with Dr. Clifford L. Kiehn, also from the University of Michigan. Ruth believes Colonel Schaefer arranged meetings just to see how she was faring. One day, Dr. Kiehn asked Ruth to accompany him to his headquarters. On the way, they stopped and had tea and biscuits with the colonel. "It was just the three of us," Ruth remembers. "We had a good time talking about Michigan and a little bit about what we did."

Other times, Colonel Schaefer called Ruth to ask her to make an appointment with a dentist who was on staff. She told Ruth not to let the head nurse know, because she didn't want the red carpet treatment. "She'd say, 'I just want to sneak in and sneak out' and I'd agree. Maggie was keeping tabs on me. I really appreciated it, and I think she appreciated the time we had. I never had time to piece it together until I got home."

For six weeks, Ruth worked at a station hospital in Ireland in the operating room. She then returned to England to the 193rd, which had moved into a tent, before being transferred to the 117th General Hospital in Frenchay Park near Bristol, England. "Bristol was a seaport town, so hospital ships could come in. We could put patients on them to be sent back to the United States." At this time, the hospitals seemed to be preparing for some big event.

At the 117th, Ruth worked in the plastic surgery ward. "A few were on the ward when I arrived," she says. "Then the war got more intense. One night, I received fourteen patients in one fell swoop. We worked the rest of the night, then all the next day getting them situated and removing their dressings to determine the extent of their injuries." Because the wounds were fresh, Ruth and her staff had to set up a burn procedure. "It was a real learning process as we went along. To remove the dressings, the patients had to bathe to soak the dressings off. With only three tubs for this part of the process, removing the bandages from all the patients took days. We were working fourteen-hour days. That was about all you could put up with without taking a break."

One Tuesday, Ruth was unable to accommodate a colonel's weekly inspection. When pressed for an explanation, Ruth gave him a tour of the ward and what she and her staff were up against. "We had two nurses and three corpsmen, but there wasn't much patient care I could do because of my duties to run the ward," Ruth says. "Five people and we had to take care of eighteen patients twenty-four hours a day. It was just too much." The colonel must have agreed, because Ruth received several nurses to get the situation under control. "I don't know where they came from or where they went, I was just glad to see them.

"Sometimes following surgery," she continues, "these patients had to have casts on to stay immobile for three weeks. It was pretty hard for those guys, because it was really uncomfortable. We had some excellent results, though. We were able to save arms and legs that would have been amputated in WW I because this procedure didn't exist. It was a real thrill to see a badly damaged leg or arm covered with pink flesh. I only lost three patients during my tour of duty." Ruth served eighteen months overseas.

Ruth remembers a special patient in the fall of 1944. Dr. Kiehn notified her that she would receive a five-year-old British boy on her ward. An American army truck had struck the boy in Bristol. One of his legs was injured so badly that the English doctors considered amputation but decided to consult Dr. Kiehn first. He determined the leg could be saved and requested the boy be sent to the 117th where he would arrange the surgery.

After the surgery, Ruth put the boy in a private room next to her office so she could keep her eye on him. His name was Robert Day; they called him Little Robbie. "The ambulatory patients on the ward would stop in and visit with him. I got some children's books from somewhere. The soldiers read to him and gave him gum and stuff like that, spoiling him rotten." Ruth and her staff cared for Little Robbie and got him through his next round of surgery, and then he left the hospital. "I never did hear how he fared after that. I arranged for Dr. Kiehn to see him one more time, but I didn't get to see him at that time."

Before Ruth arrived in England, Bill Prengle had been an aviation engineer there building airstrips for B-24 bombers. Ruth was able to contact Bill and saw him a few times before he was moved to a staging area to train as a soldier again. They were supposed to meet one night. "Bill and I had a pact," she says, "that if he called me and said, 'I can't make it tonight,' I'd know they were going." This coincided with the preparations at the hospital. Ruth didn't know what was going to happen, just that it was something important. "Well, I got the call. I knew he was gone. I didn't sleep very well that night.

"One morning," Ruth says, "I got up early and rode my bicycle to

Central Supply to roll bandages or something. I had turned on the radio to listen to some news when I heard General Eisenhower's message that the invasion, later called D-Day, had started. I was on pins and needles for a while." Midafternoon the first day of that invasion, Ruth's hospital received patients wounded in combat.

"A day or so later, some enlisted men from the post office came over to Central Supply," Ruth says. "They said to me, 'Hey Lieutenant, is your husband Captain Prengle?'" Ruth responded that he was and asked why they wanted to know. "The men said that they'd heard on the radio that Bill captured five Germans and took them prisoner. I thought they were just pulling my leg but found out later they were telling the truth." After a while, Ruth received airmail from Bill. "It was just a couple of words to let me know he was still around," she says.

Ruth remained in Bristol until July 1945, when she was moved to a staging area to be sent home for a month's leave for rest and relaxation. Afterward, the nurses were to regroup for shipment to Japan. "On the boat home, we got the news the first bomb was dropped, and then the second bomb was dropped." Ruth was in Times Square on August 14, 1945, when V-J, Victory in Japan, Day was declared. "I wasn't the nurse that got kissed, though," Ruth laughs, referring to the now famous picture of a sailor kissing a nurse. "None of us could believe the war was really over," Ruth says. "We wondered when the next shoe was going to drop. We wondered if we could really celebrate."

They docked in New York on a hot and muggy day. Still in their wool uniforms and carrying gear, the nurses sweltered in the heat. "We had to bring all this stuff back with us," Ruth says. "I had half a tent, a heavy coat with wool lining, a gas mask, and mess gear. We stood on the boat a long time before we could get off." As they disembarked, the Red Cross gave the nurses some cold milk to drink. "Oh, that was wonderful," Ruth remembers, "because we weren't allowed to drink milk in England. Their cows weren't tested for tuberculosis. That cold milk on such a hot day was just wonderful."

The nurses boarded buses for Fort Dix, New Jersey, where they turned in their gear before receiving orders for leave. "We had to go here and turn that in and go there and turn this in." Afterward, Ruth went home and rested. "I just laid around and began to feel more like a human being again," she says. "I needed that month off. I don't think I would have

*Ruth in fatigues.*
*Photograph courtesy of Ruth Hamilton Prengle*

survived if I had stayed." After a month, Ruth received orders to report back to Fort Dix.

"We were put on troop trains at Ft. Dix and sent to Gaston, Alabama. If you don't think that wasn't a fiasco," she says. "It was hot and humid, and of course there was no air conditioning. The nurses kept their pajamas on the whole time. The food was terrible. We were crammed in, and our train was often sidetracked to let a faster train through. It took us three days to travel from New Jersey to Alabama." Once in Alabama, "we had to sit and wait until they decided what was going to happen to us," Ruth says. "Of course we knew we weren't going to Japan, which was really a relief. Finally, we got orders to report to Battey General Hospital in Rome, Georgia, for tests and so forth. They gave us physicals exams and checked us out really well. Then I got my discharge papers and went back home."

When Bill was discharged, he returned to college, eventually earning

*Bill and Ruth Prengle, Austin, Texas, 2002.*
*Photograph courtesy of Ruth Hamilton Prengle*

his Ph.D. They moved to Houston in 1947 where he taught chemical engineering at the University of Houston. They have a daughter and a son.

One day in 1992, Ruth received a letter that began with these words, "I don't know if you remember me or not, but. . . ." Ruth knew immediately who it was from. "I thought, 'oh my gosh! It's from Little Robbie.'" The letter was indeed from Little Robbie. Later that year, Ruth attended a reunion in England of another General Hospital out of Michigan University to celebrate the arrival of the hospital there in WWII. "Little Robbie and his mother came to the banquet that night," she says. "He had one little spot on his leg that didn't heal well, but he played soccer growing up," she says proudly. Ruth and Big Robbie have stayed in contact ever since.

# 7

# BUENA "MAC" McQUEEN LEHMAN

*Army Nurse Corps, 79th Field Hospital,*
*England, France, and Germany*

"I enjoyed every minute of my service."

The whistle shrilled loudly, the engine hissed, and drivers strained against the huge steel wheels of the train as it inched forward and then picked up speed. Buena McQueen waved goodbye to Charlie, her husband of one week, until he was only a dot in the crowd at the depot. She settled back into her seat for the long journey back to her assignment at Fort Bliss in El Paso, Texas. *I wonder when I'll see him again. I wonder if I'll see him again.* Tears stung her eyes as she tried to hold them back. No matter how hard she tried to think of other things, thoughts of Charlie kept returning. Soon, he would be shipped overseas to parts unknown. Within weeks, Buena, an army nurse, would also board a ship going overseas. Her unit, the 79th Field Hospital, received casualties in England, France, and Germany.

Buena McQueen wanted to study nursing in order to become an airline stewardess. Passengers often became sick from the turbulence of low altitude flights, so airlines often required hostesses to have a nursing degree. "My father thought it was a disgrace that I wanted to be a nurse or with the airlines," she says. She received her RN degree in May 1941 from the Appalachian Hospital Training School for Nurses in Johnson City, Tennessee. The school was near her hometown of Butler. Upon graduation, she decided not to become an airline stewardess and started a career in nursing instead.

Her first position was in urology at Johns Hopkins in Baltimore, Maryland, and she was there when the United States entered the war. "Another nurse, Eva Knapp, and I were the youngest ones there," Buena says. "They

*Army Nurse Buena "Mac" McQueen.*
*Photograph courtesy of Buena "Mac" Lehman*

were calling older nurses back because the young ones were joining the service. That's where all the action was." She and Eva decided they wanted to go where the action was, too, so they enlisted in the Army Nurse Corps and received commissions as first lieutenants.

Assigned to Fort Bliss, Buena worked in the William Beaumont General Hospital. Although she cared for many patients, Buena especially remembers one officer. "We had this officer in a private room, and he was married and was a very nice patient. He'd had some fingers taken off plus many other troubles," Buena says. "He asked me if I would stay and talk with him that night after my shift ended. I can't remember his name, but I remember what he looked like."

Buena explained that she had been on her feet all day and needed to rest. She also had to prepare her uniform for work the next day. Although she had a nagging feeling that she should stay, she also knew she needed to be rested in order to take care of her other patients properly the next day. "He'd never asked me that before, and we'd had him about a week. I thought it strange that he wanted me to be there." When she reported for duty the next morning, she learned that the officer had expired during the night. Buena thinks about the officer frequently. "Maybe he had a feeling that that would be his last night. I don't know, but I still remember that."

On the way to the officer's club on Saturday night in El Paso, Buena and two other nurses were standing on a street corner waiting for the light to change. Two male lieutenants joined them and struck up a conversation; one of them was Charlie Lehman. Buena and Charlie fell in love and, after a two-week courtship, were married in Galveston, Charlie's hometown. They had their picture taken. Buena was beautiful in her white wedding gown, and Charlie wore his tall brown boots that he'd worn as a cadet at Texas A & M University. Five days later, Charlie was ordered to Camp Polk, Louisiana, for shipment overseas. On that very day, Buena was called to return to Fort Bliss. However, she was able to get a three-day extension to go with Charlie. Afterward, Buena boarded the train alone for the trip back to El Paso.

At that time Buena requested overseas duty. Training was at Fort Knox, Kentucky. "Training included road marches of up to ten miles," she says, "plus gas mask training, and climbing Jacob's ladder. I did this without any trouble. Some of the girls couldn't make it, but I did because I was young and in shape." In high school, she had been a starter on the basketball team. "We set up tents and slept in them," she continues. "I almost froze because it was so cold."

The previous year, Charlie had graduated from Officer's Candidate School at Fort Knox on November 6, 1943, as a medium tank platoon leader. Buena probably walked down the same roads at Fort Knox as Charlie had. Throughout her service, Buena and Charlie would continue this pattern of never being at the same place at the same time until she got to Germany. Buena had retained her maiden name, and they communicated by writing to APO numbers. Charlie carried their wedding picture everywhere in his wallet.

From Fort Knox, Buena went to Camp Kilmer, New Jersey, for processing before going to New York City to board a ship for Europe. She departed on Christmas Eve 1944. While crossing the Atlantic, destroyers with their convoy dropped depth charges to sink a German submarine, which was nearby. Buena felt the concussions from the explosions. "We got a jolt. Two GIs got broken arms because they fell from upper bunks." Several weeks later, Charlie left New York, also bound for Europe. Buena

*Buena and Charlie Lehman, wedding photo.*
*Photograph courtesy of Charlie and Buena Lehman*

landed and worked briefly in Bournemouth on the southern coast of England. Later, Charlie's convoy dropped anchor between Bournemouth and the Isle of Wight to wait for nightfall to cross the English Channel.

By late 1944, Germany was clearly losing the war. The allied armies were advancing through France and the Low Countries, pushing back the Germans. In desperation, Hitler launched an attack to retake territory taken by the Allies. Although they fought intensely and temporarily created a bulge in the Allies' line, the Americans and Allies held and pushed back the enemy.

Fought from December 16, 1944, to January 28, 1945, the Battle of the Bulge would prove a crucial victory to winning the war. More than a million troops were involved including 600,000 Germans, 500,000 Americans, and 55,000 British. Casualties of the battle were 81,000 Americans with 19,000 killed; 1,400 British with 200 killed; and 100,000 Germans killed, wounded, or captured.

In England, Buena worked in the operating room as well as being in charge of a post-op ward. She traveled across the channel with a detachment to assist a field hospital in the Battle of the Bulge and certainly where there was plenty of action. "We'd get them first," she explains. "Medics brought them right in from the battlefield. We kept them only so long because they'd be bringing others in from the field hospital, they'd go to a station hospital where they would have the necessary things done. If they needed surgery, or required a long time to get well, they were sent to a general hospital and eventually back to the United States.

"It was pitiful to see strong young bodies so torn up in battle, even for a nurse," she says. "In addition to dealing with wounds, some of the wounded lay unconscious in the snow so long their feet froze before they were taken to the field hospital. I helped the surgeons amputate lots of toes."

Upon her return to England, Buena remembers one soldier in particular. "I remember this one little guy," she says. "He had the most beautiful cheeks, almost like a girl's, and blond hair and big blue eyes. He was so sweet. One night, he gave me a card to write to his mother. She'd sent him cards that were already addressed. All he had to do was write something on it. However, his arms were bandaged up and he couldn't write, so he asked me to write something." The patient's condition created a dilemma for Buena. "He was critical, and I didn't think he was going to recover, so I couldn't write his mother and tell her that her son was getting along well or had a comfortable day or night, then have someone from the service knock on her door to tell her that her son had expired."

Buena didn't write the card. "I don't know if he recuperated or not, but I've often had him in my mind since then. I don't know if I did right. One time I think it was right. No news is good news as they say. The next time, I think it was wrong."

Although their head nurse discouraged them from doing so, Buena and a friend, Ludke, decided to go see the sights in London. The Germans were trying to set London afire with unmanned flying buzz bombs. These bombs were particularly unnerving because one couldn't tell when or where they would fall and explode. The first night, they were sleeping in a Red Cross facility when one exploded nearby. "Ludke was normally a slow-talking

person, but she jumped out of bed and yelled, 'What the hell was that?'"
Buena told her that it was one of those bombs the head nurse had warned
them about. They returned to the hospital without delay.

When it was safe to cross the English Channel, Buena's unit, the 79th
Field Hospital, left England for Le Havre, France. As they traveled across
France, she worked and lived in tents without floors. Sand was everywhere,
including their food. She remembers one tent had a piano in it. "My friend
Bradle and I never knew why we would have a tent with a piano in it."

Her unit crossed France into Ludwigshafen, a town on the Rhine
River, in western Germany. Charlie's company arrived in Mannheim,
directly across the river. Buena's unit took over a hospital in a nice building
vacated by the Germans. The allies had spared the hospital—clearly marked
with white crosses on the roofs and sides—when they bombed the town.
This was a Catholic hospital and the nuns were still there. "They couldn't
do nursing," Buena says, "but they stayed and did our laundry and cleaning.
They lived in the basement." The first night, the Germans bombed the railroad station in nearby Ludwigshafen.

In the German hospital, Buena remembers a practical joke American
GIs played on the nuns. "Our GIs were kind of naughty. They taught the
nuns to say bad words. They taught them that *goddamn* meant *nice and clean.*
So when the nuns brought in the pillowcases and things, they would say,
'Here are the goddamn linens.' I tried to tell them that wasn't what it
meant."

Buena had told the people in her unit to look for signs pointing to
Charlie's unit, but the GIs liked to tease her, too. They would tell her they
knew where Charlie was when they didn't. "They told me so many times,
I always discarded it," she says. "I think they liked to come to my door and
knock because the nurses would sometimes give them liquor that the officers brought from the German cellars." One day, a GI seemed very serious
when he told her he knew where Charlie's unit was. "He begged me to
believe it, but I had heard that before. Anyway, he was so serious, I got the
chaplain." From the GI, the chaplain found out where Charlie's unit was
and went to find him. When he located the unit, Charlie was not there, but
the company commander had already dispatched a messenger to tell Charlie
where Buena was.

Charlie drove all night without headlights to Buena's unit. Once there,
he wasn't allowed to see her because his ID card read *Lehman,* and he was
asking for his wife Lieutenant *McQueen.* Suddenly, Charlie remembered the

wedding picture in his wallet and showed the corporal in charge. Convinced, the corporal let Charlie in to see Buena. Her commanding officer gave her the rest of the day off so they could be together.

Charlie returned several weeks later, and the nuns saw him leaving her room before daybreak. "The nuns thought I was immoral," she says. "They wouldn't speak to me. They finally got word that Charlie was my husband, then they brought me strawberries and flowers to apologize." The nuns also finally realized that Buena had told them the truth when she told them *goddamn* didn't mean *nice and clean.*

The hospital accepted enemy and Allied casualties as well as American. One day, she sent a Russian patient to do work in the kitchen; at the same time, her friend Nellie McGrath sent a German patient. "I heard this commotion because the diet kitchen was close by. I went to see what it was about. The German and Russian were chasing each other. That taught us a lesson to not send a German patient and a Russian to do KP at the same time. That just doesn't work."

She recollects another bizarre incident involving a Russian soldier who died in the operating room. "They took him to the morgue where he revived and sat up on the stretcher," she laughs. "That happened three times before he finally died for good."

*Buena "Mac" Lehman and Charlie Lehman in May 2002.*
*Photograph by Cindy Weigand*

After V-E Day, Buena had enough points to leave the military, but Charlie did not. The 79th was scheduled to go to the south Pacific, but Buena did not want to go with them. Transferred to the 53rd Hospital Train, she returned to the United States by way of Marseilles. She was in Marseilles when the bombs were dropped on Japan, ending the war. Concerning her time in the military, Buena says, "I enjoyed every minute of it. I would've stayed in if I hadn't met Charlie."

Discharged from the army in 1945, Buena joined Charlie in Fort Jackson, South Carolina, where they stayed for a short time before moving to Bryan Station so Charlie could complete his education. After graduation, Charlie worked for Sears Roebuck & Company for thirty-four years. They have two children.

Charlie still has the same wedding picture he carried in his wallet throughout Europe and showed the corporal that morning in Ludwigshafen. He had the photo propped up on the television next to the portrait of Buena when I arrived in their home. His tall brown boots stand next to a wall, as polished and shiny as the day he and Buena were married.

# 8

# DORIS McCRAW COBB

*Army Nurse Corps, European Theater of Operations*

"I fought the battle of transportation."

The steel wheels of the forty-and-eight, a railroad car designed to carry forty people or eight horses, screeched and then lurched to a halt. Army nurse Doris McCraw and her colleagues jolted forward. They heard the clanking of their car being disconnected from the ones behind them. With a swoosh of steam being released, the engine started backing, pushing the car to a siding. A collective moan spread through the car, for this had happened many times before. As they traveled to Marseilles to join troops and other nurses going to the Pacific theater, the French government had once again interrupted their progress. Cattle and other freight destined for Paris was deemed a higher priority, so they pushed the car with the Americans to the side to wait for another train.

The passengers sat in the car, talking among themselves, waiting. Suddenly, swarms of French people gathered outside the car and called to them. "Mademoiselle, puis-je acheter votre chemise [could I buy your shirt]?" asked a woman in a tattered shirt. "Combien pour vos chaussures [how much for your shoes]?" a man asked, pointing to his feet. "Mademoiselle, puis-j'avoir seulement un paquet de nourriture [could I just have a package of food]?" asked a waif, looking up hopefully (and hungrily) at the group.

"This happened many times on our trip," Doris says. "We didn't have enough clothing to sell them any. We were only given enough K rations per day for the trip, so we didn't have much food, either. However, we did trade them soap for wine. Sometimes, they had fruit or other food they wanted to trade for something. If we had any, we gave them candy bars. We certainly got in communication with the people of France." Possessing

*Army Nurse Doris McCraw in 1945.*
*Photograph courtesy of Doris McCraw Cobb*

a clear, smooth complexion, Doris appears ten years younger than her age. Sixty years after the fact, Doris still looks upon her service during WWII with amusement.

Doris McCraw was born in Hopewell, Virginia, in 1922 and graduated from high school in 1939. "At the time I graduated, the choices for a career were either to be a teacher or be a nurse," Doris says. "I thought I could be a nurse and a teacher. As it turned out, I was able to do both." She attended nursing school at Petersburg Hospital School of Nursing and did a student affiliation in Philadelphia.

In 1943, while a senior at Philadelphia, Doris joined the Student Reserve of the American Red Cross. Because of a projected nurse shortage, the ARC was recruiting nursing students for the military. By joining the reserve, Doris agreed to be *willing* to join the military. "When I graduated," Doris laughs, "I received a letter asking me *which* branch of the military I wanted to join, not *if* I would join, so I joined the Army Nurse Corps." Upon hearing she had passed the state board exams for licensure, Doris became eligible for active duty in January 1945, thus starting her battle of transportation.

For basic training, Doris reported to Billings General Hospital, Fort

Benjamin Harrison in Indiana, from February 15 to March 15, 1945. Next, she reported to Fletcher General Hospital in Cambridge, Ohio, where she stayed for almost two months. Upon receiving orders to report to Indiantown Gap, Pennsylvania, she joined five hundred nurses gathered there from the eastern and midwestern parts of the United States. While there, the government had an odd requirement of them. "We had to have two pair of four-buckle arctics," Doris says. "These are the kind of galoshes that go over your shoes. They didn't tell us why we had to have them. I never got over trying to find two pair of four-buckle arctics."

From Indiantown Gap, Doris went to Camp Kilmer, New Jersey, to prepare for shipment overseas. "They didn't tell us where we were going but did tell us to prepare for cold weather. We were what they called 'casuals' because we weren't with a special unit as those already in Europe were. We were going over there as replacements wherever we were needed." On May 1, 1945, the five hundred nurses boarded the ship the *Isle de France* at Fort Dix, New Jersey, for the trip to Europe. "At that time," Doris explains, "there was a feeling that the war was over, but we didn't know that for sure, so we zigzagged across the Atlantic. We landed in England on the tenth of

*Doris McCraw in fatigues.*
*Photograph courtesy of Doris McCraw Cobb*

May, one day after the war in Europe ended. Needless to say, nobody was happy to see us."

Doris remembers a comical incident on the trip over. "While on ship," she continues, "we met a British major from the Royal Air Force who considered himself to be a hypnotist. He did hypnotize two nurses, one of whom was a friend of mine. He told them that when they awakened, they would go down and play the piano. Now, I knew that my friend could not play the piano, but sure enough, when he awakened them, she went to the piano and started to play "My Country 'Tis of Thee," but to the British, it is "God Save the Queen." Many of the troops on board were RAF officers who had been in the United States training. One of them, not aware of what had taken place, went over to the women and asked them to "please play something else so they would not have to stand.""

They docked and then went by train to Bath near Southampton, England. "They gave us three packets of K rations, one for breakfast, lunch, and dinner," she says. "I thought that was pretty neat because I'd never seen K rations." Southampton was where the nurses finally found out why they were required to have two pair of galoshes. "The first thing they did was take one pair away from us to give to the people returning to the United States," she says. "The other pair we kept for our own use." While in Southampton, they were housed at a base set up for a specific reason, but they didn't know what. "I don't know why, but we were not permitted to go out for quite a while. Finally, they did let us go to Bath to see a different part of England."

After two weeks in Southampton, the military sent Doris to different organizations throughout England. "The first was Cirencester," Doris says, "but when we got there, they were all packed up ready to go back to the United States. They were not happy to see us." The group at Cirencester was celebrating the victory in Europe, and Doris was able to participate. "They had this big bowl of something so I had a glass," she laughs. "I found out later it was martini. I went back to my room and wrote my parents," Doris laughs. "They saved the letter for me. I learned the lesson to never write your parents when you've had a martini."

After a week, the military then deemed Doris's services were needed at a Station Hospital near Bury St. Edmonds where she stayed from late May to mid-July, and then she was transferred to France. "Supposedly, we were going to France to get ready to go to the Pacific," she says. "I went to the

189th General Hospital where I stayed about two weeks. They didn't have anything for us to do, so I got a pass and went to Paris."

While in Paris, Doris met some celebrities. "I went to see the Follies," she says. "Bob Hope and Jerry Colonia, who were on a USO tour, were there the same evening. Later, we went to an officer's club. I danced with Jerry Colonia who was introduced to me as General Colonia. I laughed and remarked, 'I didn't know you were a general,' to which he replied, 'I am a General Nuisance. How would you like to be my straight man?'"

When the group returned from Paris, they found out they were being transferred to another hospital, the 173rd, at a camp called Camp Maurmelon. "On the ship going over," Doris says, "there were five hundred army nurses, two hundred WACs, and about six thousand troops. There were about twenty of us in a cabin designed to hold only one or two passengers. We were stacked four-high. Since I was small, I was on the top bunk."

Doris was at Maurmelon about two weeks and then got ready to go to Marseilles. With the war in Europe over, troops were staging in Marseilles for shipment to the Pacific Theater of Operations. "Well," Doris says, "I got to Marseilles to join the 173rd General Hospital to go to the Pacific. Of course, they didn't have enough ships to take everyone, so I got a pass, called TDY, to the Riviera. Good living." It was on the way to Marseilles that their travel was often interrupted for goods going to Paris or other parts of France.

When Doris returned from the Riviera, she received more news. "The war in the Pacific had ended," she says, "but there were people at the port in Marseilles who had been there for several years waiting to go home. We'd been there for approximately three months, so they weren't about to send us home."

Doris went first to the 50th Field Hospital at Soissons, France. This hospital had gone in with the 101st Airborne into Normandy, having followed them throughout the war in Europe. The doctors, nurses, and enlisted men had been at the port of Marseilles for a year, since D-Day, June 6, 1944. From Soissons, Doris was ordered to go to the 98th General Hospital in Munich, Germany. "The hospital had had twenty direct hits on it during the war. It had been a Catholic Hospital for children. We worked with the nuns who were still there. Some of them were wonderful; others were like the nurses in nursing schools, kind of on the crabby side. In Munich, we had the normal nursing care that you give any patients. Most of our patients had injuries and diseases that people get when they are in foreign countries. I worked primarily on the dermatology ward.

"Munich had been bombed terribly during the war," Doris continues. "By the time we got there, it had almost been completely destroyed. We had to admire the work ethic of the German people, even though they had been our enemy. They were out with wheelbarrows, buckets, shovels, pick axes, anything they could get a hold of trying to rebuild."

While in Munich, Doris again had the opportunity to do some sight-seeing. "We went to Garmisch and Bavaria. I first learned to ski in Garmisch," she says. "I finally got some boots to fit—with three pairs of socks. They taught me to go up and down the slope. Due to the altitude, and the fact that I hadn't eaten breakfast, I fainted on the slope. A handsome French officer picked me up and took me back to the lodge. A friend of mine hurt her knee, but no one even offered to carry her skis. If you skied, you were expected to carry your own skis."

In April 1946, Doris received notice that she could stay in the army for an indefinite period, get out as soon as she wanted, or extend her tour for another year. "I had already been accepted at Western Reserve University to get my baccalaureate degree," Doris says, "so I decided to get out.

*Doris McCraw beside one of her means of transportation.*
*Photograph courtesy of Doris McCraw Cobb*

In May, about twenty of us boarded a Liberty ship and came home. We had to go to Fort Dix to get separated from the army."

"While I was being separated from the service," Doris says, "they had decided to do a study to determine what size the average American woman was for some reason. To do that, they measured every fifth woman. I was one of the fifth. I had always told everybody I was five foot two. I had blue eyes, so I was five two with eyes of blue, but they measured me at four feet, eleven inches tall. The sergeant told me everybody else had grown, but I was the only one who had dried up." She never learned the full results of the study.

In May 1946, Doris separated from the service at the rank of second lieutenant. She attended college at Western Reserve and the University of Virginia and received a B.S. degree in nursing education. During this time, she became engaged but decided against marriage. In the years that followed, she taught nursing and was the director of a school of nursing. Returning to school, she earned a master's degree in nursing service administration from Columbia University in 1955. While at Columbia, three classmates, one each from the army, air force, and navy, convinced Doris to return to active duty.

Entering as a captain, Doris had tours of duty in Boston, Massachusetts, Okinawa, Washington state, Georgia, Thailand, Virginia, Texas, and Europe. Her last assignment was chief nurse at the 130th Station Hospital in Heidelberg, Germany, for two years. In 1974, she retired with the rank of

*Doris McCraw Cobb in 1991.*
*Photograph courtesy of Doris McCraw Cobb*

colonel and established residence in San Antonio. For eleven years, Doris was married to Blethyn C. Cobb, Jr. The marriage ended in 1978.

"I always say my World War II experience was the battle of transportation," she laughs, "because I was moved to so many places. I think I rode in the back end of every vehicle that the army had—truck, ambulance, you name it—except a tank. I probably could have arranged that if I'd wanted to. It's not that it wasn't enjoyable, because it was, but most World War II nurses stayed with one unit the whole time."

Doris stays active in the Women's Overseas Service League in San Antonio, having served as national president from 1990 to 1992. She's also active in the Army Nurse Corps Association (formerly the Retired Army Nurse Corps Association), which she helped establish as well as serving as the first president. She retains membership in the local American Legion and in women's activities at her church. Doris also enjoys attending theater productions, playing bridge, and reading.

## 9

# MARION K. KENNEDY

*Army Nurse Corps, 20th General Hospital,*
*China-Burma-India*

"We were proud of the medical care we gave."

Marion and a group of medical personnel walked down the gangplank into the town of Perth, Australia. On their way to India, their transport ship had been detained until an escort ship arrived to accompany them on the next leg of the journey. Glad to be off the ship for a while, they laughed and talked as they meandered down the street, looking curiously in shop windows along the way. Passing an inn, they decided to stop in for a drink. Inside, they placed their orders and continued their merriment, enjoying the Australian beer. Marion surveyed the scene around her. Music blared from somewhere in the back of the room. Soldiers stood at the counter, arms around attractive young women, whispering in their ears.

Suddenly, a sailor from their ship rushed to the table, interrupting their conversation. "Get the nurses out of here, pronto!" he demanded.

Hastily and without a word, the gentlemen in the group escorted the women out of the bar.

"It seems we'd stumbled into a house of ill-repute," Marion laughs. "That was the first of several adventures in Perth."

Marion carries herself with the dignity of a high-ranking officer. She speaks softly and deliberately. Born in Allentown, Pennsylvania, Marion served two and a half years in the Army Nurse Corps in the China-Burma-India Theater of Operations. Her unit, the 20th General Hospital, was located near the air bases from which airplanes flew over "The Hump," the Himalayan Mountains, to take supplies into China. Also nearby, the army was rebuilding the road, called Ledo Road, as an overland supply route. Her

*Army Nurse Marion K. Kennedy by bamboo hospital ward in India.*
*Photograph courtesy of Marion K. Kennedy*

journey to the area took over two months of sailing across the south Pacific, which was heavily patrolled by Japanese ships and submarines.

"I had just finished my basic nursing program at the Hospital of the University of Pennsylvania when the Japanese bombed Pearl Harbor," Marion says. "The university had the outline of a reserve unit on paper. They were asking people to sign up so that the unit would be well composed of personnel from the hospital—surgeons, medical men, doctors, lab people, a dietician, and nurses—when the unit was activated. Quite a few of us signed up including doctors we had known since they were medical students."

The unit was activated on May 15, 1942, and left with great fanfare. "We got on the train at the 30th Street Railway station in Philadelphia complete with band, families, and all sorts of reporters," Marion laughs. "Forty-eight hours later, we arrived at Camp Claiborne, Louisiana, to heat and humidity, for indoctrination. We were in barracks that had been built hastily for the expansion of the army. Although we were in civilian clothes, we really felt like we had joined the army. We wore civilian nurse's uniforms on our first duty days but received army uniforms in due course."

In January 1943, Marion's unit left for California for shipment overseas. They sailed on the *Monticello*, an old Italian cruise liner in poor condition that had been confiscated from the Italian government. "We traveled alone in zigzag fashion. Two weeks later, we woke up and were in the beautiful harbor of Wellington, New Zealand. Scuttlebutt came out that this was not our final destination. We were there two days to have the ship refueled and get provisions. There were about three thousand troops and several medical units on board."

Departing from Wellington, New Zealand, the ship zigzagged south of Australia for two weeks until it reached Freemantle, the port for Perth, Australia, on the west coast of the continent. "The military thought we needed an escort for the rest of the journey, so we stayed in Perth for four days waiting for an escort. We were permitted to leave the ship each day for excursions. The people were apparently accustomed to the Americans doing this because they were very friendly and very helpful."

From Perth, small Dutch ships, called corvettes, escorted the *Monticello* into Bombay, India, on the western coast. They landed on March 3, 1943. "All of the men were taken to a replacement depot, but we ladies were fortunate, we were taken to Poona nearby. This was a place that the British military had used for many years as sort of a resort area. It had a rather nice hospital set up there. Several of the wards were empty of patients, and we were housed in those wards of the hospital. The British officers on R & R, rest and relaxation, were just delighted to escort us to various activities in the evening, so we had a nice time in Poona.

"The British held dances and other events in order to raise money for the British Red Cross in India," Marion continues. "We were fortunate, we felt, in getting involved in a lot of very pleasant activities, and it gave us something to do during the day. Aside from that, since we had no transportation, there was nowhere that we could go."

About a week later, Marion and the other nurses boarded an Indian narrow gauge railroad for the trip across India to Gauhati. "We stayed a couple of days at an American Baptist mission school. The government had rented the school minus the students, of course, as an area in which to house us. After three days, we got on another even more narrow gauge railroad for twenty-four hours and got off at a little Indian village nearly at the end of the rail line. That was the beginning of the road they called the old Burma Road."

In the spring of 1942, the Imperial Japanese forces had severed the Burma Road, China's last supply link to the Allied world. Unless the Allies continued to provide the Chinese with essential military provisions, Japan would eventually overwhelm China's conventional military forces. Marion explains, "This was done to supply the Chinese to keep them active in the war. They felt the more Japanese they kept in China, the fewer troops they would have in the South Pacific. Eventually, the Allies hoped to invade Japan." So important was getting the Ledo Road built and reestablishing a land route over which to transport supplies, fifteen thousand troops were assigned to the area.

"This is where we set up a hospital," Marion continues. "In the beginning, we had five wards we took over from a MASH unit that had been working there for several months. There was an operating room, an x-ray area, and several wards in bamboo buildings. As the engineers, the quartermaster, and all the support facilities came into that basic area, I think it was called base number three, our patient load increased. We arrived there in mid-March, just before the monsoon rains came.

"With the rains came a lot of mud to negotiate, and mosquitoes," Marion continues. "With the mosquitoes came malaria and dengue fever, and there was a very limited supply of quinine. We used it to treat only the more severely ill men. By early fall, the hospital received a supply of atabrine, a medication used to prevent malaria. All of us were scheduled to take the medication until we left the area. Atabrine had a yellow dye in it that gave our skin a definite yellow tinge."

Initially, the conditions under which the nurses worked were primitive. "There was a limited amount of electricity," Marion says, "so it went to the operating room, of course, and to the x-ray unit. We used kerosene lanterns for light. Eventually, we got more and stronger generators. By the time we left, we had plenty of electricity.

"Also, we didn't have running water," she continues. "The first water we got was out of the river and it was muddy. What little hospital linen we had was washed in that muddy water so it was almost khaki colored rather than white. Things gradually improved. I would rather have them improve than vice versa which is what happened to the POWs in the Philippines." Over time, support troops were sent to the area and a laundry unit was sent from the United States.

After a few months, the hospital started getting Chinese patients so the hospital was divided into two sections, one for Americans and one for the Chinese. "The Chinese were on a different menu than we were. Also, we didn't have nursing personnel on duty in their section during the night. Enlisted medical personnel took care of these patients. That fall, we started to get a few combat casualties because the engineers and the infantry troops were getting farther up the road. As they advanced deeper into the jungle, they encountered more resistance from the Japanese.

"When I first arrived in mid-March, we had about 125 patients. A year later, we had well over a thousand. At two years, I think we had a little over two thousand patients at one point. Each ward was a separate bamboo building with about thirty to thirty-five patients in each structure."

Jungle warfare created difficult situations for the nurses. "We got patients with 'dirty wounds' because they had occurred either in accidents or in combat in the jungle and were well contaminated," she says. "For these patients, we adapted some IV bottles and tubing into a drainage system to drain their wounds. There were also some very ill patients with a disease caused by a jungle mite called 'mite-typhus fever' because it resembled typhus. As a matter of fact, if a soldier of about eighteen to twenty years old caught it, he might become very ill, but chances were he would recover. If a soldier of about thirty to thirty-two caught it, his chances of recovery were much less. Nothing seemed to help but to treat the symptoms."

The increased number of patients necessitated the construction of new buildings in addition to the five original ones. "What they would do when we needed another ward," Marion says, "was clear the ground and natives would sit down and split the bamboo and weave matting that became the walls. Then they cut down palms and they became the roofs. It was no trouble to have a ward erected in less than twenty-four hours. Later on, we got more sophisticated. They poured a slab of concrete for the floor, but that came much later. Before then, we got corrugated tin roofs because the palm leaves dried and wouldn't be sufficient. Tin roofs became the fashion of the day."

The nurses were also housed in these bamboo dwellings. "Our quarters were similar to the hospital. About twenty-eight to thirty of us were in one building. We slept on a type of Indian bed called a charpoy that had four posts, the outline of a bed, made of some kind of wood, and then the Indian hemp was woven for the springs."

While the army constructed the Ledo Road, pilots flying C-47s, C-46s, and C-54s flew supplies over the treacherous Himalayas into western China. "It was difficult for them because these were the days before planes were pressurized and also before pilots had much in the way of oxygen. They had to go so high they often got into sticky situations. We sometimes had patients come in from plane accidents, but more often than not, if they had an accident high in the Himalayas, they were not recovered in time."

Marion stayed at this location until the summer of 1945. Of her experience and service she says, "The university had sent a unit, the 20th Base Unit, to France during World War I. We thought we had a very good standard of medical care. The surgeons really had a good basic foundation in medicine and surgical care, and the medical people correspondingly.

"We were proud of the medical care and surgical nursing care we

*Col. Marion K. Kennedy at retirement.*
*Photograph courtesy of Marion K. Kennedy*

gave," she continues. "Because we knew what the protocols were, we followed through with taking care of those patients much as we had done in civilian life. By the time we left, we'd gotten some very good equipment considering it was World War II and we were about as close to the end of the supply line as you can get."

Discharged from the army in the fall of 1945, Marion reentered in August 1953, toward the end of the Korean conflict. She was assigned as an instructor to an enlisted specialist program at Walter Reed Army Hospital in Washington, D.C. Afterward, she went to Germany for two years, then returned to Fort Sam Houston in San Antonio, Texas. For a time she worked for the Department of the Army in Washington recruiting personnel, then returned to Fort Sam Houston for several years until she retired at the rank of colonel.

# 10

## PATRICIA "PAT" D. COSTELLO HUTCHINSON

### (JANUARY 8, 1919–JULY 20, 2002)

*Women's Army Corps (WAC), Southwest Pacific Theater of Operations, Brisbane, Australia; New Guinea; Leyte and Manila, Philippine Islands*

"Your conscience just catches up with you—I felt that there was something I had to do."

*Author's note: Sadly, after we had two brief conversations, Pat Hutchinson passed away on July 20, 2002. During the war she wrote many letters to her sister, Eleanor, who kept them along with WAC newsletters and news clippings. The letters are a remarkable record of Pat's experience as a WAC in the Southwest Pacific Theater of Operations. Pat's story is told through excerpts of these letters. I express my appreciation to Pat's husband, Dayton Hutchinson; daughter, Gail Tausch; and son, James Hutchinson, for generously making these available.*

From the deck of the *West Point*, Pat Costello looked excitedly over the ocean and inhaled the salt air. The warm sunshine on her face was almost intoxicating. She remembered the ocean voyage she took with her family as a child. Seeking a climate more conducive to her father's health, they sailed from New York State to the Port of Houston. From there, they traveled inland headed for Arizona but only made it as far as Uvalde, Texas.

This journey on the Pacific was calmer and warmer than she remembered the Atlantic being. Life had been exciting since she joined the Women's Army Corps. Now she was on her most thrilling adventure yet, overseas duty. She wondered what lay ahead for her in Australia when the

*WAC Patricia Costello.*
*Photograph courtesy of Gail Tausch*

roar of the ship's engine suddenly stilled. After moving forward for a few minutes from momentum, the boat stopped.

Pat hurried back to her cramped cabin. *Is this it? Will we be torpedoed or will we escape unharmed?* Japanese submarines had been spotted in the area, and all the Americans could do was drop anchor and wait—without a sound, in the dark, for who knows how long—wondering if they would be attacked.

After drifting in the ocean for three days, the captain determined that they were not in danger at the moment, and they proceeded on their journey. Stopping in the middle of the ocean would happen two more times before they reached their destination, Brisbane, Australia.

Patricia Costello had been assigned to the Southwest Pacific Theater of Operations (SWPTO) to replace civilian workers employed by the American government there. Having narrowly escaped from the Philippines two years earlier, Gen. Douglas MacArthur, army commander of the forces in the SWPTO, was making good on his promise to return. Fighting had started in New Guinea, so he moved his command closer to the area to divide his time between Brisbane and Moresby, New Guinea.

The government of Australia forbade its women to move forward with the troops, necessitating WACs be assigned to this area. Officially, Pat was with the United States Armed Forces in the Far East, USAFFE. She first served as secretary to the general purchasing agent for general headquarters in Brisbane, in Hollandia, Netherlands, New Guinea, and in Leyte, Philippine Islands. While in Leyte, she was reassigned to the Enemy Property Custodian Office.

This EPC's mission was to take custody of enemy property confiscated by the Japanese and dispose of the property in the best interests of the war. Pat developed all office procedures and records to fulfill this mission. Duties included administration of properties such as plantations and manufacturing companies, as well as small businesses such as bakeries. "From just two of us in the office in the beginning," she says, "there were several hundred by the end of the war." For excellence in performing her duties, Pat was recommended to receive the Bronze Star.

In what was known to be a difficult theater of war, Pat endured the heat and humidity, monsoon rains, mud, and mosquitoes associated with the tropics. Often, there was inadequate food, clothing, and water. Many times she retreated to foxholes when the Japanese bombed the area.

After her childhood in Uvalde, Pat attended Sul Ross State College in Alpine, Texas, and the University of Southern California, Los Angeles. She enlisted in the Women's Army Auxiliary Corps on March 19, 1943, as a second lieutenant. When asked why she joined, she responds, "Your conscience just catches up with you. I felt there was something I had to do." The WAAC were to work with, but weren't a part of, the regular army. "Not long after I joined," Pat says, "Congress passed a law that made us a part of the army. This made us eligible to go overseas." Passed in September 1943, with this law the organization became known as the Women's Army Corps, WAC.

Basic training was at the Fifth Camp Training Center at Camp Polk, a former prisoner of war enclosure near Ruston, Louisiana. At that time, the Americans had taken few prisoners and it was one of the few training centers available for the women. After completing basic training, Pat was stationed at Fort Riley, Kansas, as personnel clerk and secretary to the director of military personnel. She spent several months in early 1944 recruiting in Wichita, Kansas.

Pat applied and was accepted for overseas duty. She reported to Fort Oglethorpe, Georgia, for training in August 1944. Once training was completed, Pat waited. "We weren't told whether we were going to the European or Pacific theater. We didn't know until the day before we left which we were going to."

Early in September 1944, Pat reported to Camp Stoneman, near San

Francisco, point of embarkation to the SWPTO, with Brisbane, Australia, the first stop. "There were times we had to drop anchor in the middle of the ocean and just wait because submarines had been sighted. No lights. No noise. I guess at age twenty-three, I thought it was adventurous. Thank goodness for youth." She worked for the adjutant general while on the ship. After a few brief stops in New Guinea along the way, Pat arrived in Brisbane where she worked as secretary for the general purchasing agent for general headquarters. From Brisbane, she writes her first letter home.

Brisbane, Australia
October 31, 1944

Dearest Eleanor,

I have just been here about a week, but I like the job I was assigned to very much and the camp we live in is very nice. We live six to a tent-like hut, have a large shower, laundry room with irons and washing machines, a sewing-room with three machines, an open-air theater, and just about anything else you could ask for.

. . . Please write me soon. The army places mail next to food as a morale factor, but I place it ahead of food. . . .

> All My Love,
> Pat

From Brisbane, Pat flew to Tacloban, on the island of Leyte, in the Philippines. In October, General MacArthur had launched an attack on the Japanese there and established troops. Pat was among the first group of approximately sixty WACs to arrive at the island.

Somewhere in the Philippines [Leyte]
2 December 1944

Dearest Eleanor,

Was this one of the places you imagined me to be! Well, I have been here several days now—was one of the first small group to arrive here. I was in New Guinea for about two weeks before coming here, as I flew down there from Brisbane (I think I last wrote you from there). Then my job moved up here and I, of course, moved with it. It was really an experience! We flew up here and when we got off the plane, a newsreel man started taking pictures of us. We rode to our quarters in a truck and he followed on the bumper of a car, taking pictures along the way. The soldiers and Filipinos cheered us as we went by. Some of these soldiers had never seen WACs and could hardly believe their eyes.

Well, this place is pretty rough, but I like it because I like my work so much and feel as if I am really "in the war." This is the rainy season and it pours three or four times a day. They have no pavement or sidewalks, so you walk in the streets which are knee-deep in mud the consistency of chocolate pudding. Every once in a while, you fall in a hole and almost disappear from sight.

It's also very hot here in more ways than one. The Japs take great pleasure in chasing us out to our foxholes two or three times a night (by bombing), so our sleep is pretty fitful. In fact, to get enough rest, you have to go to bed very early. It really isn't as dangerous as it sounds, though. Most of the danger is from flak which we can escape by taking to our foxholes. Besides, it's a great show to watch the fireworks.

We had water tonight for the first time in two days and I really enjoyed my shower and shampoo. It really improves my morale to get cleaned up after walking through this mud all day. You really learn to appreciate the little things in life over here. We live in a former Catholic Institute and there is a beautiful chapel right next door, so don't worry about me. Thank you for your prayers. Everyone over here does plenty of that. . . . If you get this before the holidays, a Merry Christmas to you all.

Marjorie Dubose (a friend from Alice, Texas) is right here with me, and that makes everything just about perfect.

I Love You,
Pat

In a 1994 interview for New Braunfels's *Herald-Zeitung,* Pat says, "We arrived in Leyte just 36 days after the combat landing of MacArthur and his troops. There were approximately sixty of us in the first group of WACs, and after we arrived, fighting got so hot that MacArthur doubted the wisdom of bringing women forward that soon and stopped all further movement for a time."

Leyte, Philippine Islands
8 December 1944

Dearest Eleanor,

This is to ask you if you haven't already done so, don't send my letter to Mother or mention such things to her. Please don't ever get too optimistic about the war being over soon—it would take a miracle for that to happen.

We still walk around up to our ankles in mud, but I am sort of getting used to it and don't mind so much. It rains every day and the other day we had a regular flood. Marjorie fell in a ditch and almost drowned. One day, I got bogged down in the mud and couldn't move either foot. What a terrible feeling! A fellow had to come along and pull me out with all his strength. Of course, Marjorie and I were having such hysterics that we never would have gotten out.

> All My Love,
> Pat

About this time, Pat writes a letter for the War Department, by request of the Public Relations Office, concerning her assignment in the Philippines. Following the letter for the War Department, she writes a letter to Eleanor relating some of the same information, but her wording is not so guarded.

Sgt. Dorothy P. Costello
A-807647
5205 WAC Det, GHQ (Atchd)
Home town: Uvalde, Texas

Hear I am in the "Pearl of the Pacific," the Philippine Islands, although at the present time you would have to dig deep in mud to find anything resembling a pearl. I was in the first group of WACs to enter the Philippines and it was a wonderful experience and one I will never forget. We flew down from New Guinea and arrived here around noon. The GIs, some of whom had never seen a WAC before, gave us a royal welcome, even stopping their trucks along the road to get a good look at "an American girl." Before we had gone very far in our drive from the airstrip to our quarters, one of the fellows in the truck told us to put our helmets on. Thinking of our "coiffures," we laughingly refused, so the second time he told us he made it an order. About that time we heard three shots, the signal for an air alert with which we have become so familiar, then a lot of what we at first thought was thunder and then realized was ack-ack. In all this confusion it started to rain and by the time we had our raincoats on the excitement was over. The people all along the road ran out of the Nipa huts to wave a welcome to us. All of the small children would hold up their fingers forming a "V" and shout, "Mahboohay," or something like that, which evidently means "Victory." We finally arrived at our quarters which are an old Catholic Institute converted into a barracks. There is a statue of the Holy Mother in front and a small chapel next door which always give me a feeling of safety during an alert. We are very comfortable and it is very nice to live in a building with a roof over your head instead of a tent top. We also have a shower house and a place to do our washing. For the most part though we send our laundry to the Filipinos, as we don't have much time for anything outside the office. We eat three meals a day at the enlisted men's mess and wade through the mud for about four blocks each meal to stand in a long weaving line (always reminds me of the snake dances at football games) with our mess kits in hand waiting for our portion of bully beef or Spam, depending on which day it is. The food really isn't too bad though, considering the amount of people they have to feed and the always present problem of supply in this theater.

The Filipinos are very gracious people and I have been to several "Filamerican" parties and also to a party given by a Filipino doctor and his wife. They are, of course, very glad to see the Americans and can't do enough for you. Our quarters are always infested with small, barefooted boys who will clean your shoes—a dreaded job to us—for a bar of candy or a stick of gum. The GIs here have also been wonderful to us—a welcome change from the ridicule and the resentment felt in the States—and every evening some organization has a dance or dinner for us. Sometimes fellows will walk four or five blocks out of their way just to talk to a girl from back home. When that happens I always get a lump in my throat. Of course Marjorie and I being from Texas are always on the lookout for a fellow Texan and we have found a number of them.

We couldn't imagine what Christmas would be like with rain and mud and heat in our thoughts in place of ice and snow and sleet, but considering the fact that we are so far from home, we had a very enjoyable time. Christmas morning we had a party for about two hundred Filipino children. There was a Santa Claus, a magician, a tree and stockings filled with candy and gum, and a toy for each child. When the children saw Santa Claus, they started shouting "Mickey Mouse," and nothing we could do or say would change their identification, so you can see what an influence Walt Disney is to them over here. They simply stormed the tree, Santa Claus, and a number of the girls who were distributing the toys. That night we had a dance and also had a dance on New Year's Eve. For the first time since we came overseas we were allowed to wear skirts and shirts or off-duty dresses (the lucky few who had them), and we got a big kick out of getting acquainted with our legs all over again. We went caroling Christmas Eve and while we were out got caught in a raid and couldn't find a foxhole to dive in, so we stood on a porch and watched the show, and it was quite a show! It is the first Christmas that we haven't had to buy our own fireworks. This year the Japs furnished them for us but we gave them a sample of ours, too.

I have left my job until the last because it is of the greatest importance. It is just the sort of thing I have always wanted in the Army and I can't believe my good luck in getting it here. It is certainly worth coming half way across the world for. I am a secretary to a Colonel who is very pleasant to work for and the work we do in our office is very interesting. It gives you a feeling of satisfaction to know that your presence here is warranted in a small way at least.

Must close as I owe lots of letters and since they are the most important thing in one's life there, I must get some of them answered.

All My Love,
Pat

3 January 1945
Leyte, Philippine Islands

Dearest Eleanor,

[I] am sitting here with four of your letters in front of me—the last one dated December 12th. Thank you for writing so often. I know you are busy, and I certainly enjoy your letters. Thinking about the Christmas holiday in the Philippines, I have a lot of things to be thankful for and I realize it more every day.

Christmas morning, we gave a party for 200 Filipino children. We had a tree, burlap stockings with candy, gum, etc., a magician and a Santa Claus. When the children saw him, they yelled "Mickey Mouse!" and we couldn't talk them out of it.

Christmas Eve, we decorated and had carols, and there was a fifteen minute radio broadcast to the United States on a national hookup. We sang on the back porch. When they bombed, we didn't go to the foxholes. We just stood there and watched the bombing like idiots, I guess. About that time, one of our fighters shot down a Jap bomber. We couldn't help be glad, because that bomber was trying to kill us.

Christmas night, we had a dance and since it was Christmas, we were allowed to wear skirts. It was the first time we have been out of trousers. . . . We kept looking down at our legs as if they were strangers. We had a grand time—a G.I. orchestra, Coca-cola (with flavoring) and cake. . . . You can imagine the rush this group of WACs got. Some of these fellows have never seen WACs before. They are certainly grand to us over here.

Haven't had much sleep for the past two nights. The Japs seem to be starting the new year off with a bang. Then too, there is a full moon which always means trouble. You get to where you hate moonlight here. The other night, besides a couple of alerts, we had a slight earthquake. Anything to make life more exciting!

It' still very hot here, but the rainy season is slackening—thank goodness. Now we just go ankle-deep in mud. . . . I'm still enjoying my work very much. It is a wonderful change to have an interesting job. I'm in the Enemy Property Custodian Office.

> All My Love
> Pat

On January 2, 1945, General MacArthur's army forces landed on the island of Luzon, Philippines, on which Manila, the capital, is located. By February, American forces had recaptured the city and he set up headquarters. On February 4, troops liberated Santo Tomas Internment Camp. Some of the former prisoners were taken to Leyte for recuperation.

Leyte, P.I.
31 January 1945

Dearest Eleanor,

Haven't had any mail to speak of for over two weeks and haven't written many letters. I would like to request some things, but I have just received one Christmas package so far. . . . There are several things you could enclose in a letter, such as a flat package of aspirin or vitamins (these I really need—all I can get), a small flat bottle opener (occasionally we get a beer ration).

. . . I got some Mexican food that Ruby sent me. Marjorie and I heated it in our mess kits over a candle! You'd be surprised how hot it got. It was wonderful. . . .

A fellow told me he saw me in a newsreel one night. We were getting off the plane and into a truck. Hope you get to see it.

The war certainly looks good in this theater. The Luzon invasion has been so successful it almost scares me. Of course, we have visions of going into Manila before too long. Maybe after the Japs are run out of the Philippines, the rest of the war won't take too long. . . . The Japs have been too busy elsewhere to bother us much lately—thank goodness!

I Love You,
Pat

Leyte, P.I.
25 February 1945

Dearest Eleanor,

We have been busy and it is so hot, you are tired out by the time you get home and rush out to get a shower (four times out of ten, there is water). . . . The rainy season is just about over—so now we complain about the terrible dust, and pray for a shower.

I received your Christmas package that week. I am crazy about

the beautiful slip. You have no idea what it did to my morale. . . .
When I get to Manila—soon I hope—it will be just the thing to
wear with my off-duty dress. We are supposed to get some up
there. I got a Christmas package from Mother, Ruth and Alice.
. . . They sent a lot of cosmetics, bedroom slippers, a book, cake,
and Mexican candy, and such wonderful things as cold cream and
Milk of Magnesia tablets (those are some of the nicest Christmas
presents I've ever had!).

I have talked to several boys who were POWs in Manila for
three years. They are in a replacement camp here, where they
outfit them, feed them wonderfully, let them rest, drink iced beer,
meet WACs, and in general, learn to live all over again. Of course,
they are sending them home as fast as they can. In the meantime,
MacArthur says, "Give them anything they want!"

Some of their stories aren't very pretty, and the scars of those
three years will probably always be in their hearts as well as their
bodies. They were, in general, like a bunch of kids at circus while
up here, or maybe more like someone who has been deaf and
dumb for three years and suddenly comes out of it.

I read a letter by a boy who went up to Luzon in the invasion.
. . . He was present at the liberation of Santo Tomas prisoners and
his letter made you weep unashamedly. I think the greatest tragedy of all was the people who were killed in the fight, just as they
had been liberated. They were so sure we would return. In fact,
the boys said they used to lay bets on when it would be.

The fellow who wrote the letter said that as they neared the
prison, they saw a gray-haired, middle-aged woman, unmistak-
ably American, inside the enclosure. She was running up and
down, grabbing the fence and peering out, yelling excitedly,
"They are coming! They are coming!" Can you imagine her feelings?

Our bombings have ceased. Guess they are too busy elsewhere.
I am very anxious to move on. I've been here three months
tomorrow. Marjorie has moved to a camp about eighteen miles
away, as she is with a different organization. She has been gone
almost a month and I've seen her only once. It is hard to get
around here. When we move again, I hope we'll be together.

I Love You,
Pat

From Leyte, Pat's group moved to Manila. In an August 1995 interview for New Braunfels's *Herald-Zeitung*, she describes her arrival. "We were put on trucks and trucked through the city," she says. "Homes had been shelled and whole families had been taken outside and shot in cold blood—old people, little babies, everyone."

Pat stayed in a Catholic college, the de la Salle College for boys, while she was in Manila. "We were told to stay away from a certain section of the college. Being women we were going to go in the other part to see why we couldn't go there. Walking down a curved staircase, I came upon a Filipino woman and a baby—they had been bayoneted through." There were many bodies of dead Filipinos that had not been taken from the college before their arrival.

Manila, P.I.
6 April 1945

Dearest Eleanor,

Haven't had but one letter in the past sixteen days, so you can imagine the state of my morale. Besides that, I haven't received about five Christmas packages and have lost my barracks bag with my tropical worsteds and new shoes and a lot of personal stuff in it. . . . I shipped it from Brisbane in November and haven't seen it since.

I would give ten million dollars to be able to walk in home right now and find all of you there. Well, the war news looks so good now, that for the first time in two years, going home holds a little reality instead of just being a dream to live on. By the time you get this, maybe the European war will be over. . . . Oh God! If it would only end all over the world by at least Christmas!

There is a new regulation that WACs can go home if their husbands are in the States or are returning from overseas. Too bad I didn't get married. . . .

One of the presidents of a Philippine province told his people, "Liberty is like a house—if you are careless and improvident, it is soon mortgaged and lost." Nothing comes free. Certainly not freedom, and we are learning that the hard way.

Easter Sunday, we had . . . high mass. A memorial service was held for the dead comrades of this particular infantry outfit and they blew taps. This outfit has been over here three years, so you can imagine their buddies who have died. The sermon was given by a priest who was bayoneted twice at the time seventy people were murdered there, and it is a sermon none of us will ever forget. He was thrown at the bottom of a heap of dead bodies, and it took him ten hours to extricate himself and crawl upstairs . . . ten survivors . . . hid behind the altar for four days until the Americans came.

I sat there and thought of all that happening right there less that two months before and thanked God for being so good to us and keeping everyone at home, safe from such horror.

[Running short of personal items, Pat then asks her family for hose, a housecoat, and powder.]

> I Love You,
> Pat

Manila, P.I.
27 May 45

Dearest Eleanor,

Have been working like a true Trojan lately, and am kind of worn out. Would like to take my points (49) and go home, but am afraid to get too much hope up. . . . When I get home, I'll have the WAAC ribbon, Good Conduct ribbon, Southwest Pacific ribbon with three battle stars (one for each combat area I have been in), the Philippine Liberation Ribbon, and I think a citation for our headquarters. Just watch my smoke!

Did I tell you I went out boating and went aboard some Japanese half-sunk vessels out in the harbor? Had a wonderful time. Am going again next Sunday if it doesn't rain.

> I Love You,
> Pat

Manila, P.I.
23 June 45

Dearest Eleanor,

[The same detachment, USAFFE, becomes AFPAC, Army Forces in the Pacific.]

This has been my bad luck month. First, I sprained my right thumb, then I got heat rash everywhere except my face, and almost got infected, then my office got transferred to another headquarters and I will soon have to leave all my friends. . . .

Everyone has had a touch of war nerves here lately. We got all worked up over the point system. They called us in three times to ask us "yes" or "no." We signed and initialed things, but nothing has happened. The program was to start in June. . . . Just wish I could get home for Christmas! Wouldn't it be nice to all spend Christmas together again? It doesn't seem possible that it is almost two years since I last saw all of you.

Our food has been pretty rotten lately, but is improving now. I lost seven lbs this month, but don't tell Mother that. I feel fine though, so don't worry about me. I think it was the hot weather as much as anything.

Well, darling, must close as I have things to do as usual. We have water indoors (usually) now, and taking a shower in a smoke-stained shower stall is a real luxury. . . .

> I Love You,
> Pat

On August 6, 1945, the atomic bomb was dropped on Hiroshima. Japan surrendered August 15.

Manila, P.I.
26 Aug 45

Dearest Eleanor,

As you can imagine, things have really been chaotic around here lately. The best news I've had is that all WACs with 44 points or over will be sent home in September, so I will probably get home sometime in October—as a civilian, I hope! "When I get home." Everything now begins with those words. When the war was still dark-looking, no one ever mentioned going home because they couldn't let themselves think about it. Now that it is almost a reality, it's all we ever talk or dream. . . .

I know I've probably changed, Eleanor. I look bad now as I was sick for awhile and lost a lot of weight (don't tell Mother this!). I've started on the upgrade though, and just knowing I'm

*Patricia Costello in 1947.*
*Photograph courtesy of Gail Tausch*

going home soon makes me feel better. One thing wrong with me is that I'm dead tired—physically and mentally.

Things were comparatively quiet here when the war finally ended, although I know I'll never forget it. We had three false alarms and by the time it was official, everyone had spent so much emotion they were worn out and I still can hardly believe it, even when I saw the crowd, the photographers, the M.P.s, etc at the City Hall when the Japanese envoys arrived. . . . Everyone here is talking about going to Tokyo. None of that for me, thank goodness.

All My Love,
Pat


Manila, P.I.
20 Sept 45

Dearest Eleanor,

In a week, I move out to the Women's Disposition Center, a terrible place about seven miles from Manila, where I will be "processed"—records checked, clothing checked, etc. Then I will sit out there and wait for transportation, am going by boat, and no one seems to have any idea how long we'll have to wait. You can imagine the transportation problem here!

If I have to wait too long, however, I'm going to write a nasty letter to my Congressman and ask him to explain why it is that thousands of American are waiting here while the *Lurline* took 750 Australian wives to the States last month. The stock answer to that is they've been waiting eighteen months. Personally, I don't give a damn if they have to wait thirty years. I think every military person has a right to return home before the taxpayers of the U.S. foot the bill for Australian wives' passage. I've been waiting for two and one-half years to go home—one year of it in the tropics while they have been waiting eighteen months with their own families in their own homes. . . . I don't mind waiting months while internees and combat men go home, but I don't want to wait *one minute* for an Aussie to leave before me.

Anyway, looks like if I'm at all lucky, I'll be home sometime in November.

All My Love,
Pat

*Pat Costello Hutchinson with sister Eleanor in 1995.*
*Photograph courtesy of Gail Tausch*

On November 1, 1945, Pat received her long awaited discharge (honorable) at Fort Sam Houston, Texas. In the 1994 interview, Pat says, "I contracted infectious hepatitis and was hospitalized in Santo Tomas Prison hospital so was not a pretty sight on discharge in the States."

After a few months' recuperation, Pat went to Washington, D.C., where she had a civil service position at the Pentagon. In February 1948, she traveled to Berlin, Germany, and worked at the office of the Consulate General until August 1949. Afterward, she returned to Uvalde. She was working at a bank when she and Dayton Hutchinson married in 1951. They lived in Uvalde until 1963 when they moved to New Braunfels. In New Braunfels, Mr. Hutchinson had a feed and seed business while Pat worked at various positions in town.

# 11

# DOROTHY DAVIS THOMPSON

*Army Nurse Corps, Philippine Islands*

"They had no plans for what to do with us but to lock us up."

The huge tires on the 2.5-ton truck crunched on the gravel as it slowed, then halted. Against orders, Dorothy removed her heavy metal helmet. It was February 9, 1945, yet streams of perspiration ran into her eyes. The sweat-soaked bush jacket and men's trousers she wore clung to her body. The official orders had read, "unknown destination," but Dorothy recognized her surroundings. Her convoy was approaching Santo Tomas Internment Camp near Manila in the Philippines.

*What has happened in the sixteen months since I left? Are Father and Eva still alive?* The road back to the camp had taken sixteen months, but in a matter of hours, Dorothy would learn the fate of her father, sister, and friends, if the armed escort made it through enemy lines. The boom of the howitzers clearing the way for them brought Dorothy to her senses. She replaced her helmet, fastened the chinstrap, and braced herself. The truck engine roared, and they started rolling along the road pocked from previous shellings.

Formerly a university, the Japanese converted the sixty-acre walled facility of Santo Tomas into an internment/prisoner of war camp for foreign nationals when they seized control of Manila. Dorothy tells her story in an even voice as if narrating a documentary, often in present tense. Indeed, hers is a story worthy of a documentary.

Specific incidences stand out more vividly than others. At times, she laughs softly, amused at the irony of a particular situation. For nearly two years, Dorothy was also a POW in Santo Tomas Internment Camp, STIC. Interned with her mother, father, and sister, Dorothy was repatriated

*2nd Lt Dorothy Davis*

because of health concerns. Her mother was allowed to accompany her back to the United States. Sixteen months later, Dorothy returned as a member of the Army Nurse Corps sent to assist in the liberation of Americans, including her sister and father, from the prison.

Dorothy was born in China to an American businessman and his wife. While growing up, her family visited the United States infrequently. Dorothy attended Shanghai American School from kindergarten through twelfth grade. The school was developed by missionaries and business people to educate Americans in China. Upon graduation from the school, Dorothy decided to attend college in the states.

Intrigued by the experiences of an aunt who served in World War I as a Red Cross nurse, Dorothy decided to study nursing. Her aunt had served in France with the British Expeditionary Unit from Presbyterian Hospital,

New York. "The stories my aunt told me were exciting and I thought they were pretty neat," she says. Accepted to Columbia University in New York City, Dorothy left Shanghai in April 1937 aboard a freighter destined for New York.

Later that year, the Japanese bombed and overran Shanghai, then blockaded the city for six months. "My father couldn't send me money or letters," she says. "It was quite traumatic. I didn't know if they were even alive for weeks, but my father had many business connections and was able to get a cable out telling me and my sister that he and Mother were okay."

Her sister, Eva, already in New York, greeted her when she docked. "At least I had someone to meet me," Dorothy say, "but she wasn't allowed to help me come through customs. I was really afraid of that. I'd heard a lot of weird stories that they would make me pay tariffs for things purchased in China. Everything I had was made in China. I didn't have any money and didn't know what I was going to do if they made me pay tariffs."

Eventually, Dorothy's family moved to Manila in the Philippines. A manufacturer's representative for electrical appliances and wiring devices, her father's territory had covered that part of the world. Dorothy joined them after graduation, arriving in December, one year before the Japanese bombed Pearl Harbor.

Dorothy took and passed the exams to be licensed in the Philippines but never worked in a Filipino hospital. Instead, she worked at Sternberg General Hospital as a nurse with the civil service. A U.S. Army facility, Sternberg had wooden barracks and was a 450-bed hospital built in a quadrangle located on the south side of Manila. Immediately, she filled out the necessary documents and took the physical to join the Army Nurse Corps. While she awaited word of her acceptance, Dorothy worked with corps nurses performing the same duties.

Suspecting an attack, dependents of army personnel had been sent home. However, business people and their families stayed. "My father was solely on his own," Dorothy explains. "He had no big company he could go back to and work for. He had to take care of himself."

On Sunday, December 7, 1941, the day Pearl Harbor was attacked, it was already one o'clock in the morning, December 8, in Manila. Dorothy and the nurses heard practically nothing. On Sunday, she and her fiancé, Donald Childers, had gone on a picnic with Dorothy's friend, army nurse Phyllis Arnold, and Phyllis's fiancé. Both men were in the army and had commands in the Philippine Scouts. "The boys didn't say anything, but they did know something was going on I'm sure," she recalls. "They took us home that evening. I never saw Donald again." Her friend, Phyllis, did see her fiancé again. "They were married on Bataan, but he, like Donald, didn't make it through the war.

"The Japanese bombed Manila about one o'clock in the morning," Dorothy continues. "Japanese planes came in by what seemed like the hundreds and hit their targets—Cavite, then Nichols Field—without losing a single plane. The planes at Nichols Field were destroyed. Clark Field was also bombed, leaving the U.S. Air Force powerless and unable to defend the city. We lived about a mile from Nichols Field, so we took shelter. The only shelter we had was the basement. There was no such thing as bomb shelters." Although she hadn't received official notification of acceptance into the Army Nurse Corps, Dorothy immediately headed for the hospital at daylight. "I knew that things would really begin to happen."

The next three weeks were a nightmare. Dorothy was on night duty. Beds were made available to civilian nurses who didn't live in the nurses' dormitory, but sleep was nearly impossible. No one got much rest.

After bombing the islands, the Japanese invaded Manila on December 10, 1941. Three weeks later, on December 22, Gen. Douglas MacArthur declared it an open city. Dorothy explains, "When an open city is declared, all military troops must move out. The Japanese wanted to save the city so they could make it the headquarters for their armed forces. The United States didn't want to harm the Philippine civilians living in the city. The hospital was full as were several other buildings in the city that had been taken over for the wounded. Army nurses and other hospital personnel were needed in Bataan and Corregidor, where American troops had retreated, to set up Field Hospitals. The war continued on Bataan and Corregidor.

"Because I was a civil service nurse," Dorothy continues, "I was chosen to stay with the patients they could not move. The patients were really antsy, as you can well imagine, because they were military and they knew the law." The Japanese, if they chose, would even shoot wounded soldiers. Dorothy was the only American nurse left at the hospital. "I really felt deserted," she says. She also had to disarm soldiers that were admitted, then unload and hide any weapons they had. "I hadn't been given any instructions in weapons," she laughs. "I knew how to unload a 45 mm but was not familiar with other weapons. I can still see myself standing there looking at this thing with it pointed to the floor, wondering what I should pull to get the magazine out. Anyway, I didn't shoot myself or anybody else."

On New Year's Eve, 1941, three officers returned with orders to triage and evacuate the remaining patients on three interisland boats. Those able to resume duty within two weeks were to go to Bataan; those who would take longer to recover were to go to Corregidor to a hospital located in the Malinta Tunnel system. The third group, those not returning to duty, was to board the *Mactan*, but their destination was unknown.

Dorothy describes the situation, "When the trucks bearing the patients arrived on the dock, the whole dock was on fire," she says. "The warehouses where army equipment was stored were being burned, so the Japanese couldn't use U.S. equipment. The boats tied to the docks were endangered by the fire. The men responsible for the patients didn't have time to sort the patients and put them on assigned boats. All the boats got away, one to Bataan, the second to Corregidor, and the third, the *Mactan*, found its way to a safe place where the patients could be cared for. Three months later, the boat arrived safely in Australia."

Dorothy was left at the hospital, the only American nurse. "Again, I felt deserted," she says. "One thing that really stands out in my mind is that they had told me I must stay until morning in case someone needed help, then I could go home." As daylight neared, Dorothy went to the balcony as she had done each morning during the long hours of night duty from December 8 to December 31. She looked forward to the few minutes of solitude before reveille, the sounding of the bugle to start the day. The American flag was raised while "The Star-Spangled Banner" vibrated through the air. "I stood there waiting for the music," she says. "I knew it wasn't going to come, but I kept thinking, somehow, it would and maybe there would be a flag. But there was no flag and there was no music. It really hit me." Manila was no longer under the control of the United States. The island of Luzon and other islands would soon fall to the Japanese.

There was no one around when Dorothy started her walk home to join her family who had not seen her since December 8. During this time, Dorothy knew nothing about the fate of her family, and they knew nothing about her. "They had no idea where I was or what I was doing because we had no way of communicating. When I finally got there," she laughs, "I must have looked like the wrath of God because I hadn't got any sleep since the first bomb fell. They were pretty happy to see me, and I was so relieved to see them that I was finally able to sleep."

Aware the Japanese were on the march, Dorothy's mother had stockpiled canned goods and other things. "We didn't know whether we would be allowed to use them or anything else, but this was something to do, so they were doing it."

The Davises heard little of what was happening for two days after Dorothy arrived back home. The Japanese didn't bother them until January 4, 1942. They went to every residence of Americans and other aliens. "They gave us thirty minutes to pack. They didn't tell us where we were going. They did tell us we only needed to take food and clothing for three days.

"They took us to Rizal Stadium to 'register' us," she continues. "Toward evening they brought trucks; we were loaded up and taken to Santo Tomas. It was almost dark by the time we got there. They obviously hadn't made any plans for what to do with us except lock us up." There was nothing in the buildings except for a few cot-like beds left by the Philippine Army. The family was assigned to three different buildings. Dorothy went alone. "We were assigned to rooms, but most of them didn't have beds. We hadn't taken bedding because they said 'food and clothing.' I slept on the concrete floor. It wasn't very comfortable, but we were pretty tired by then."

The family reunited the next day, and they were very hungry. "There was no place to heat any food or to cool it. So anything you opened but didn't eat right away, spoiled. Consequently, people started getting ill within twenty-four hours." As a nurse, Dorothy started looking for a place to set up a clinic and to look for doctors and other nurses. At that time, there were no military nurses in the camp.

In addition, the need for the internees to remain orderly became apparent the first night. "We were told that anyone caught trying to escape 'will be shot.' We had to develop a scheme to keep order among the people. Without that, we would really be putting ourselves in jeopardy."

A leadership emerged, a simple government developed, and a mayor was elected. The "officials" assessed what needed to be done and duties were assigned. Jobs assigned to internees were garbage collector, plumbers to build more showers (the camp had one shower and one toilet for each floor), plus other jobs. Within days, the camp also established a school for children and university classes for adults.

Dorothy's assignment didn't make her popular among the internees. "My job was to confiscate all the liquor anybody had brought in. They chose me to do it because they figured we would need a little 'medicinal spirits,'" Dorothy laughs. "I can still see myself standing at the sink just pouring bottles of liquor down the drain."

Despite the warnings and the efforts to maintain order, some tried to escape. "Three men tried to escape and were shot," Dorothy says. "Not too many people made attempts to get out of the camp."

All the while, Dorothy continued her search for a room suitable for a clinic. "We would find an empty room, clean and fix it, and scrounge around to find some furniture, then the Japanese would come around and say, 'Empty room. Ha! Twenty-five people, seventy people' and fill it up." Eventually, she found a building with two wings. Dorothy envisioned that one could be used for male patients, the other for female. The building had a bonus—a small room with a Bunsen burner. "Ah, we have a kitchen," she says.

After cleaning the room, a group was sitting outside the door talking. "I heard the clanking of their sabers," she said. "You always knew when they were coming. I knew they would take over the space we'd just cleaned." Dorothy thought fast and came up with an ingenious solution. "We have very sick patients," she told them, "extremely contagious. Venereal disease." The soldiers backed off and didn't return.

In addition to assigned duties, Dorothy remembers volunteers stepping forward for unlikely jobs. A former playboy offered to cook for the hospital. The proprietor of an exclusive men's clothing store carried patients with severe diarrhea to and from the one toilet and cleaned them if necessary. Others offered their assistance as aides in the hospital.

As an internee in the prisoner of war camp, Dorothy stayed busy with her nursing duties but remembers "there were always people around. No privacy." At full census, Santo Tomas, a sixty-acre walled campus, held nearly four thousand prisoners.

The Japanese also had not made many provisions to provide food for the internees. When a kitchen opened a few weeks later, they provided a watery gruel for breakfast at seven in the morning that was edible only when coarse sugar or coconut milk was available to put on it, but those soon disappeared. The last meal, a cup of diluted soup that might have a tiny bite of meat in it, was served at 4 o'clock p.m.

To supplement the meager portions the Japanese provided, the internees also cleared land and planted a vegetable garden. For a while, Filipino servants on the outside brought food to their employers and lowered it over the wall. A wealthy internee could obtain more food than others.

Early in her imprisonment, Dorothy had heard rumors of internees to be repatriated. Finally, the Japanese told doctors to choose four people who needed special treatment for life-threatening conditions. Dorothy's name was on the list.

Army nurses from Bataan and Corregidor had arrived in July, and once again Dorothy worked alongside army nurses, and they formed strong bonds. However, the workload at the hospital was heavy. "I was pushing myself pretty hard, not getting much sleep, and not eating very much. I finally got sick. The doctors thought I had bacterial endocarditis. At that time, there was no cure."

On September 26, 1943, twenty-one months after entering STIC, Dorothy, accompanied by her mother, boarded the *Teia Maru*, a former Japanese luxury ocean liner, on the first leg of her journey back to America.

Large rooms that had formerly housed social gatherings had been converted to accommodate repatriates who were not assigned to cabins. The room to which Dorothy was assigned held seventy-five repatriates. They slept on pallets on the floor. "I measured it so I know," she says. "They were only five foot eight (inches) long, I'm five feet nine, and twenty-three inches wide. The only way you could lie on the pallets and not get into somebody else's area was to lie on your back with your arms to your side. If you turned over, your feet would move over onto the next pallet. Everyone got pretty jealous about their space." They were allowed one small bag of belongings. "These were piled up on the sides of the rooms, so clothes didn't get changed. Nobody had a bath, and this trip was five weeks long."

For toilet facilities, the seventy-five women were told they had two commodes and two washbasins. "We thought we could maybe make that work, but then we were told that the water would only be turned on for thirty minutes in the morning and again for thirty minutes in the afternoon. Seventy-five women can't even get their teeth brushed in that length of time!" Dorothy had to contend with more than physical discomfort. "I had not wanted to leave Santo Tomas and my conscience was really bothering me."

October 18, after five weeks at sea, the *Teia Maru* docked in Mormugao, Portuguese India, near the Swedish ship, the *M. V. Gripsholm*, the ship that would take them back to the United States and freedom. Even though the Japanese ordered them not to, Dorothy watched the workers pile fancy leather luggage and other expensive belongings on the deck. She thought of her own small bag in the mountain of other bags, near the pallets lined up side-by-side, end-to-end, with no space in between. Dorothy remembers thinking, "are they going to be surprised because we're going from *bad* to *good,* and they are going from *good* to *bad.*" Possibly, the Japanese knew their prisoners had been treated better than they had treated the prisoners of Santo Tomas and didn't want the former prisoners to know.

Along with the twelve hundred Americans from various parts of the Southwest Pacific Theater of Operations to be repatriated were three hundred Canadians and Latin Americans. The exchange of prisoners took three days. Dorothy looked forward to the good food in adequate quantities she knew would be on the *Gripsholm.* She envisioned bathing well for the first time in months and changing clothes that were on the ship for that purpose.

However, Dorothy, an ill former prisoner of war who had just completed a five-week voyage without bathing, could not immediately board the ship. "Before we could board, we had to sign promissory notes for $575." The bill was issued by the Department of State, Washington, to pay for passage on the *Gripsholm* and repatriation. "We didn't have that kind of money, but they made us sign a note and, believe me, they collected every cent of it from me."

In addition to the promissory note, further surprises were in store. "We were all American citizens with passports, but before we could get into the United States, we had to fill out a questionnaire in which we had to write every address that we had ever lived at. We also had to give six references."

Upon docking in New York, after a journey that had taken months, the passengers were again detained. "Not one person was allowed off that ship until every single person was interviewed by the FBI, the army, and the navy. And believe me, they had called all six of the people I put down for references. They even knew the grades I had gotten while I was in nursing school!"

As she prepared to leave the ship, Dorothy was handed a telegram from Col. Florence Blanchfield, chief nurse for the Army Nurse Corps, telling her to report immediately. Penniless and with little clothing, Dorothy reported to Colonel Blanchfield who greeted Dorothy warmly and gave her some good news. "She told me that I'd been accepted into the army two years before. Then she handed me a copy of the cable and told me to go down to the finance office and get paid."

However, Dorothy's hopes were soon dashed. "I got to finance and the officer looked at it and told me, 'I'm sorry, I can't pay you. You never took the oath of office.' And that was it." Although upset for Dorothy and furious over the situation, Colonel Blanchfield could offer no assistance. Dorothy eventually got paid for the two years she worked as a civil service nurse, but she lost time for a promotion in the Army Nurse Corps.

In the weeks that followed, Dorothy reported to the Pentagon for debriefing. "I looked around the room, which was a very large room, and they were all generals. They had *no* information about what was going on in that area. They did not know if any of the army nurses were still alive. Fortunately, I had gotten all their names and addresses and had contacted their next of kin."

During this time, she received an interesting phone call. "It was about 11 o'clock in the morning, and Eleanor Roosevelt's secretary was on the line," Dorothy says. "She told me, 'Mrs. Roosevelt would like to have lunch with you today. Can you come at one o'clock?'" Dorothy faced one small problem. "I had one skirt that was respectable, and one blouse and a little jacket that were barely respectable, but I didn't have a hat. Back then, ladies never went out to lunch without a hat." Fortunately, Dorothy had an aunt and uncle who lived in New York. Without asking, Dorothy borrowed "an absolutely hideous hat" from her aunt and had lunch with the president's wife.

Mrs. Roosevelt had heard about Dorothy's plight and offered to ask the president to call for a special act of Congress to get her paid with rank. "An act of Congress!" Dorothy laughs. Dorothy graciously declined, saying she would just take the oath and get on with life.

At every opportunity, Dorothy asked for an assignment in the Philippines, hoping and praying she could help liberate STIC and her family. Finally, she received orders for the Philippines, but the exact location wasn't specified. "I found out later that orders had gone ahead of me to every place in the southwest Pacific. If a group was going to that area, I was to be included."

Dorothy boarded a ship in San Francisco that docked in Hollandia, New Guinea. Early one morning, while anchored in the harbor waiting for transportation on the next part of the journey, they heard a loud blast. Water poured in the porthole above Dorothy's bunk. The ship had been torpedoed. "Apparently it was from far out," she says. "Nobody really knew from where, but it damaged the ship."

There was a staging area for nurses, so they went ashore. While there, they received uniforms deemed more appropriate for the area, men's pants. Dorothy chose an Australian bush jacket instead of a shirt. The Signal Corps Company, having heard that forty nurses had arrived, decided that a party

*Dorothy Davis taking the oath*

was in order. The men spent the whole day putting a wood floor down in the mess hall so they could call their party a dinner dance. Dorothy and nine other nurses attended the dance in their new attire. Here, Dorothy met her future husband, Jack Thompson.

Eventually, a hospital ship came through bound for Tacloban, Leyte, an island southeast of Manila. The ship docked on February 3, 1945, the same day the U.S. Army burst through the gates of Santo Tomas. "They had apparently sent out an SOS for medical help," Dorothy says. "A medical clearing company, part of the First Calvary unit that fought their way into Santo Tomas, was trained to stabilize wounded soldiers, then evacuate them to a field hospital. None of the wounded or the internees could be evacuated. Only Santo Tomas was liberated; it was still surrounded by Japanese troops and the shelling continued. A clearing company only consists of a doctor and a few well-trained corpsmen. They were overwhelmed. The fighting was not over, plus they had four thousand internees in very poor health to take care of."

At Tacloban, Dorothy observed nurses preparing to leave. "I just intuitively knew they were going somewhere that was important to me," she says. "I was really angry that I had been too late to get on it." Dorothy went to bed that night, not bothering to unpack or get undressed. "I just stuffed my duffel bag under my cot and fumed all night long." At six o'clock the next morning, she went to the latrine. There she met the chief nurse. "She asked me 'How long will it take you to get ready to leave?'" to which Dorothy replied, "I'm already ready!" She had only fifteen minutes, but she was the first nurse to the plane. "She didn't tell me earlier because she was afraid I'd tell the other nurses what was going on."

Dorothy and the other nurses flew in C-47s to the island of Luzon. "We could look out the window and see ack-ack bursting underneath us all the way," she says. "You know, it didn't bother me a bit. I was so intent on what we were doing." There was no airstrip, and the Japanese still held Clark Field, so the pilot landed in a field next to a couple of tents for wounded soldiers waiting to be evacuated. The men assigned to care for the wounded did not expect company, but they were so glad to see some nurses. In a small amount of time, the men fed the nurses and put up a large tent for them. As the nurses were getting ready for bed, they observed soldiers digging a trench around them and putting machine guns in the trenches. "They told us that the Japs were just a quarter of a mile down the road and to run to the trenches if they attacked."

By the next morning, the nurses still had not been told their destination. "We were told they were going to send us down in 2.5-ton trucks," Dorothy says. "They said they didn't know if we'd get there or not but to dive out of the truck and get under it if anything happens. Then they filled our canteens, issued us C rations, and loaded us on the trucks."

While they traveled down the dirt road, artillery howitzers fired ahead of them. "We didn't know what they were firing at," she says. "We found out later that was how they intended to get us through Japanese lines." Dorothy started to recognize her surroundings but was told not to tell anybody anything. Then, they were at the front gate of Santo Tomas.

As they entered, Dorothy's heart sank momentarily. "The place looked desolate," she says. "It was almost disheartening. I was just really emotional. . . . I knew something had happened, you could see the damage, but nobody was around. This leaves you sort of eerie." The sound of the trucks drew people out of the buildings. "I began to see people I recognized, and they recognized me," she continues. "They let the word go. The nurses gathered, they were all nurses that had rushed out to see what was going on."

Then Dorothy heard someone call her father and sister to come to the

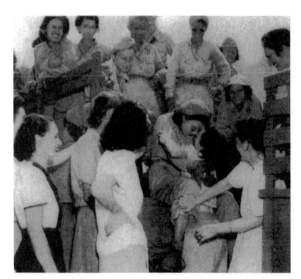

*Dorothy Davis (on back of truck) greeting army nurse internee*
*Rita Palmer inside Santo Tomas Internment Camp, February 1945.*
*Photograph courtesy of Dorothy Davis Thompson*

front courtyard. "My sister got there first, then my father came. It was . . . it was something," Dorothy says. The chief nurse allowed Dorothy a few minutes with her father and Eva and then told her to report for duty. The Japanese were still shelling Santo Tomas. "They had all these injured people and the internees to take care of," Dorothy continues. "The army nurses were doing what they could, but after all, they weren't in all that great a shape either. They had been working very hard during the last two nights." Dorothy didn't see her family again until much later when the family returned to the islands from the United States to resume business.

The shelling became so intense, Dorothy couldn't make it to the hospital. "There was a little aid station in the main building. I stayed there because they were having injuries brought in, makeshift as it was." Dorothy and the medical crew had little to work with that night. They had a sterilizer, but the electricity went off and she couldn't sterilize anything, so they depended on the few things that had been wrapped. "We worked the whole night by the light of a Coleman lamp. It puts out a good light," she says, "but it can't be directed into a wound. I don't know how many surgeries we did. These were abdominal wounds. We mended gut, we cut out gut.

*Dorothy Davis receiving the Bronze Star, Manila, July 1945.*
*Photographs courtesy of Dorothy Davis Thompson*

Then there was no place to put the patients but in the filthy beds of the internees. They were just cruddy. The internees put out of their beds slept on the floor.

"During the next few weeks," Dorothy continues, "we cared for civilian men, women, and babies as well as American soldiers injured during the brutal battle for Manila between the Japanese and the United States Army and Navy. We delivered babies conceived in Santo Tomas. We also cared for hundreds of sick internees and Filipinos for lockjaw, gas gangrene, and other infections seldom seen in American soldiers."

The shelling continued but gradually eased as American troops recaptured the islands. The workload became lighter. Dorothy found out later that a plane had landed on the main street in Manila to evacuate the army nurses. They were the first POWs to leave. Evacuation of the rest of the internees took weeks.

Once again, Dorothy pushed her body beyond its limit and she became ill. "We were still working very hard, and my body began to object to the lack of sleep and so forth," she says. "I finally got pneumonia and was in the hospital for almost a month." She returned to duty but got a bad case of diarrhea. "I had both bacillary and amoebic dysentery and was running a very high fever." Her condition was so bad, doctors decided to evacuate her by air back to the states.

The process was slow. Dorothy spent much time waiting for an airplane to take her on the next part of her journey home. In the planes, she was placed on a stretcher attached four-deep to the sides of the plane. Eventually, Dorothy made it to Letterman General Hospital in San Francisco where she spent three weeks waiting for a hospital train to take patients to an army hospital as near to their home as possible. Finally, Dorothy boarded a hospital train bound for New York.

Still running a fever, she was taken to Rhodes General Hospital for further evaluation and treatment. "They were just sure I had malaria, but all tests for malaria were negative," she says. "After four months of treatment for other problems, I begged to go back on duty."

Dorothy was assigned to Walter Reed General Hospital, then managed to be sent back to Manila. While Dorothy was in the hospital, Jack had made his way up to Manila from Zamboanga on the island of Mindanao. He was the first to greet her and take her to her parents' house. They were married three months later. She was stationed at the 10th General Hospital

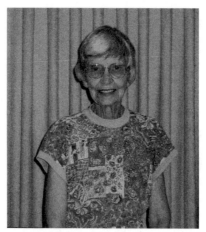

*Dorothy Davis Thompson in April 2002.*
*Photograph by Cindy Weigand*

at Fort McKinley, seven miles outside of Manila. When Jack received orders to return to the United States, Dorothy got orders to Okinawa but wanted to return to the states with Jack. With enough points to do so, Dorothy resigned from the Army Nurse Corps in 1947 as a captain, and she and Jack returned to the United States.

Dorothy and Jack have three children, five grandchildren, and three great-grandchildren. Dorothy's sister, Eva, lives in a nursing facility nearby.

In her book, *The Road Back: A Pacific POW's Liberation Story,* Dorothy tells her remarkable story in more detail.

# 12

# H. R. BRANTLEY

*Army Nurse Corps, Manila, Bataan, Corregidor,*
*Philippine Islands; Santo Tomas Internment Camp, Manila,*
*Philippine Islands*

"When an enemy soldier with a bayonet says get off the truck,
you do what he says."

H. R. listened to the clump, clump, clump of the hobnailed boots and
the clank of the sabers of the Japanese guards as they walked across
the hospital ward, out the door, and faded into the darkness. Once out of
earshot, she waited a full minute more to make sure they didn't return. All
she heard was the breathing of patients and the rustle of their palm-fiber
mats as they slept restlessly in their beds.

Satisfied her patients were asleep and the guards were gone, H. R. hurried to her bed, slid out the hemp bag, and pulled out the rope ladder. Her
friend, Edith, met her at the window as they always did on the nights they
were told food would be waiting. Without a word, they hung the ladder
securely from the windowsill and H. R. climbed down. On the ground, she
ran to the fence, grabbed the package of food that a contact on the outside
had placed there, and then sneaked back to the ladder. After tying the package to a rope Edith had lowered, H. R. scrambled back inside.

While Edith hid the packages of food in the laundry room, H. R. put
the rope back in the hemp bag and slid it under her bed. The next day, the
packages would be picked up with the dirty laundry, and then taken to the
kitchen to be distributed among the internees.

"It's a wonder I didn't get caught and decapitated," she says, "but if
you get hungry enough, you'll do anything."

H. R.'s voice is high pitched, almost squeaky, from disuse. During our

*Army Nurse H. R. Brantley in 1942.*
*Photograph courtesy of H. R. Brantley*

three-hour long conversation, she has to clear her throat often and takes frequent sips of first her morning coffee, then water. As she tells her story, I realize the weakness of her voice disguises a tremendous strength of spirit that enabled her to survive a horrendous ordeal as an army nurse during World War II.

As a prisoner of war, H. R. Brantley spent three years in Santo Tomas Internment Camp in the Philippines. Her capture followed months of nursing duty under extreme combat and physical conditions. H. R. and a band of nurses followed the American army as it retreated first from Manila, to the Bataan Peninsula, and finally to the island of Corregidor before surrendering to the Japanese in May 1942.

Born in 1916, H. R. lived on a farm near Jefferson in Marion County with her mother, father, and seven siblings. They raised cattle and grew a large vegetable garden, using mules to work the land. The family harvested vegetables and then peddled them in Jefferson.

In town, H. R.'s father got magazines for his children. "I read about the frontier nursing service in Kentucky," she says. "The nurses rode horseback in the mountains and delivered babies. Delivering babies didn't interest me much. I'd lived on a farm and knew all about the animals and their deliveries, but I wanted to ride a horse. I decided that I could ride a horse if I became a nurse, so I headed in that direction. I drove a Model T Ford to high school in Jefferson."

After she graduated, H. R. chose to attend Baylor School of Nursing in Dallas, but she wasn't old enough. "I was seventeen, but had to be eighteen to go to nursing school. My father didn't believe in idleness. He insisted I go back to high school, so I did. I studied chemistry, biology, and other subjects that were helpful in nursing."

In 1935, H. R. entered school to study to be a nurse. "Actually, the student nurses were the workforce for the hospital in those days," she says. "I think there were sixty-five of us that went in that year, but they dropped out like flies." Determined to finish, H. R. woke up every morning and said to herself, "I'm going to finish this. I'm not going to quit." She wanted to go back home to the farm when she graduated, but times had changed by then, and she decided not to.

During nursing school, they studied various areas of service available upon graduation. Frontier nursing no longer interested H. R. She really only considered one area. "Most of the nurses did private duty because you got *five* dollars for twelve hours," she laughs. "Private duty nursing didn't appeal to me nor did public health, then I read you had to have two years' experience to go into the army." H. R. decided that's what she wanted to do. "They still had the cavalry in those days, so I thought I could ride a horse and also see the world." She worked at Baylor two years, then applied and took the required physical at Fort Sam Houston in San Antonio.

Called for active duty in June 1939, she took the oath of office in Dallas, officially entering the Army Nurse Corps as a second lieutenant, then traveled back to Fort Sam Houston. "We lived in a dormitory," she says. "It was riches to me. I had a room to myself and I shared a bathroom with only one other person. I had wonderful meals. Three a day, which was just fantastic." She was assigned to duty on a medical contagious ward.

At that time, no basic training was required for the Army Nurse Corps, nor was there an official uniform. "About a week after I started," she says, "the chief nurse said to me, 'Miss Brantley, next time you're at the PX, buy yourself a gold bar and a caduceus and put it on your uniform.' This was basic training, you see. My uniform was my white dress uniform. At the time, ranks weren't used when addressing each other. I put on the caduceus and bar, and I was in the army!"

Also working at Fort Sam Houston was a girl who had been to the Philippines. "It sounded wonderful. It was light duty and tropical." The girl traveled via ship from San Francisco to Hawaii, then to the Philippines. When her tour in the Philippines was over, she went by ship to China, then back to the port of New York. "She had circumnavigated the world, which is exactly what I wanted to do," H. R. says. "That's where I headed."

In 1941, H. R. and five other nurses received orders to report to the Philippines. In San Francisco, the nurses boarded the USS *Pierce* with troops and doctors. First stop was overnight in Hawaii. "We had a great time. We saw the hula dancers and all the beautiful sights of Hawaii," she says. From Hawaii, they continued their journey until they reached the south Pacific. Japanese steamships were in the area. "They told us to put on bright clothes and go up on the deck and be engaged in games and so forth," she says. "If the Japs looked at us, they'd think this was a pleasure cruise. Soldiers were not to be seen."

In the Philippines, H. R. was assigned to Fort William McKinley, a station hospital about seven miles outside of Manila. They were quartered in old wooden barracks. "Duty was light," she says. "We had tropical diseases like malaria and dengue fever and lots of infections. If a soldier got hurt, he was bound to get an infection due to the heat." Because of the heat, they worked either mornings or afternoons, or they worked from seven at night until seven in the morning. "This was a solid month duty," she says. "If you were assigned to night duty for a thirty-day month, you worked thirty days in a row."

Off-duty hours were often filled with pleasure. Fort McKinley had a post pool, a bowling alley, golf course, and movie theater. The base had a streetcar to carry the personnel to their desired destination. "One of the girls had a car, so we went shopping in Manila," H. R. says. On the south side of Manila was Sternberg Army Hospital.

Huge Cavite Navy Yard sat thirty miles south of Manila with the U.S. Navy Hospital at Canacao nearby. Across Manila Bay to the west, on the 1,735-acre island of Corregidor, was Fort Mills. Two hundred miles north of the capital, Camp John Hay was located near Baguio and the Cordillera Central Mountains, a popular getaway for the wealthy because of the cool, dry mountain air.

Seventy-five miles north was Fort Stotsenberg and Clark Air Field, the main base of the U.S. Army Air Corps in the Pacific. The base offered polo games and opportunities for horseback rides in the hills nearby. "It was just a picnic," H. R. says. "Nobody thought anything about war." Upon occasion, she rode horses on her days off. Little did she know that in a few months, she would have to eat horses to survive.

Earlier that year, the government started sending the dependents of the military back to the United States. "This didn't send a warning to anybody. Sending dependents home should have alerted somebody," she says. In October, the army issued the nurses a World War I helmet and a gas mask, and then trained them how to use it. Around her waist she wore a pistol belt on which she hung a canteen. Her white dress was still the official uniform.

At breakfast on December 8, the chief nurse spoke to the nurses. The Philippines were across the International Date Line, one day ahead of Hawaii. "She told us that Pearl Harbor had been bombed," H. R. says. "Well, we were twenty-eight days from Hawaii. That's how long it took us to get there. She went on to tell us that they're not going to bother us and to go about our duties."

H. R. and her friend had the morning off, so they went golfing. "The war has started, and we're playing golf," she says. "That was in the days when you had to fold bandages and all that. We could have been doing a million things, but no, we went out and played golf because the chief nurse said to."

That night, they heard firing in the distance. "We climbed out of bed and crawled under the bungalow, which was on stilts, and waited for the bomb to hit us," H. R. says. "Finally, I told the girls I had one dying ambition and that was to die in bed, so I went back to bed. And that was the way the war started for us."

At approximately 8:15 a.m., the Japanese bombed Baguio and John Hay hospital and then headed toward their primary target, Clark Air Field. Scores of unmanned bombers and fighters were lined up on the runway but not one plane was in the air to repel the enemy. In a 1997 interview to record her oral history for Texas Woman's University (TWU), H. R. describes the situation. "The pilots went out and flew around all morning. They saw Japanese planes merely passing by. Finally, they came back at 12:00 and landed. Just as they went in to lunch, here came the Japs."

At 12:35 p.m., Mitsubishi Zeros screamed in, essentially destroying the principal fleet of the Army Air Corps in the Pacific. "They destroyed almost all the planes and killed most of the pilots," H. R. says, "because they were in the mess hall. Just a trap! A trap!" An hour later, a second wave of Zeros machine-gunned the field, and the attack was over. "That was the end of the war right there as far as we were concerned."

All the buildings on the grounds—barracks, hangars, officer's quarters, machine shops—were leveled. Bits of aircraft littered the field, fires burned. Stotsenberg Hospital was nearly destroyed. Wounded and dead lay everywhere. Casualties were taken to Manila, so the army moved the nurses to Manila.

"We took over public buildings like the jai alai stadium, which is a type of indoor ball game," H. R. says, "and set up a public hospital, then waited for casualties. I was in charge of a three-hundred-bed unit, but we didn't admit one patient. Clark Field was bombed, and there were many injuries. Sternberg was the active army hospital, and many were taken there. Later, they evacuated some on the *Mactan*."

The nurses were also housed in the public buildings. "I was quartered in the Spanish Club. We walked the streets and went to Sternberg to have our meals," she says. "About December 23, the commanding officer told us we were going to Bataan the next day. Bataan! We'd never heard of Bataan and didn't know where in the world it was. He said to wear and take our white duty uniforms, nothing else. Well, we had riding clothes, boots and jodhpurs, and golf clothes. No, he said to take your white duty uniforms."

On December 22, forty-three thousand enemy troops had landed on the shore of Lingayen Gulf in northern Luzon Province, headed for Manila. On December 24, seven thousand reinforcements landed on the southern side of Manila. Gen. Douglas MacArthur had ordered everyone to Bataan, a peninsula across the bay, west of Manila. Off the coast of Bataan lay Corregidor island, guarding the entrance to Manila Bay.

The next morning, the nurses boarded public buses headed for Bataan. "The yellow convoy starts out of town, well, guess what happens? The Japs come and bomb it," she says. "We get out and lie in the ditches in our white duty uniforms. The trip took all day. We got to Limay on Bataan, which was an old Philippine army training ground. There were these long, native buildings built with slat floors, thatched roofs, and wide-open windows. No such things as screens or glass." After having to seek shelter in ditches in white duty uniforms, "Santa Claus came to the hospital," H. R.

says. "It was a supply truck and they gave us air corps coveralls, all size 42. We also got boots."

In nearby warehouses, they found cots and surgical instruments that had been stored since World War I. The newspapers they were wrapped in were dated 1918. Thankfully, the surgical instruments had been stored in oil to prevent them from rusting. "I think we put about fifty cots in each of these buildings, and we started admitting patients," H. R. says. "When the Japanese landed in Lingayen and started down, there was some resistance. Americans tried to blow up bridges and deter their progress, but it didn't take long for them to get there." Set up on December 24, Christmas Eve, the hospitals soon filled.

The nurses and doctors set up the operating room in a corrugated tin building. "We became Field Hospital #1," H. R. says. "We got the casualties, performed surgery, and did as much resuscitation as we could. Pretty soon, we were so full, they needed another place." The army went farther down the peninsula and bulldozed down trees to make an opening. "The bulldozers cleared paths along a river and they set up beds out in the open," she continues. "This was Field Hospital #2. The Japs had planned to arrive in the dry season. They had enough sense to know what they were doing." The nurses at Hospital #2 slept out under the trees, also.

Meanwhile, Manila was declared an open city. "Anybody that wasn't a German or an Italian was considered American responsibility," H. R. says. "They were told to go to Santo Tomas and 'register.' They weren't allowed to go back home."

At Hospital #1, H. R. and the other nurses checked their patients. "If anyone could tolerate transfer, he was moved to Hospital #2," she says. "We'd clear out every day and every night, we'd fill up again, see? By the time Bataan fell, there were about five thousand patients in Hospital #2."

Early in January, the Japanese attacked a barrio near Hospital #1. No one was seriously wounded, but the attack worried the doctors, so the hospital was moved west, more inland. "We had to move even farther down the peninsula," H. R. says. "We bypassed #2 and went to a place called 'Little Baguio.' There were wooden buildings for us to live in. We bathed in the stream." The doctors and orderlies slept in tents set up around the buildings. One building served as the operating room (OR).

Near Limay, the fighting was fierce. The Japanese artillery lobbed volley after volley, pilots strafed the beaches, and the infantry marched in. Casualties poured into Hospital #1 any way they could be carried—trucks, buses, mules, cart. One report states that on January 16, 1943, Hospital #1 performed 182 surgeries in the hospital's OR, a 14-by-40 foot room.

Fierce fighting and heavy casualties weren't the only concerns. The officer in charge of provisions informed MacArthur that they would run out of provisions in sixty days. The army was sharing food with up to two thousand civilians as well as feeding soldiers. MacArthur ordered that the soldiers' food be cut to two thousand calories a day. GIs scrambled in the jungles for anything to eat. Carabao, water buffalo, and horses were slaughtered. "We got two meals a day. We had breakfast first thing in the morning, then an evening meal," H. R. says. "Our chief nurse, Josie Nesbitt, looked out for us. She made every effort, by hook, crook, theft, or murder, she had something for the girls to eat."

General MacArthur tried to rally the troops, but President Roosevelt ordered him out of the Philippines. On March 11, 1942, he, his wife Jean, and their son Arthur boarded a torpedo patrol boat on Corregidor's north side. He and key staff members escaped to Australia. General Jonathan Wainwright replaced General MacArthur as commander of the troops on Bataan. Before leaving, he told the troops a convoy with supplies was on the way, and he vowed to return.

The shelling abated somewhat. "At this time, there was more bombing on Corregidor, they were concentrating on Corregidor," H. R. says. "In April, they sort of let up because they had to regroup. April was a fairly quiet month. Toward the end, all hell broke loose again and they bombed us daily, day and night."

Hospital #1 was getting so many casualties that the nurses were told to go set up another ward. The engineers built triple-deck bamboo beds. "We had about a hundred of these," H. R. says, "and I arranged this area away from the main hospital. The Japanese bombed the ward I'd just left. It was a direct hit." When the group first arrived, they had put a red cross on a hillside to indicate that a hospital was there. "They used that for bombing practice," she says.

In the TWU interview, H. R. says the day the hospital was bombed, a nurse went out looking for her. "They thought I'd been killed. When she found me, we sat out there and talked a long time just by ourselves," she says. "We couldn't go back to the area of destruction." This memory sparks another, and H. R. stops speaking momentarily. "Oh my! She just died last year, and I miss her so! We had stayed friends during all those times."

H. R. was not hurt, but others were. "There were two nurses injured

that day, but not seriously, it was minor, you know, just shrapnel wounds."
According to sources, these two nurses were probably Rita Palmer and
Rosemary Hogan. Both nurses were later awarded the Purple Heart.

On other bombings, H. R. usually remained close to her work.
"There wasn't anyplace you could hide," she says. "We had trenches along
the edge and you were supposed to get in them, but I had liquid knees. I
never did go anyplace, I just sat down where I was by some GI's bed and
held his hand and let him hold mine. There wasn't anything you could do
but get down and hope the shrapnel didn't get you."

The hospital also cared for the enemy. "We had a Japanese ward," she
continues, "where we put any Japanese prisoners that were taken. There
were very few, of course, they'd commit hara-kiri rather than be captured.
Most weren't injured anyway, they were just being incarcerated."

"Things went from bad to worse," she says. "We were on two meals
a day, and they weren't all that substantial. Everybody was up, though.
Every day somebody would climb a tree and look out to the bay and say
that he didn't see the convoy that MacArthur had promised, but it's coming.
It took us twenty-eight days to get there, but the next day we're looking
for that convoy. Faith. You never give up hope, and, of course, you keep a
sense of humor. You never give up hope and keep your sense of humor for
survival. A sense of humor and a sense of hope."

The hospital had a radio on Bataan and H. R. remembered President
Roosevelt saying in a speech, "I hate war," pronouncing war like *wo-wuh*.
"Every time things would get really tough, or we were in a bind, somebody
would say, 'I hate wo-wuh. FDR hates wo-wuh. Eleanor hates wo-wuh.'
It made everybody laugh. It broke the tension and we worked and contin-
ued to work."

MacArthur radioed from Australia that there should be no thought of
surrender.

On April 8, the commander told the nurses to take what they could in
their hands and get on some buses. "We said that we couldn't leave our
patients who numbered in the hundreds," she says. " 'What's going to happen to them,' we asked?" The commander told them to get on the buses,
and they headed south. Without another word, the nurses had the most
difficult task of all—leaving their patients behind. Troops were sent north
to meet the enemy.

"It was dusty and hot," H. R. remembers. "You could not see for the
dust. It took hours to get down there. There were fires in the area. We

worried about Hospital #2 because they were closer to the enemy." About two or three o'clock in the morning, they reached the coast. "We all got on a barge-type thing, others got on anything that was available, canoes, rafts, whatever, to go to Corregidor in shark-infested water," she says. "We all got there safely—one of the miracles. The Hospital #2 nurses didn't get there until about daybreak the next morning. When all those nurses came in, it was a time for rejoicing and thankfulness."

On April 9, American forces surrendered Bataan to the Japanese. Exact numbers are not known, but the enemy may have rounded up as many as 70,000 stranded soldiers, including 12,000 Americans. The Japanese made American troops—severely weakened by battle, nearly starved to death, and demoralized—march fifty-seven miles under the blazing sun to prison camps. The march became known as the "Bataan Death March."

On the way, the Japanese shot the men, or they lashed them to trees and either beheaded or eviscerated them. Others were bayoneted, bludgeoned, or beaten to death. The crimes the Japanese deemed worthy of such punishment were dropping behind or fainting or an officer protesting the treatment of one of his men. Other crimes were resting or taking a drink. About fifty thousand completed the trek. Those who made it were forced into slave labor.

The army nurses set up a hospital on Corregidor, in an elaborate tunnel complex called the Malinta Tunnel. Built around 1910, the system consisted of a long central tunnel with laterals off to the sides. If it could be seen from the air, it would resemble open books. Heavily fortified, the medical team could continue to work even though the island was being bombarded. "I was glad I wasn't stationed on Corregidor before the war because it was so confining," H. R. says. "I didn't care about being on an island." Yet she ended up on the island with eighty-four army nurses, twenty-six Filipino nurses, and one navy nurse.

"They moved the patients from topside," H. R. says. "There was a topside, bottom side, middle side. The hospital was on topside and it had been blown to smithereens the first few days of the war, so they moved their patients inside the tunnel. It was a safe place, but that was about all you could say for it. There were patients there, so we were able be on duty right away." The nurses lived in a smaller lateral. "We had one bathroom. No shower, no nothing. Sometimes the water would be off for a long time," she says. They were allowed outside the tunnel for brief periods in the evenings and in the morning.

In the Malinta Tunnel was a supply depot. "They issued us men's uniforms, men's khaki shirts and pants and that was nice, mostly they fit," H. R. laughs. "It was better than the coveralls, which were okay for most of us, but the little nurse that weighed ninety-eight pounds, we didn't find her for several hours after she put hers on."

With Bataan under their control, the Japanese concentrated their efforts on Corregidor. They set up large guns on Bataan and lodged shells on the island, plus they bombed from the air. "It was bomb, bomb, bomb. Just bombs," H. R. says. "Well, we were in the tunnel and were safe, but you can imagine the repercussions and the echoes. And the water would go off and the lights would go off." Casualties mounted. "We set up more beds along the tunnel sides and had them everyplace. We had enough beds," she says. "I don't know where they all came from, but we had them. We had very few linens and mattresses, though."

H. R. remembers General Wainwright well. "I'll never forget him. He was a wonderful person," she says. "He would come to the hospital area and have corn meal mush with us in the morning. Walking down the corridor, he'd slam something with that riding crop he carried and say, 'They're giving us hell today, aren't they?' We loved General Wainwright. He was marvelous."

General Wainwright soon realized that the surrender of Corregidor was imminent, so he desperately tried to get the nurses safely off the island. On April 29, two U.S. Navy PBY seaplanes were to sneak through the blockade to deliver supplies and take out personnel to Australia. Twenty nurses were chosen to leave. "They said they intended to get us all out eventually, but it was not possible," H. R. says.

The seaplanes flew in on schedule. "They chose the nurses that were sick or had been on there a long time. Some were just ineffective," H. R. continues. "There was one who just sat like she was in shock. Some had been there quite a long time." H. R. was comfortable with those chosen to leave. "I've always said, and I don't mean it as a braggadocio or anything like that," she says, "but if I had been selected to go out, I would have felt that I wasn't worthy of the team, you know? I did not want to go. They told us to write letters to our family. Well, I couldn't write a letter. What was I going to say?" One of H. R.'s close friends, Lucy Wilson, made it out and called H. R.'s family when she returned to the United States.

One plane with ten nurses aboard made it to Australia. The other plane was damaged on takeoff and had to be repaired. Forced to go ashore, the passengers hid from the Japanese in various locations. When the plane was ready to leave, they couldn't be found, so the plane left without them. The passengers were captured by the Japanese.

Later, a small submarine, the USS *Spearfish,* managed to get through the minefield in the bay and evacuated eleven army nurses, one navy nurse, twelve staff officers, a civilian dependent, and two enlisted men who were stowaways.

On May 5, 1942, an officer came to the nurses' lateral. "He told us the Japs had landed and the end was here," H. R. says. The nurses continued to take care of the several hundred patients and run the hospital. Corregidor was surrendered on May 6, 1942. "Fortunately, the Japanese commander who took surrender of the hospital had been trained in UCLA," H. R. says. "He spoke perfect English. He understood a little bit about the American way of life. He told the commander that we should continue to take care of our patients and stay out of sight."

The Japanese decided to move everyone out of the tunnel and take them to the topside hospital. "The hospital had been completely destroyed, but we put cots and beds up there and moved patients up there," she says. In June, the Japanese decided to move everyone into Manila and herded the prisoners down to a pier where a ship stood waiting. "We watched them load our patients into the hold and then they directed us onto a deck." H. R. remembers the Japanese officer in charge. "He served us tea and told us what he was going to do when he got to Chicago. He told us that when they landed in San Francisco, he was going to go to Chicago."

Before the nurses left Corregidor, they tore a piece of muslin from a sheet and each one wrote her name on it. One of them said, "We wanted to leave a record in case we disappeared."

The ship docked in Manila in early July 1942. "We watched them off-load our patients into trucks, then they directed us off," she says. "By this time, we're just horrible looking. We got on open-air trucks and rode through the streets of Manila. The Filipinos gave us the *V* for victory if no Japanese were in sight. If the enemy could see them, they didn't dare do it. We were their friends, and they were our friends.

"They drove us into the grounds of Santo Tomas," H. R. continues. "Well, we had heard about Santo Tomas Internment Camp where civilians were incarcerated, but internment is too nice a word. It was a prisoner of war camp. We told the Japanese that we were military and wanted to go take care of our patients. Well, when someone with a bayonet tells you to get off the truck, you have a tendency to do what he says.

"They herded us into a private room and there was pineapple and tea. I'll tell you what, nothing ever tasted so good in my life. Fresh pineapple and tea." It wasn't long before the nurses asked to use bathroom facilities. "That was an excuse to get out, you see, because they weren't letting any of the internees have any contact with us." As they walked down the hall to the bathroom, they exchanged bits of information with the prisoners.

The nurses were quartered on the second floor of a convent outside of Santo Tomas. "I don't know how many acres it was, but it was a fairly large area with a native rock fence around it," H. R. says. "They'd put barbed wire over the top of that so there was no way to escape except through the gates. The building we were quartered in had a fence around it, too. We had beds, cots, anything they could put in there. Some with mattresses and some without, and a mosquito net above. Of course, a mosquito net was an absolute necessity.

"In all," H. R. continues, "there were sixty-seven army nurses who were prisoners, and eleven navy nurses, by the way." The army nurses were from various hospitals throughout the Philippines. One of the nurses, Ruby Bradley, came from Camp John Hay. When she died in 2001 at age ninety-seven, she was the most decorated person in the army.

Somehow left behind at Canacao, the eleven navy nurses were moved to various places in Manila until taken to STIC when it first opened. These nurses and civilian nurse Dorothy Davis Thompson set up a clinic and did the best they could with what they had. After spending several months at STIC, the navy nurses moved to another internment camp, Los Baños, to the north.

The army nurses were kept in the convent for a month to recuperate. "It's a good thing, because we were yellow, thin, and pukey looking," she says. "We could go outside twice a day for exercise and fresh air. They brought our food from Santo Tomas. They brought us soup at noon, and sometimes we got fresh fruit, sometimes a banana. We had two meals a day, such as they were." Ironically, being inside a prison camp was a relief for the nurses. "We weren't under fire and not in danger, so we just took advantage of the rest and recuperated. I learned to play bridge."

Civilians inside the camp were able to supplement what the Japanese provided by having Filipino servants bring them food. This was called the package line. Notes with news from the outside were also passed in these packages, but H. R. knew no one. "There was an old army nurse named Ida Hube who had worked in Manila," she says. "She had married a German, so she wasn't incarcerated. Hube was real wealthy and twice a week she came to the gate with food. She saved our lives."

By the time H. R. and the nurses arrived at STIC, the camp was well organized. The internees were treated to two hours of music a night. There was a public address system over which they announced the day's activities or gave the internees an update on the war through coded messages. For, instance, when the Americans landed in Leyte, someone over the loudspeaker said, "Better Leyte then never." A wealthy businessman even offered the nurses loans while they were in the camp. H. R. received twenty-five pesos a month.

To keep people busy, they were required to do two hours of work a day. Some tended a small garden where they grew a few vegetables, including a native plant in the spinach family called talinum that matured quickly. One chore the women did was to clean the worms out of the rice. "I'd say, 'Leave them in,'" H. R. says. "It's protein. When you get hungry enough, you'll eat anything."

In August 1942, the nurses moved to the main campus of STIC and resumed their nursing duties "with a little bit of nothing," H. R. says. They even performed surgery if absolutely necessary. Very ill patients were sent to hospitals outside the camp. "I chose night duty with four other nurses," H. R. says, "so I could be away from people and have a little privacy; to get away from the crowd. There wasn't anything to do, so we'd sleep all day and work all night, from seven at night until seven in the morning. You learned to sleep through the war."

H. R. and the nurses had rooms separate from the other internees. "My bed was a wooden bed that someone had made. It had wooden slats on the bottom with spaces between the slats. My mattress was a bath towel." H. R. spent three years in Santo Tomas. "For years afterward, I had marks on my back where I had slept on those slats. There were fourteen in our room. I can name you everybody in that room. They were all such special people and we were all such good friends."

One day, a businessman with contacts on the outside told H. R. that he could have food brought to the back of the hospital if someone could get it. "I volunteered," H. R. says. "He gave me a rope ladder with hooks on it. In the Philippines, all the windows have a metal ornate shelf on the outside." When food was available, the man gave H. R. a special sign. "I climbed out that window, down that rope ladder, went to that fence and got the package, and brought it back. My friend, Edith, had brought a rope, I'd tie the rope on the package and she'd pull it up. We'd hide it in the laundry room. It was prearranged that it would go out in the dirty laundry the next morning and be taken to the kitchen to be distributed among the internees. We did this many times."

H. R. kept the ladder in a native hemp bag under her bed. There was also a radio in camp to get the latest "scuttlebutt" from the outside. An electrician bolted the radio to the bottom of a five-gallon can and arranged to have it moved daily.

The Japanese performed inspections periodically and became aware of the radio. One day, H. R. had to go to the restroom, but a Japanese guard was at the door and waved her back in, then they called all the nurses out and searched the room. "When I returned to my room," she says, "they had pulled that bag from under my bed, taken the ladder out and left it there. I just knew I'd be decapitated right there, because I know they saw it. Thank goodness it didn't register with them what it was for."

Of all the starving people in the camp, H. R. remembers one group in particular. "It was especially hard to see the children go hungry," she says. "Of course, they tried to give them three meals, at least some food, three times a day. There was no such thing as milk, but there were coconuts. They made milk by grinding the meat of the coconut and watering it down. At least it had a few vitamins."

For ten months, Dorothy Davis Thompson and H. R. worked together in the hospital until Dorothy was chosen to be repatriated and left for the United States.

Early in 1944, conditions went from bad to worse at STIC. Formerly under the management of the Japanese Bureau of External Affairs, the Japanese put the camp under the control of the War Prisoners Department of the Imperial Japanese Army. The new commandant told the internees he would dismiss the internee-elected government, isolate the camp from any contact with the outside, and put more severe regulations in place.

The package line was shut down. Nothing from the outside was allowed into the camp including the packages of food from Hube to the army nurses. Guards took roll and counted people. Inspections became more frequent. The commandant promised ample supplies of food, but the provisions that arrived were usually meager in quantity and spoiled.

According to records kept by internee Peter Richards, the daily cereal ration for internees had been reduced to three hundred grams per person through September 1944. One metal paper clip weighs approximately one gram. By December 20, they reduced the daily cereal ration to 187 grams.

The malnutrition suffered by the internees led to such diseases as inflammation of the nerves, numbness in hands and feet, ocular pain with blurred or double vision, skin rashes, sores on lips and swollen tongue, and anemia. Bone rubbed against bone so that their joints creaked when they walked.

In testimony before the American War Crimes office, H. R. told investigators:

> At frequent intervals during 1944 . . . I witnessed the slaughter of cattle by the internees for consumption of the Japanese; no part of this meat was allowed to the internees, but occasionally the internees were given the bones of the cattle. . . . I had frequent occasions to witness the Japanese sentries eating meals that had been brought to their posts and these meals during this entire period included a sufficiency of fresh eggs and citrus fruits and an abundance of rice; part of this rice was frequently thrown away.

Aside from the illicit radio transmissions a few minutes each night, the prisoners had no contact with the outside world. "We didn't get any mail until 1944," she says, "and I got a Christmas card from my mother that said 'Papa died in 1943.' It had been almost a year before I got that news. After that, I didn't care if I went home or not because my father was such a special person."

The news of her father's death injured H. R. emotionally, and then her mother poured salt into the wound. "Mama blamed me," she says. "Mama said I killed him because he worried so about my being gone." H. R.'s parents hadn't heard about her fate. "I was captured in July 1942, and it was February 1944 before they got word from the government that I was alive in Manila," she says. "It took that long. Of course, all that time, they didn't know what happened." However, the United States government had not forgotten the people in the Philippines.

General MacArthur was making good on his pledge to return. Having regained control of other islands in the Pacific, American planes bombed Manila. "In September of '44, we saw the first planes and the wonderful star on the wings instead of the 'fried egg' as we used to call it," H. R. says.

"Of course, they announced immediately, 'we're having maneuvers. Stay away from the windows.' It was wonderful seeing those planes, but it hurt when I saw one of our planes shot down. I thought 'that man is giving his life for me. He's trying to save me,' but. . . ." H. R. stops talking as she relives that moment and then says, "Oh, terrible."

In October, troops had landed on the island of Leyte. On December 25, airplanes flew over STIC and dropped leaflets that offered the internees further hope. On the leaflet was the following message:

> The Commander-in-Chief, the officers, and the men of the American Forces of Liberation in the Pacific wish their gallant allies, the people of the Philippines, all the blessings of Christmas, and the realization of their fervent hopes for the New Year, Christmas 1944.

Meanwhile, inside the compound, "Things went from bad to worse," H. R. says. "They immediately cut our rations. We had less than three hundred calories a day from that time when the Americans came. They knew they were on the way out. It was pretty gruesome." According to Mr. Richards's records, the chairman of the camp medical staff was jailed by the Japanese for refusing to exclude the words *malnutrition* and *starvation* from death certificates of internees.

On January 2, American allies landed on the island of Luzon, near the Philippines. On February 3, American airplanes flew in formation over STIC. One of the pilots dropped a pair of goggles from the cockpit with a note attached that said, "Roll out the barrel. Santa Claus is coming. . . ." At nine o'clock p.m., tanks from the 44th Tank Battalion crashed through the gates.

The internees were uncertain whose tanks they were. "We had been told we weren't going to get out of this alive," H. R. says, "so we were crouched down hiding. Then a soldier in a tank raised up and said, 'Well, aren't there any Americans here?'" There were several tanks that came into the camp that night. "They looked like Greek gods to us," she says. "They were beautiful. I hugged this guy and said, 'What pretty teeth you have. Are they your own?'" The next morning, the internees had an American breakfast, "and we all got sick," H. R. says.

American tanks made it to Santo Tomas, but there was little time for celebration, because the Japanese continued to shell the compound. On February 7, the convoy with Dorothy Davis Thompson and nearly one hundred army nurses arrived in Santo Tomas in open trucks to relieve the nurses in Santo Tomas. "There was also a nurse from Baylor in one of those trucks," H. R. says. A few days later, an army C-47 landed on the main street of Manila and flew the nurses to Leyte to recuperate a little before returning to the United States.

H. R.'s family and all of America had little news of what happened to troops, army nurses, and civilians in Manila, but they had heard the horror of the "Rape of Nanking." When she disembarked from the ship that brought her home from the Philippines after enduring incomprehensible hardships for three years, H. R. said she would never forget some of the first words spoken to her. "One woman had the audacity to ask me where my baby was." H. R. pauses to reflect on the remark. "Incredible. Of course, people just can't imagine what it was like, you know, and how cruel the Japanese really were. That Bataan Death March is one of the most awful things inflicted by one human being on another. But we survived.

"It's hard to pull some of it up," H. R. says. "We were told, and it's natural, to put what happened out of your mind; to not remember, to make an honest effort to forget." The army gave her sixty days for recuperation. H. R. hated to go home because her father wasn't there to greet her, but she did return home. After two months, she was reoriented into the Army Nurse Corps and reported for her last assignment before leaving the corps. After a short, unsuccessful marriage, H. R. reentered the army.

H. R. enlisted as a second lieutenant and got an automatic promotion to first lieutenant when released from STIC. She received back pay of $70 a month and $1,007 for the meals she didn't eat in the army mess halls while interned. "Japanese interned in America were paid $20,000," she says, "but the Japanese didn't pay us a thing, and they're not going to."

She retired in 1969 as a lieutenant colonel. During her last years of service, those closest to her never knew of H. R.'s captivity. Even today, few know of these brave nurses called the Angels of Bataan. Her comment to this fact is to paraphrase a verse from the Bible, "A prophet is without honor, even in his own home."

From the time she was ordered to Bataan, through the shelling of Corregidor, until she was liberated from Santo Tomas Internment Camp, there was never any doubt in H. R.'s mind that the Americans would return. Her closing comment is a testament to her tremendous strength of spirit and the strength of those who endured with her. "We had faith, faith, faith. We never for a minute gave up hope. We'd say, 'They'll be here tomorrow.'

*H. R. Brantley in June 2002.*
*Photograph by Cindy Weigand*

"You see, you keep a sense of humor and you keep hope."

A plaque was placed at the Altar of Valor on Mt. Sumat, Bataan Peninsula, the National Shrine of the Philippines, on the occasion of the Reunion of Peace, to commemorate the thirty-fifth anniversary of the liberation of Americans held prisoner of war in the Philippines. The plaque reads:

> In honor of the valiant American Military women who gave so much of themselves in the early days of World War II. They provided care and comfort to the gallant defenders of Bataan and Corregidor. They lived on a starvation diet, shared the bombing, strafing, sniping, sickness and disease while working endless hours of heartbreaking duty. These nurses always had a smile, a tender touch, and a kind word for their patients. They truly earned the name of:
>
> **The Angels of Bataan and Corregidor**
> *Dedicated this day 9th Day of April 1980*

H. R. was present when the plaque was dedicated and made the response to the United States ambassador's speech. "It was a kite-flying day," she says.

**Other Texas Angels**
Agnes D. Barre
Clara Mae "Bickie" Bickford★
Earlyn "Blackie" Black★
H. R. Brantley
Myra V. Burris★
Bertha "Charlie" Dworsky★
Dorcas E. Easterling★
Eula R. Fails★
Verna V. Henson★
Frankie T. Lewey★
Sally Blaine Millet

★Deceased as of this writing

# 13

# MARY ELLEN ANCELIN GUAY

*Women Accepted for Voluntary Emergency Service
(WAVES), Corry Field, Pensacola, Florida*

"Our veterans deserve the support of a grateful nation."

Mary Ellen carefully checked the chamber of her .22 to make sure their were no shells, then placed her rifle in the trunk of the car. Her younger brother, Jean Hartnet, laid his .410 shotgun next to it. With their father, Remy Jean Ancelin, at the wheel, they scooted into the back seat and chattered happily about their successful hunting trip in the hill country near Kerrville, Texas. Mr. Ancelin started the motor and switched on the radio to listen to music and news while traveling home to Dallas. President Roosevelt was addressing the nation. He said, "This is a day that will live in infamy." Mary Ellen and her brother looked at each other in disbelief. That morning, while they were hunting, the Japanese had attacked Pearl Harbor. America was at war.

"When we heard that," Mary Ellen recalls, "my brother and I looked at each other and said, 'Well, we've got to sign up.'" Only sixteen at the time, Mary Ellen was too young to join the military. Even if she had been older, Mary Ellen could not have entered the service. The law permitting the Women's Navy Reserve wasn't passed until July 1942. The women were called WAVES, acronym for Women Accepted for Voluntary Emergency Service. "Most women at the time were expected to marry well, have a family, and be socialites," she says. "That was never in my plans. I wanted to be an adventurer."

The first time we spoke, Mary Ellen was recuperating from major surgery. Always a go-getter and a joiner, she was frustrated by her inability to get back into the swing of things as quickly as she would have liked. While

*WAVE Mary Ellen Ancelin.*
*Photograph courtesy of Mary Ellen Guay*

her voice was strong and energetic, the tone of the discussion was often serious. Upon subsequent conversations, as her body and psyche healed, Mary Ellen exhibited a quick wit and great sense of humor. Also evident are a deep-abiding faith and indomitable spirit.

Mary Ellen Ancelin was born in Dallas, Texas, on May 11, 1925, into a military-oriented family. Seeking a life free from religious and political persecution, her father's family emigrated to Weatherford from France in the 1890s with the Franco-Texan Land Company. The family spoke French when at home. Her father's ability to speak the language was prized during World War I. As a corporal in the U.S. Marine Corps, he served as General John J. Pershing's interpreter when the American expeditionary forces went into France.

Mary Ellen is the oldest of five children. "My dad always wanted a girl. He got the girl he wanted, but then he raised me as he would a son so that I learned to obey," she says. "He was a strict disciplinarian, but it was a loving discipline for our own good. We were expected to do the chores assigned to us on Saturday, which we didn't like. My father was a Red Cross lifesaver instructor so we learned how to swim. I learned how to shoot and I was a pretty good shot. We had a well-rounded education that would prepare us for almost anything."

Mr. Ancelin was an early member of the American Legion, so Mary Ellen grew up active in Post 275 in Dallas. As a junior auxiliary member, she was the drum majorette for the Sons of the American Legion drum and bugle corps of which her brother was a member, and she helped pass out poppies at Veteran's Day parades and other events. At eighteen, Mary Ellen joined the Ladies Auxiliary. "We had a strong sense of family unity," she says. "I learned about the flag and had patriotic feelings about everything. Of course, we met the veterans of World War I. The legion is like an extended family. That's why Bud and I wanted to join up when we heard the president's speech."

Restless, yet still too young to join the service, Mary Ellen did what she could. "I joined the Civil Air Patrol," she says, "because I thought I needed to learn how to fly. I never have been very good at math. However, I completed ground school and was learning to navigate, but I never got to fly. I wore my uniform, though. I never will forget that olive-drab suit. I was really very proud to wear it."

After graduating from Highland Park High School, Mary Ellen attended college. "My dad said that he would let us all have one year of college," she says, "then he told us we were on our own. I attended classes at North Texas Agricultural College, which is now the University of Texas at Arlington. I had a wonderful year and did everything college kids do."

Not yet old enough to enter the service, Mary Ellen took a year off to work before continuing her education. "I worked for the federal government because they paid more. I made the magnificent salary of $1,594 a year, but it was enough to attend college a second year." While she waited for her twentieth birthday, Mary Ellen attended Southern Methodist University her sophomore year and majored in arts and sciences and languages. "I really wanted to be an interpreter with the State Department," she says. "I thought that would be so great. I could travel and do fantastic spy work."

While attending classes, Mary Ellen continued to help with the war effort. "I was a USO hostess in downtown Dallas at the Adolphus Hotel," she says. "The servicemen there were young and lonely and going off to war." The Ancelins had a nice home, so they often provided hospitality to these men. "There were a lot of army and navy cadets attending officer training at SMU," she says. "One night, I brought seventeen of them home." The family made pallets for young men in the den. Mary Ellen's brothers came down the next morning, looked at all the uniforms, then went running to their parents' room yelling, "Mom! Dad! Mary Ellen brought the whole navy home!" The family once even had French sailors in their home. Mary Ellen also scanned the skies as a volunteer air raid warden.

May 8, 1945, Germany surrendered to the allies. On May 11, that same year, Mary Ellen turned twenty years old, becoming eligible for the military. Even though hostilities had ceased with Germany, the United States was still at war with Japan. Mary Ellen wanted to enter the service for two reasons. "The first was because I was patriotic," she says, "the other was because I needed two more years of college to get my degree. I knew you got a year of college when you signed up. The GI bill helped give me a liberal education."

The WAVES particularly appealed to Mary Ellen, but there was a family tradition. "My father was a marine, and my brother enlisted in the marines, but I was vain," she admits. "I'd been in the Civil Air Patrol and didn't think that olive-drab uniform was all that flattering." Having attended Catholic schools, she'd always worn a blue and white uniform, so it seemed natural for her to want to continue. "I loved the navy uniforms. I thought they were so beautiful."

"I signed up and was sworn in the WAVES," she says, "but didn't get an assignment right away." Reluctantly, she went back to her classes to wait for the service to call. "I didn't want to," she says, "because I was ready to go. I wanted to go before the war ended. We were still at war with Japan. I wanted to serve my country."

The navy called, and Mary Ellen was off to basic training. "I was the only girl in my peer group at SMU and of my other friends who went into the service," she says. "My best girl friend was going to enlist, but she would have had to cut her long, beautiful red hair, so she backed out. I was the only one who went. I felt like I had to represent all the people who didn't go."

Mary Ellen traveled to Hunter College in New York for basic training. "I had six weeks of intensive marching," she says. "Plus, I learned Morse code and how to identify aircraft." Officials at basic training were very strict about rules and regulations. "They were teaching us to be good navy people. We had to make our beds military style," she says. "If there was a wrinkle in it, you got a demerit. They dusted the mirrors with white gloves. If they found dust or if there was anything that wasn't perfectly in order, you got a demerit."

The consequence for getting too many demerits was to scrub the entryway to their dormitory. "I scrubbed that thing several times on what were supposed to be my Saturday afternoons off," Mary Ellen laughs. "In fact, we just went in shifts because there were so many demerits. Issuing demerits is the military's way to stress discipline. You follow orders, and you do things right. That was the best-scrubbed entryway that ever was. It was so shiny, it's a wonder we didn't get it so slick we had accidents.

"We were all gung-ho to go," Mary Ellen continues, "then we dropped the bomb on Hiroshima in August." She remembers the admiral driving around with the top of his jeep down telling everyone they could go back home, but she had different ideas. "I'd joined the navy to see the world, and I hadn't seen the world yet. I wasn't going to get out. I wanted to see what was available." She waited for an assignment.

Although Mary Ellen wanted to attend officer's school, enlistees had to have a college degree to do so. She then considered becoming an aircraft mechanic. Assigned to Corry Field, Pensacola, Florida, she found out they didn't need any. "It's a good thing, because I'm not mechanically minded," she says. "They didn't need any anyway because the war was over." However, she had skills the navy needed, but she didn't want them known. "There were a lot of men who needed to be brought back. They wanted WAVES who could type to get their paperwork done. I wouldn't admit I could because I didn't want an office job."

The situation became so desperate the chief put out an appeal. "I finally admitted I could type and was made a yeoman," she says. "I felt good about getting the work out, though. The records of the men returning from overseas were all screwed up. They weren't getting their longevity pay for being in for three years. Their personnel records weren't up to date. They couldn't get discharged until all the information was accurate." Mary Ellen's job was to interview the men and get their records in order. "I really did feel good about doing the job. I wasn't put in a situation in which I was threatened, but I was ready."

Mary Ellen enjoyed the military while at Pensacola and working with the other WAVES. Interviewing the returning servicemen instilled in her an even greater gratitude for their sacrifice to retain the freedom she enjoys today. Entering as an apprentice seaman, Mary Ellen was honorably discharged from the military as yeoman first class. "I wouldn't take anything for my military service because it's made a big difference in my life to this day," she says.

Mary Ellen married Jim Guay, a navy aerial gunner, in September 1946. They had five children—Greg, Jamie, Cathy, Mike, and Chris—who

*Mary Ellen Guay in May 2002.*
*Photograph by Cindy Weigand*

have "done us proud," she says. One son served in the Vietnam War. Mary Ellen is a field representative for the Women's Memorial and remains active in the American Legion Post 163 in Weatherford. In 1990, she was elected the first woman commander of the post. Also in 1990, the first female commander of the Department of Texas American Legion, Patsy Palmquist, appointed Mary Ellen to the department's National Security Commission, a five-year appointment. Of those five years, she was elected and served as chairman for three years and vice chairman for two. No Texas woman had served in those capacities on that commission. In 1995, she was elected Texas's State Historian, only the third woman at that time to hold the office since the legion's founding. She is also a member of the "20 and 4," the National Honor Society of Women Legionnaires.

Mary Ellen is still a pretty good shot, too. Recently, she participated in a target shoot to raise money for the post. Her two shots were so close, the man in charge asked her if she was sure she had shot twice. Mary Ellen didn't win, however. Another woman did, much to the chagrin of the men who participated in the contest.

Of her commitment to the American Legion, Mary Ellen says, "Taking care of veterans continues through my life. I feel I owe the men and women who suffered and died serving their country because I was allowed to live. They deserve the support of a grateful nation."

# 14

# GLADYS "LINKY" SOMMER BROKHAUSEN

*WAVES, Naval Air Station, Richmond, Florida*

"If you have to bail out, don't jump feet first, the tail assembly will chop off your head."

Linky finished off the ice cream her comrades had bought her, then settled back for the flight back to the air station. Her thoughts drifted to Brok, the man she was dating. They'd spent a wonderful day together while the pilots she'd flown with went deep-sea fishing. Suddenly she felt cool and shivered. *The ice cream wasn't that cold.* Looking out the window, she saw nothing but clouds, and they were climbing. The SNB Bugsmasher seaplane wasn't pressurized. *What the heck's going on?* Just then, the co-pilot came to see her.

"Uh, you don't happen to have a chart for the Pensacola area in your purse, do you?" he asked.

"No, I don't have a chart in my purse," Linky answered.

"Do you have one in your suitcase?" he asked.

"No, I don't have a chart in my suitcase."

"Do you have a chart anywhere!"

Linky nodded.

"Where is it!"

Linky tapped her forehead indicating she had the chart memorized. A few days before, Linky had an instrument check ride with her commanding officer in the very same airplane and remembered the coordinates and other figures. The pilot grabbed her hand and led her to the pilot's seat.

"After I chewed them both out for going on a flight without proper preparation," Linky says, "I put on the headset and took us home. Just as

*WAVE Gladys "Linky" Sommer.*
*Photograph courtesy of Linky Brokhausen*

we got over Pensacola, the clouds opened up. I handed the plane back to the pilot because I sure couldn't land the thing. I'd never landed anything but an Aeronca or a Taylorcraft.

"I knew it was the same plane," she continues, "because I recognized the scratches on the instrument panel. Was it unfair of me to leave them with the impression that I might have a full catalog of radio ranges in my pointed little head?"

Asked about her service in WWII, Linky Brokhausen responds, "I was part of the AEF in WWII. That's not the American Expeditionary Forces as in WWI, but Americans Exiled in Florida!" Often during her tour of duty, Linky had to prove her ability. At least once, she had to defend her honor. Whatever the situation, she kept her wits about with a sense of humor that persists today.

Linky Brokhausen was a LINK Trainer instructor in the Navy Women's Reserve, the WAVES (Women Accepted for Volunteer Emergency Service). The LINK Trainer was used to train pilots in instrument flying, and from it Linky received her nickname.

Linky was born Gladys Sommer, the oldest of three daughters, to patriotic parents in Louisville, Kentucky. "Dad always wanted a son, but he got

Gladys, Gloria, and Patricia instead, and never forgave us. He was the big-
gest put-down artist of all time. I had an ego about this big," she says, ges-
turing with her thumb and index finger a space of about an inch, "until I
got in the navy. While I wasn't Miss America, I learned I wasn't dog meat
either. I discovered that I had a brain because I got the job I got strictly
through my ability to take multiple choice tests."

Her father chased Pancho Villa in Mexico and was a veteran of World
War I. Despite being designated disabled when the United States entered
WWII, he volunteered for and was accepted in the army at age forty-five.
He served as an engineer in England. "By the time I got out, I outranked
my father," Linky says. "I had more stripes or equivalent. He never said a
word, and I didn't throw it in his face. I should have."

Linky had just graduated from high school when the United States
entered WWII. "My father was a state commander of the local VFW," she
says. "I listened to the men, took notes, and typed them up for them. From
the beginning, when Hitler started to move, they were of the opinion that
the U.S. would get into the war. So I thought, like a lot of women, that it
would be nice to help out."

Signed on July 30, 1942, Public Law 689 established the Women's
Reserve of the Navy. The WAAC, Women's Auxiliary Army Corps, was
established earlier that year. Since she lived near Fort Knox, Linky sought
out local WAACs. "I talked to some at Fort Knox, and it seemed like all
they did was desk jobs and drive trucks," she says. "Well, I was working as
a secretary at Standard Oil and bored out of my gourd. Also, I didn't drive.
The navy offered more specialties and the army's uniforms weren't all that
attractive."

Despite her desire, Linky faced a hurdle. "We could enlist at twenty
with parental permission," she says. "I knew there was no chance whatsoever that my mother would sign for me to join the navy." Soon afterward,
she got engaged to a marine and forgot about joining the military.

"He was one of those who didn't come back from the Pacific," she
says. "I moped around for awhile, then one day went down and signed up,
then I went home and told my mother. She and my grandmother nearly
brought out the sackcloth and ashes. After all, no nice girl from a good family would do such a thing as join the navy."

Since she lived near Fort Knox, people often asked why she joined the
navy instead of the army. Linky developed a standard reply: "I told them I
didn't want to wear khaki underwear."

For your country's sake today—

For your own sake tomorrow

**GO TO THE NEAREST RECRUITING STATION
OF THE ARMED SERVICE OF YOUR CHOICE**

Are you a girl with a Star-Spangled heart?

JOIN THE WAC NOW!

THOUSANDS OF ARMY JOBS NEED FILLING!

Women's Army Corps
United States Army

MINE EYES HAVE SEEN THE GLORY

WOMEN'S ARMY CORPS

ARMY OF THE UNITED STATES

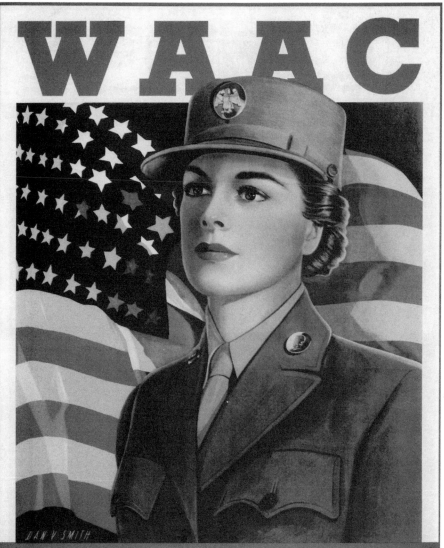

# WAAC

## THIS IS MY WAR TOO!
### WOMEN'S ARMY AUXILIARY CORPS
### UNITED · STATES · ARMY

YOU ARE NEEDED NOW

JOIN THE
**ARMY NURSE CORPS**

APPLY AT YOUR RED CROSS RECRUITING STATION

She's helping to win
*...how about you?*

Serve in the Navy...

*Enlist in the* **WAVES**

**INQUIRE AT ANY**
Navy Recruiting Station or Office of Naval Officer Procurement

Don't miss your great opportunity..

THE NAVY NEEDS YOU IN THE **WAVES**

Share the Deeds of Victory

Join the **WAVES**

APPLY TO YOUR NEAREST
NAVY RECRUITING STATION OR OFFICE OF NAVAL OFFICER PROCUREMENT

**JOIN THE NAVY NURSE CORPS**

APPLY AT YOUR RED CROSS RECRUITING STATION

"THE GIRL OF THE YEAR IS A SPAR"

ENLIST IN THE COAST GUARD **SPARS**

APPLY NEAREST COAST GUARD OFFICE

TITLE IV — WOMEN'S AIR FORCES SERVICE PILOTS

Active dut
status.
38 USC 10

Sec. 401. (a)(1) Notwithstanding any other provision of law, the service of any person as a member of the Women's Air Forces Service Pilots (a group of Federal civilian employees attached to the United States Army Air Force during World War II), or the service of any person in any other similarly situated group the members of which rendered service to the Armed Forces of the United States in a capacity considered civilian employment or contractual service at the time such service was rendered, shall be considered active duty for the purposes of all laws administered by the Veterans' Administration if the Secretary of Defense, pursuant to regulations which the Secretary shall prescribe—

Record

(A) after a full review of the historical records and all other available evidence pertaining to the service of any such group, determines, on the basis of judicial and other appropriate precedent, that the service of such group constituted active military service, and

Disch

(B) in the c[ase of] any such group with respect to which such [Secre]tary has [made an] affirmative [deter]mination th[at] the service [of suc]h group [constit]uted active [militar]y service, [issue t]o each [membe]r of such [group] a discharg[e from s]uch service [as h]onor[able].

THE SPIRIT
OF
AMERICA

JOIN

Linky reported to the Office of Naval Officer Procurement, ONOP, in Cincinnati. "They gave us mental tests first. We were settling down when an officer entered. A group of young men were taking the naval cadet exams next door," Linky recalls. "He said that there had been so many complaints about the difficulty of their tests that he wanted to try something. He wanted four or five women volunteers to take the test. If we passed, we need take no more tests. Should we flunk, we could take the WAVES' exams."

Despite warnings to never volunteer, Linky and four other women raised their hands to take the test with the thirty to forty men in the room. After a brief explanation, the officer started the timer. "There were some strange questions considering the education of women of that era," she says, "but all five women were among the first ten to complete the tests. All passed with flying colors. We learned that, in the future, whenever the subject arose, we would be held up to the men as examples to spur them on— and shut them up—especially since none of us were college graduates. That had been one of the specifications when we were invited."

Physical exams followed. "This was the first time I had gone through a complete physical," she says. "They put us through what's called the 'daisy chain.' They really went over us with a fine-tooth comb." On May 2, 1944, Linky left for basic training at Hunter College in New York City.

The navy had commandeered Hunter College and apartment buildings on the perimeter of the campus to train and house the recruits. "We had double-decker bunks in our rooms. Twelve girls shared an apartment and one bathroom," Linky says. "As I had belonged to a drum-and-bugle corps, and already knew my left foot from my right, I wound up as platoon leader. We marched everywhere. Come to think of it, the bathroom was about the only place we didn't march to."

Besides learning to march, there was one more aspect of military life she needed to learn. The first time she met an officer, she realized she didn't know how to salute. "I gave him the only salute I knew—the Girl Scout salute," she laughs. "He couldn't quite suppress a smile."

"When we got to basic training," she continues, "the only item of uniform we had was the hat, the round one with the brim and black top that indicated we were boots. Otherwise, we wore civvies, with the addition of a little folded pouch on a string to carry our money and our ID. These hung around our necks and flapped on our bosoms as we marched."

In the mess hall, Linky had her first collision with authority. "I don't know what those male cooks had against us women, but what they put in front of us was a crime." The first morning, they plopped some "horrible looking stuff" on Linky's tray. "I was unable to gag it down. As a result of leaving food on my tray, I was given extra duty polishing brass doorknobs during my free time," she says. A week later, they served the same stuff, and Linky said she didn't want it, but they put it on her tray anyway. "It looked like something that had already been eaten. I was never able to ascertain which end of the alimentary canal had rejected it. This time my extra duty was cleaning cigarette butt boxes."

The third week, the objectionable food was served again. "I said I didn't want it. When I saw it coming anyway, I jerked my tray out of the way and there was a huge plop on the deck followed by an angry and bellowing officer. Male." Linky told the officer the whole sordid story. "I told him when I saw I was going to get the food after I said I didn't want it, I took action. You know, the ensuing weeks, I didn't get anything dumped on my tray, nor did anyone else."

The women were also tested to determine their abilities. Before she signed up, Linky had decided that she wanted to be a LINK instructor. "I had a second cousin who went into the Army Air Corps," she explains. "He was one week from getting his wings when he flew into a mountain at night in Washington State and bought the farm. I had read about these funny machines they used to teach men to fly.

"However, in the military, the odds you'll get what you want are astronomical," she continues. "I think they gave us sixteen hours of multiple choice tests and you weren't supposed to finish in the first place, but I did. The woman who interviewed me told me as far as she was concerned, I could have anything I wanted because I had placed in the top ten of sixteen hundred who had taken the test." Statistics show that only one percent of the ninety thousand enlistees qualified for LINK operator training. At stations throughout the United States, they trained four thousand cadets per day.

The woman went on to tell Linky that there must be a mistake in her transcript because she took an almost perfect geometry test and that class wasn't listed. "I don't have the foggiest idea how I did that," Linky says. "Louisville was peculiar. Our high schools were segregated by sex. I attended an all-girls high school, and we didn't get higher math and science classes. One teacher even told me, 'You're a mathematical idiot. Don't try to do anything where you work with figures.'"

Her interviewer tried to persuade Linky to apply for control tower operator, but she insisted on LINKs. "It's a good thing, too," she says. "I would've washed out in a day. Taking flight lessons later, I learned that up to about twenty-five feet I had twenty-twenty vision, beyond that, I was as blind as a bat."

Training to be a LINK trainer operator was at Naval Air Station, Atlanta, Georgia. "Classes were something else," Linky remembers. "We learned the theory of flight, aneroid and gyroscopic aircraft instruments, Morse code, aerology, airway traffic control, FAA rules and regulations, and how to read a wiring diagram. They taught us to troubleshoot and repair the trainer."

The curriculum required that the women fly as passengers to witness in the real world what they learned in theory. "I was draped in a sit-on type parachute harness," she says. "I was going up in an SNB airplane known as the 'Bugsmasher,' so I was instructed on how to abandon the plane should the need arise. They told me, 'If you have to bail out, do not jump feet first; the tail assembly will chop off your head. Do not dive out as though diving into a swimming pool. The tail assembly will chop off your feet. Make yourself into a ball and roll out.' This was very soothing for a girl who had never been in a large plane!"

Linky and the crew took off into the night over Atlanta. "They had a policy of doing something to scare their female passengers, but I was a spoil sport. I fell asleep. Then the instructor asked me if I wanted to fly the plane and I said, 'yes,'" Linky laughs. "The instructor turned to the other passengers and uttered a few bleeps. Evidently, he'd been asking the girls if they wanted to fly the plane for months, and they always refused."

The instructor asked the crew what he should do. A student answered, "Let her fly. She can't do anything worse than kill us." Her first time in an airplane, Linky flew a holding pattern over Atlanta without mishap.

While Linky was stationed in Atlanta, her mother visited her and met some of the WAVES Linky knew. Her mother was so impressed that when she returned home, she removed the sackcloth and ashes and placed a blue star in her window, proudly proclaiming to the world that a family member was in the military.

After graduation, Linky went alone to NAS Richmond, Florida. Her assignment turned out to be quite a surprise. "This was the headquarters of the navy's LTA, Lighter-Than-Air, program," she says. "There were a few HTA, Heavier-Than-Air, pilots attached to Station Operation, and two or

*Linky Sommer standing on steps of barracks, NAS Pensacola.
Photograph courtesy of Linky Brokhausen*

three planes, but for the most part, all the procedures that had been drummed into my head in school went totally to waste. Although women were not supposed to be allowed up in blimps, I did go a few times and got to take the rudder control at times.

"When I went up for promotion, there was no one to test me in the trainer," Linky says. "So instead of doing my 'flying' in the trainer, I did it in a JRF 'Grumman Goose.' Much easier and more fun."

In the blimp hangar at NAS Richmond, Linky had an ugly sexist confrontation. One student, a lieutenant, junior grade, consistently made "smutty remarks" to her when he arrived for instruction in the trainer, so she always tried to have a chaperone present. One day, the lieutenant arrived when no one else was around.

"When we went into the LINK shack, 'El Jerko' locked the door behind us," Linky says. "I unlocked it. He relocked it. This happened several times. I tried to get him into the trainer, but no go. There was no doubt whatsoever what he had on his mind. He made himself very clear." Linky turned off all the power, picked up her hat and purse, and told the officer to lock the door behind him. He ordered her to stay, reminded her that he was an officer, and therefore she had to obey him, but she kept walking. Following her across the hangar, he yelled for her to return.

Linky went to the nearest door where she knew there would be people. "I figured that if there was an audience, he'd give up. Wrong!" she says. "There were five or six enlisted men who were good friends of mine because we worked weird hours together. When they greeted me, El Jerko sounded off. He said, 'Now I get it! You goddamn bitch in blue. You're so busy giving it away to the enlisted men that you have nothing left for me.'"

Linky looked at her friends, fearing they would come to her rescue. The officers present risked court martial if they did so. She decided that if this happened to anyone, it should be her, the injured party. After she placed her hat and purse on the counter, she switched rings. On her right hand she wore her mother's pinky ring, which was fragile; on her left hand was a heavy silver ring with sharp edges. (Her mother's ring is visible on her right hand in the photo at the beginning of this chapter.)

"I asked Jerko if he had said his piece, then commented that the navy may have made him an officer, but it had dropped the ball when it came to making him a gentleman," Linky says. "Then I gave him the old one-two, a left to the breadbasket, and when he doubled over, a swift right to the kisser. Don't know if it was a jab, a hook, or an uppercut, but it worked just as it had in grammar school when my father taught me that method of handling bullies. He staggered backward, hit the wall and slid down to sit in the butt box, which I thought was quite fitting. I learned later that I had not only bloodied his nose and split his lip, but broke his nose and loosened two of his incisors. I was *mad!*"

Linky immediately went to her commanding officer to tell him what she had done. Together, they went to El Jerko's commanding officer. "He was livid. He was a man with four daughters with a viewpoint to match." When the offender arrived, still in his bloodstained uniform, to start court martial proceedings, "both of the COs lit into him," Linky says. "Among other things, they told him that the young ladies who worked there were indeed ladies and should be treated as such." El Jerko was shipped out the next day. "I felt for the girls wherever he was sent," Linky says, "because he was the type who would take his revenge on any and all WAVES he might come in contact with down the line. Innocents would have to pay for my resistance."

Linky stresses that this incident was the exception, not the rule. "For the most part, I was very lucky to serve under men who would back their staff all the way down the line," she says. "In the navy, the rotten apples were known as the two percent. Almost all of the men with whom I came in contact were people I'm proud to have known." Linky remembers one bit of fallout from the incident and laughs. "Word went around NAS Richmond that should I shift my rings, head for the hills, because I had a wicked right fist."

Linky and her comrades celebrated V-J Day at NAS Richmond, but Linky says, "The air station was informally decommissioned by a hurricane which blew away and/or burned all the hangars and aircraft."

Next duty station was NAS Pensacola in August 1946. She was assigned to 4-Mike, the PBY seaplane training squadron. According to Linky, "This was quite a change from blimps. Finally, I could use what I was taught in school. It was an upgrade in many ways. I had been taught in and had used in Richmond the ANT-18, the little blue trainer with wings. At Pensacola, they had the new and larger NAV-BIT, which gave various signals automatically. The instructor didn't have to constantly twiddle dials."

The first students Linky taught were fledgling pilots followed by groups of NAVCADs-A/Ps, or student officers. The instructors took turns giving them indoctrination talks to explain what they would be doing in the department. Years later when the first seven astronauts were named, Linky recalled the names of two of the students in these talks—Alan Shepard and Wally Shirra. "Later, Alan Shepard was a student in my group, and he was really sharp, plus being very pleasant and easy to get along with. I really cheered when he drove that first golf ball on the moon."

When she went to her job one morning, she found a man curled up on top of her desk taking a snooze. She didn't recognize him as her scheduled student and noticed he wasn't an officer, so, "Being ladylike and genteel, I booted him in the rump and suggested that he move his fat can elsewhere. I got a glare from some very blue eyes. We did not care for one another at all."

A few weeks later, a roommate of his maneuvered them into a double date. The gentleman's name was Stanley D. "Brok" Brokhausen. "Neither one of us was the least bit interested in getting serious with or about anyone. We wound up having a simple wedding in the station chapel the following summer. I heard someone say, 'I give it a year. If he hasn't killed her by then, he'll at least divorce her!'"

After several months, there was a change in the way pilots qualified for instrument cards. "Some of us started putting them through the works in the trainer so that they could quickly qualify with the check pilot," she says.

"Here, the resistance to our instructing hit a new high, especially from the A/Ps. They were firmly of the attitude that no way could 'those girls' possibly know what they are talking about."

At about this time, Linky flew the students home when they had not properly prepared for the flight. Afterward, Linky noticed that the two pilots and other A/Ps didn't give her a hard time. "Guess they figured out that 'those girls' did know what they were talking about. Made it easier for the rest of the gals, too."

When the war ended, Linky resigned from the navy because she was told she had to and looked for a job. With all the men and women discharged from the military, jobs were few. She had passed the exam to be a secretary with the State Department in Frankfurt, Germany. On her way to get a passport, she passed the navy recruiting office and stopped in for old time's sake. There, she learned that her job in Pensacola was still available to her at no reduction in pay, so she rejoined.

Linky and Mr. Brokhausen married in July 1947, but Linky stayed in the navy for fifteen months after their marriage until he received a perma-

*Linky Brokhausen in March 2002.*
*Photograph by Sara McBryde*

nent position in San Diego in October 1948. Despite their comrade's prediction, Linky and Brok had been married for forty-four years when he joined the "silent squadron."

When asked if she is glad she joined the navy, Linky responds, "You betcha! I enjoyed my job so much that I would have stayed in for twenty years if I hadn't had the good luck to marry a great gentleman. Today, I could do both, but not then." She also says, "I met some very fine men and women, along with a few stinkers, of course. I went places, did things, learned things, and saw things that I probably wouldn't have had I been a quiet little mouse and stayed home. I can truly say I got an education in more ways than one."

Linky lives in a modest green farmhouse east of Georgetown. She does fancy needlework that she sells at a craft store downtown, where she also works one day a week. Other activities include attending plays and orchestra performances, bowling in a league for seniors, and being a ham radio operator. For relaxation, she works crossword puzzles and is an avid reader.

# 15

## EVELYN WHEELER SWENSON

*WAVES, Boston Naval Yard, Philadelphia Naval Yard,*
*Naval Purchasing Office, Chicago, Illinois*

"Admiral Nimitz didn't want women in the navy, but then there was a shortage of men."

The railroad car lurched to the right, and Evelyn Wheeler grabbed the back of a seat to steady herself. "I can't wait to get off this train," she said, more to herself than anyone around her. "Three days is enough." The young women within earshot merely nodded agreement. The last one to step inside the women's railroad car, a member of the Shore Patrol, locked the door behind Evelyn. *I'm stuck in here until we get to Northampton, Massachusetts.* She went to the bathroom to wash her face; the faucet gurgled and a few drops of water trickled out and then stopped. *Drat. Still no water.* She returned to her seat and slumped down. Coal dust fogged around her when she did so. She looked out the window into the darkness; the kr-thunk, kr-thunk, kr-thunk of the wheels lulled her to sleep. "Northampton, Massachusetts," the Shore Patrolman shouted from the back of the car, and Evelyn looked up from her slumber. Finally, they had arrived. She looked at her watch—it was two o'clock in the morning.

"One of the memorable experiences was that trip to Northampton," Evelyn says. "We were not allowed on or off the train, and they locked the doors at either end. Breakfast was at 5:00 a.m., lunch at 10:00 a.m., and dinner about 5:00 p.m. The rest of the time we were stuck in our car. The last day, we had no water except what we got to drink in the dining room."

More than three days before, Evelyn and twenty-five other women accepted into the WAVES boarded the troop train in Dallas for the three-and-a-half-day journey. Three of them, including Evelyn, were headed to

*WAVE Evelyn Wheeler, Boston, Massachusetts, 1944.
Photograph courtesy of Evelyn Wheeler Swenson*

Smith College for officer's indoctrination. The other women were going to Hunter College, New York, for basic training. "When we got there," she says, "they handed us sheets and told us to go to bed as quickly as possible. I told them I was going to wash my hair because I'd been on the train for three days and it was black from the coal dust. They consented only because the three of us were officer candidates and would be put in a room by ourselves, with our own showers, and wouldn't disturb the rest." After boot camp and throughout her time in the navy, finding a place to live was often difficult for Evelyn.

Evelyn is a quiet woman with warm and pleasant smile. She was born in Tilden, Texas, and attended the University of Texas in Austin, graduating with a degree in nutrition. She was working in a chemical plant in Arkansas when she enlisted in the navy in June 1944. "I wanted to go into the navy because I'd had friends, both male and female, join the navy," she says. "My mother was concerned about me working in the chemical plant, so she considered the navy an improvement."

The morning after their arrival, Evelyn was up at 6:00 a.m. The first order of the day was to get a physical. "As I remember, we had no covering whatsoever," she says. "Not even a sheet. We just went from one cubicle to the next. After our physicals, they took us to a shoe shop in Northampton where we were fitted for shoes. After lunch, we went to the drill field. None of us knew how to drill. I got to giggling so the officer in charge said, 'Get up here and take control.' The only command I knew was 'Forward March.' We marched off the field and she had to run after us.

"Following drill, we had classes until late in the afternoon each day," she continues. "Some of the courses were history of the navy, naval identification of ships and airplanes. On Saturday, we had to stand at attention while the commanding officer came and reviewed us. We were issued wool skirts and short sleeve shirts and it was hot. I remember one girl had sweat dripping off her nose and the CO made note. She told me later it was all she could do to keep from spitting in the officer's face. Some of the girls fainted on the field and had to be taken away in an ambulance."

The officer candidates started as plebes the first month of training, became midshipmen the second, and graduated as ensigns in the United States Naval Reserve the end of the second month. Following graduation, Evelyn and two other ensigns were assigned to Supply Corps and went to Boston Navy Yard for duty. The navy had made no arrangements for accommodations.

"We had to find our own places to stay," Evelyn says. "We could only stay at the YWCA three days. One friend and I went up and down Beacon Hill trying to find something at that time. In some places, the bedroom would be on the third floor and the bathroom in the basement or something terrific like that. One of the girls knew a family whose son was in the army. Finally, we looked them up and rented out his room for two months."

At this assignment, the women sometimes had night duty. "The officer in charge never let me go out into the warehouses by myself," she says, "but my roommate had to."

Following Supply Corps duty at Boston Navy Yard, Evelyn attended Harvard Business School, which the navy had taken over for Supply Corps School. While at Harvard, she and the other women stayed in dormitories at Radcliffe. "We had to march to classes," she said. "The men could proceed 'at ease,' or walk, but we had to march." For three months, she studied disbursing and supply before going to the Philadelphia Navy Yard.

"In Philadelphia, we had no place to stay," Evelyn says. "They'd made provisions for enlisted WAVES but not officers. Three of us got a third-floor apartment in a row house on the west side. I worked as the priorities officer in the contract section of the supply department at the Philadelphia Navy Yard. I relieved a girl going to Hawaii. They had just been allowed to go overseas. At first, it was a concession for us to even be in the navy. Admiral [Chester] Nimitz didn't want women but decided he needed the men and we could replace them."

At the navy yard, barges were being built in preparation for an invasion of Japan. "The plan was for the barges to be towed to ships and airplanes that needed repair. Since I was priorities officer," Evelyn says, "they had to go through me to get their priorities upped to get the materials sooner. All contracts were assigned a priority as they went through the contract section. If they wanted it sooner, they had to come to me and I called Washington, D.C., to get permission to up their rating.

"While in Philadelphia," she continues, "there was a German submarine that had been captured and brought into the yard. A friend of mine was in salvage, so we boarded it and were given some things. I took canned butter and canned bacon because they were still rationed."

According to the Navy Military History website, the submarine that Evelyn refers to was probably the *U-505*. Captured on June 4, 1944, off the coast of Africa, it was the first enemy vessel captured by a U.S. naval vessel since World War I.

"The war ended in August 1945 while I was in Philadelphia," Evelyn says. "We all went down to Broad Street. It was just full of people, no cars, celebrating the end of the war. I never thought it would end. It just seemed to me it was going to go on forever, you know?" The end of the war also ended the need for Evelyn as priorities officer. "We had to get rid of all this stuff that we'd contracted for and hadn't been delivered.

"They sent me to War College in the Pentagon for six weeks," she continues. "Lawyers taught the course in contract termination, and I didn't understand a great deal of what they said." While in Washington, Evelyn again stayed in an apartment with other WAVES. "The girls were in communications and had to serve around the clock. I never knew which bed I could sleep in. It was whichever one was on duty that night."

Evelyn then went to the Naval Purchasing Office in Chicago. There, she met her future husband. "He was terminating contracts at the Naval Purchasing Office, also. I was the first WAVE they'd ever had in the office," she laughs. "They weren't sure whether they were going to invite me into the coffee room where they settled all sorts of high-minded questions. They also told jokes and thought my presence might stifle conversation, but they finally invited me in. It turned out to be a nice duty."

While in Chicago, Evelyn once again had trouble finding appropriate housing. "I finally found a room in a boarding house in north Chicago," she says. "The other girls and I were told never to go down in the basement, but my roommate and I were adventuresome and had to see what was down there. Well, there was this table and one of the women who owned the boarding house was a doctor. We figured out she was doing abortions. That's why we weren't supposed to go down there."

*Evelyn Wheeler Swenson in 1991.*
*Photograph courtesy of Evelyn Wheeler Swenson*

Evelyn and her roommate were invited to have Thanksgiving dinner with a fellow WAVE and her family and told them what a terrible place the boarding house was. "Our friend's father was a lawyer and found us a room in a residential hotel. It was very small. I had a Murphy bed that folded down out of the wall. It's a good thing we didn't have many clothes. We only had our uniforms, and not very many of those."

By June 1946, Evelyn had enough points to leave the navy. "I was discharged at Great Lakes and came back to Texas. The navy was a wonderful experience for me," she says. "It was no hardship at all as far as I was concerned. It was mostly hard finding a place to live. Frantically."

Evelyn went to social worker school at Columbia University in New York City for a time before she married. She volunteered at the San Antonio YWCA because of her gratitude to the organization for providing housing when she so desperately needed it. In 1990, Evelyn organized a national WAVE unit in San Antonio, Texas. She meets friends at national WAVES conventions whenever possible.

Evelyn married Lt. Sigurd Swenson, a career naval officer, on April 12, 1947, and had a very interesting life living in many cities throughout the United States and in Oslo, Norway. They have two children, Dr. Peter C. Swenson and Dr. Anne Swenson, and two granddaughters, Karin and Meredith.

# 16

# MARGARET "PEGGY" PECK BAROS

*WAVES, Fleet Postal Service, New York, New York, San Francisco, California*

"I treasure all the memories of my tour of duty."

Margaret "Peggy" Peck stood at attention in front of the captain alongside her WAVE comrades. The uniform against her sunburned skin hurt and she wanted to squirm, but she dared not. She was in enough trouble. After what seemed an eternity, the captain told them their punishment and dismissed them.

"Some of us had gone to Coney Island over the weekend," Peggy laughs. "All we wanted to do was to have fun and get a suntan, but we got a sunburn and had to go on sick leave. We went before a Captain's Mast, which is like going before a judge with a traffic ticket. He didn't have much sympathy because we'd brought it on ourselves, but we had fun. He gave us demerits, confined us to quarters, and gave us extra duty. We were more careful next time."

In the coziness of her spotless kitchen, Peggy spoke fondly of her time as a WAVE. She was born in New Kensington, Pennsylvania, on the Allegheny River near Pittsburgh. With support from her mother (her father was killed when she was a small child), she signed up for the Navy Women's Reserve. When she went to get her physical, she faced an unexpected problem. "You had to weigh a hundred pounds to get in," she says. "At the time, I didn't, so I went home and ate bananas for a week. I gained enough weight to get in." Peggy entered the navy on August 15, 1943, as an apprentice seaman. "A friend went with me to join," Peggy says, "but she backed out."

*WAVE Peggy Peck.*
*Photograph courtesy of Peggy Baros*

Basic training was at Hunter College in New York for thirty days. "I learned to march right, left, and to the rear, and how to stand at attention and parade rest," Peggy says. "It was a wonderful experience, and I met some fine girls." At the conclusion of this phase of her career, she received the rank of seaman second class.

From Hunter College, she traveled to Cedar Falls, Iowa, in late September for Yeoman Training School. "I hadn't wanted to do office work when I got in the service," she laughs, "but they found out I had experience and got it anyway. One memory I have of that time was waking up one morning to people screaming and laughing. I got up to see what had happened. It had snowed overnight and the southern girls were carrying on because they had never seen snow."

With a rating of yeoman third class, Peggy then reported to the Fleet Post Office in New York. "We didn't censor any mail," she says, "we just sorted the mail and got it to where it was supposed to go." After a week of this activity, the girls were ready for some fun. Besides other *uneventful* excursions to Coney Island, they attended shows on Broadway and enjoyed other sites in New York City.

Peggy was in New York on May 8, 1945, V-E (Victory in Europe) Day. "I was in Times Square when the war ended in Europe. That's something I'll never forget. Everybody just went wild. The excitement was just unbelievable." Peggy also remembers President Roosevelt's funeral procession in New York.

With the war over in Europe, the Fleet Post Office wasn't needed in New York, so the group transferred to San Francisco. They traveled by troop train across the United States, into Canada, and down to San Francisco. Peggy jokes about passing through part of Canada. "We laughed that this was our overseas service."

Upon her arrival to San Francisco on July 4, 1945, Peggy's rank was yeoman second class. "I was in the middle of San Francisco when the war was over with Japan. Another great memory," she says. No longer needed in San Francisco, she was transferred to Shoemaker, California, Naval Separation Center. As a yeoman first class, she assisted with discharging sailors from the navy.

While in Shoemaker, she met Texan Charles Douglas. After a whirlwind romance of six weeks, they married on November 28, 1945, and she

*Peggy Baros today.*
*Photograph by Cindy Weigand.*

was discharged from the navy on December 7. The couple had three sons. She and Mr. Douglas divorced in 1969. In 1972, she married Clyde Baros and moved to Gonzales. Peggy stays active in a group of former WAVES that meets regularly in San Antonio. Of her time in the service, Peggy says, "My navy career was exciting for me, and I treasure all the memories of my tour of duty."

# 17

# JUANITA MANG GOSCH

*Navy Nurse Corps, United States Naval Hospitals, San Diego, California; and Sampson, New York; NAS DISP, Norfolk, Virginia*

"It was rough seeing that much trauma in men so young."

Juanita Mang watched as the corpsmen unloaded wounded sailors and marines from the ambulance, wincing when one of them cried out in pain. She shook her head in sadness. *They go in so gung-ho and come home so badly wounded.* She then hurried to her ward to care for her patients.

"We got patients from the Pacific theater, strictly the Pacific," Juanita says. "They came from the Philippines, Guam, Iwo Jima, and Tarawa. My brother was killed in Tarawa. They were badly wounded and really hard to care for, but we did the best we could."

Quiet and modest, Juanita is a woman of few words. Perhaps her story lies not in what she said when we spoke, but more in what she couldn't express in words. Maybe there are scenes and memories that mere words are insufficient to describe. Juanita was a navy nurse in World War II.

A young woman when she finished nursing school, Juanita was thrust into the position of caring for the badly wounded from land, sea, and air battles of the Pacific Theater of Operations. She went from nursing school straight to the wards, but surely nothing in her schooling could have prepared her for the carnage of such a brutal war.

"We cared for burns, patients with legs blown off, and brain damages. Just a variety of things," she says simply. Imagine seeing hundreds of these patients brought into the hospital. Picture yourself in a similar situation at twenty-one years of age. For a year, more than likely, six days a week, Juanita cared for the wounded of war. "I was young, I had the stamina, but it

Navy Nurse Juanita Mang.
Photograph courtesy of Juanita Gosch

affected you emotionally sometimes," she admits. "You had to be a bright person for them."

Born in Charlotte, Texas, Juanita Mang graduated from the Santa Rosa School of Nursing in San Antonio, Texas, in 1943 when the war was at its peak. In desperate need of nurses, the American Red Cross was recruiting for the military, so Juanita decided to join the service. "Attending Santa Rosa, I saw a lot of military and they were always army," she says. "I decided I wanted something different, so I joined the navy." Juanita enlisted in the Navy Nurse Corps and traveled to Corpus Christi for a physical and "sort of an indoctrination." She returned to San Antonio to wait for an assignment. While waiting, she performed private duty nursing.

Called to active duty on January 26, 1944, Juanita reported directly to the U.S. Naval Hospital in San Diego, California. "My three years at Santa Rosa were my basic training. We didn't march or do any sort of military formations. We were strictly nurses," she says. "The wounded we saw came from the Pacific. It was really rough seeing that much trauma in 18- and 19-year-old boys," she says. "They went in so gung-ho, and then they were wounded."

Juanita provided nursing care for these men until she was transferred in January 1945 to the U.S. Naval Hospital in Sampson, New York. She worked there for six months. After seeing so much trauma in San Diego, the transfer provided some relief. "The nursing in Sampson was mostly routine," she says, "and the hospital wasn't nearly so big.

"We always did the best we could for the enlisted men, and they were all enlisted men," she continues. "Officers got top priority treatment. You did the best you could, but you could tell the difference in the care. I always resented that because, after all, they were all fighting the same battle."

With the war in Europe over and winding down in Japan, Juanita was transferred to U.S. Naval Station DISP in Norfolk, Virginia, until the defeat of Japan. "We stayed up all night celebrating," she says.

When she had enough points, Juanita mustered out of the navy in June 1946. Of her time in the service, she says, "My navy career was a wonderful time for me, and I treasure all the memories."

*Juanita Gosch today.*
*Photograph courtesy of Juanita Gosch*

# 18

# DORIS BAKER HOWARD

*Women's Reserve of the Coast Guard–SPAR,*
*Washington, D.C.*

"I had just one chance to be in the military. Just one."

Doris Baker stood at attention with the sixty other SPARs. The occasion was somber, yet she was thrilled to be there and a chill went down her spine. *What an honor!* Just then, she saw the pallbearers exit Union Station carrying the flag-draped coffin that contained President Roosevelt's body. Doris blinked back tears. *Sailors don't cry.* Carefully, solemnly, they placed the casket on the caisson and the procession moved forward, then down Pennsylvania Avenue toward the White House.

"When we got to the circular drive," Doris says in a warm southern drawl, "they took his body in and we went on. I was in the funeral business with my mother for a while after the war, and President Roosevelt's funeral was in the funeral books. I know where I'm standing in the photo. When they showed newsreels of the funeral at the movies, the man at the local theater would stop it so everyone in Gonzales could try to find me." Doris served in the Coast Guard during World War II. The women were known as SPARs, an acronym for the first letters of the coast guard motto, *Semper Paratus.*

Public Law 773, signed November 23, 1942, established the Women's Reserve of the Coast Guard Reserve. The recruitment slogan, "Don't Be a Spare, Be a SPAR," sought women to sign up for this smallest branch of the military. Doris answered that call. "I'd always heard about the coast guard," she says. "You know, it's the oldest branch of the service. I was very interested in it."

The nucleus of the women's coast guard, including the director, Doro-

SPAR Doris Baker.
Photograph courtesy of Doris Baker Howard

thy C. Stratton, came from the navy, which also recruited for the coast guard. By July 1943, SPAR recruiters were on the job in all district offices. By the end of 1944, eleven thousand women had signed enlistment contracts.

"The local recruiter, Annabelle, was a friend from a nice family in Austin," she says. "My parents, my mother in particular, objected to the WACs, so when Annabelle came along, why, I just felt I had to join the coast guard. My people had been in the military way back to the Revolutionary War and the War of 1812. My grandfather was in the Confederate Army. I had just this one chance to do it. Just one."

Born in Eagle Pass, Texas, on October 11, 1919, Doris's family moved to Gonzales when she was sixteen years old. "I've lived here most of my life," she laughs, "but I'm still considered a newcomer." After enlisting in February 1944, Doris and six other girls traveled to Palm Beach, Florida, for basic training.

The first group of SPARs had trained with the navy at Hunter College, in the Bronx, New York, before the training facility in Florida was established. "We lived in the old Biltmore Hotel while I was there," Doris says. "It wasn't as fine as it looked in the pictures, but it was nice. I had yeoman training there.

"One of the worst things about boot camp was that I was assigned to scullery duty. That's dish washing. There were eighteen hundred girls there in the Biltmore, so that was a lot of dishes. My friend and I tried to volunteer to work on stage for a play they were doing so we could get out of scullery duty, but we had to do it *and* be stage hands."

Doris's assignment after basic training was in Washington, D.C. "I was in Coast Guard Headquarters in the Morale Division," she says. "Mostly, I did secretarial work, but one Christmas, we took orders for the boys in service. Macy's Department Store had sent them catalogs, and their orders came back through us. We also dealt with lots of complaints and things like that."

While in Washington, D.C., Doris stayed in public housing until barracks were built for the women. "They were very nice and the food was good. It was safe," she says, "and we had a curfew. My life wasn't rough and tumble like Mama was afraid of, and we didn't get any more horrid duty like scullery.

"We also did lots of sight-seeing," she laughs. "I didn't do any sleeping. I went every chance I got. I still don't waste time sleeping if I can do something more interesting."

While a SPAR living in Washington, Doris remembers the strong

*Doris Baker Howard today.*
*Photograph courtesy of Doris Baker Howard*

bonds she formed with three friends. "There were four of us who were extra special friends and had wonderful experiences," she says. "We still get together every two years or so."

As wonderful as her time in the service was, it was brief. She returned to Gonzales in June 1945. "I was discharged early because my father had a stroke," she says. "I probably would have stayed in if I hadn't had to come home. If I hadn't joined, I would have always been sorry. I really enjoyed every bit of it because I was just dying to serve my country and be in uniform. That was wonderful."

After Doris returned home, she had intended on going to college to become a schoolteacher but became a funeral director instead and ran the family business with her mother. "It was different, but it had to be done, so that's what I did," she says. After operating the funeral home for a number of years, she sold it. Now, Doris owns and manages a ranch. At the time we talked, her hired man had just baled hay, and she was looking to sell it for the best price.

# 19

# JANIE "TEX" SHEPPARD

*Marine Corps Women's Reserve, Henderson Hall,
Arlington, Virginia*

"We heard taps as many as twelve times a day."

Janie Sheppard took the reel of film out of the container labeled "Saipan" and carefully cleaned off the sand, grit, and dried blood. Visions of atrocities she'd seen on other films passed through her mind as she threaded the film through the projector. *It can't be any worse than I've seen before.* The film ready, Janie sat down to wait for the officer from Naval Intelligence.

Promptly, he entered the room and sat in the chair next to Janie. After turning off the light, she clicked on the projector and watched in horror as scenes from the war in the Pacific passed before her eyes. Janie cringed at the sight of an American soldier hanging from a tree.

"Stop the film and cut that out," the officer snapped.

Obediently, Janie stopped the projector, cut out a strip of celluloid, and then handed it to the officer. After taping the film back together, she clicked the projector back on.

"We had film sent in every day," Janie says. "After we got it set up, Naval Intelligence would come in and watch it. When they saw a part they wanted cut out, they'd make us stop and cut it out right then and hand it to them, then we'd tape it back together. Sometimes we'd go to a movie and see the same newsreel without the parts we cut out."

Janie served her country in the Marine Corps Women's Reserve. There is no catchy acronym for this group. Like their male counterparts, they were simply referred to as the marines, sometimes as WMs for women marines.

"Oh, the men had nicknames for us," she laughs. "They called us

Marine Janie "Tex" Sheppard.
Photograph courtesy of Janie Sheppard

BAMs, for broad-ass Marines, so we called them HAMs, half-ass Marines. Only the marines could get away with it, though. No one else. If navy men tried, we called them flat-chested WAVES. That shut them up most of the time."

Like the branch of service she served in, Janie is no nonsense and to the point. She wastes no time or words telling her story.

Born on a farm in Midlothian, Texas, on April 23, 1922, Janie is from a family of ten. She was working at the Consolidated plant, manufacturer of the B-24 Bomber, in Fort Worth when she decided to join the marines. "My folks couldn't figure out why I wanted to join the service and make $50 a month," she says, "when I was making $50 a week at the plant. I just felt like I had to join the service and do my part.

"I joined the marines because I hadn't heard anything bad about them," she continues. "Besides, I had two brothers in the army and one in the air force. I wanted to be different. I liked their uniforms, too."

She signed up in Dallas on April 12, 1943, and joined the first class at Hunter College, New York, for basic training. The first class trained with

Navy WAVES and Coast Guard SPARS. Later, training was moved to Camp Lejeune, North Carolina. "Boot camp lasted six weeks," Janie says. "We studied the foundation of the Marine Corps, and they told us what they expected of us and things like that. We had some weapon training, but we were in the middle of World War II. They didn't have time to give us too much. They just gave us what they had to.

"Learning to drill was no problem," she continues, "because I was a farm kid. Many passed out because of the heat. It was hot at Hunter College. You'd start to do an about face and your foot would stick to the asphalt."

Following basic training, the marines chose certain women for specialized instruction. "They experimented to see if women could be plumbers, carpenters, and electricians," she says. "I was chosen to attend electrician school, which was six weeks long at Camp Lejeune, North Carolina. Well, you can't learn how to be an electrician in six weeks, but we learned not to get a hold of any hot wire. They had us pulling 220 volt wires into the Quonset huts to wire them."

Janie was then assigned to Henderson Hall in Arlington, Virginia, near the Pentagon and Arlington National Cemetery. "The only thing between us and the cemetery was a three-foot concrete wall," she says. "Horses pulled the caissons to the cemetery. We heard taps played ten, twelve times a day."

As an electrician, Janie learned how to show movies for the men that came home for R and R. She also had a somber duty associated with film. Janie received 16 mm film from the Pacific theater for reviewing and editing. "Before we could look at it, we had to clean it up because it had sand and grit and blood in it. We had film sent in every day. After we got it set up," she says, "Naval Intelligence would come in and watch it. When they saw a part they wanted cut out, they'd make us stop and cut it out right then and hand it to them, then we'd tape it back together. If some American boy was hanging from a tree hung there by the Japs, we'd cut that out, but if Japs were being burnt out of a cave, we left that in. They sat right by us and we handed it right to them. The worst one was from Saipan."

At this point, Janie pauses to contemplate what she saw on that film nearly sixty years ago. It's obvious she sees it clearly to this day when she shakes her head slowly and says, "Oh, the Japs were brutal. We had to cut a lot of that one out."

A memorable event while Janie was at Henderson Hall was the death of President Roosevelt in Warm Springs, Georgia. Janie was chosen for an all-service group of women to escort the caisson from Union Station. "They wanted the platoon to be as uniform as possible," she says, "so they went through the record books and found everyone five feet, seven inches tall. His body lay in state for three days. That's how long we had to practice for the funeral march. We drilled all day long for it.

"We met the body at Union Station and marched to the White House," Janie says. "If you've ever heard a funeral march, there's no way you can keep time with it. They had to yell cadence constantly to keep us in step, but it was an honor to be chosen."

Janie also saw the military as her only chance to get a college education. After the surrender of the Japanese on September 2, 1945, Janie signed up for one more year. "If we signed up for another year, we got an extra stripe. I could also go to college on the GI bill, so I stayed in to help with the discharges of all the others."

Accepted to Texas Christian University, Janie was discharged from the military in August 1946. "I was too late for the fall semester, so I had to wait till January. I knew no one would give me a job. Think about it. Nobody was going to hire a woman electrician. The government had what they called the 52–20. If you couldn't find a job, they paid you $20 a week for 52 weeks. I did that until I started school. I got my bachelor's and master's degrees in education in four years. It was good."

After completing her college education, Janie taught school for thirty-one years in the Kennendale and Lake Worth school districts. In addition to

*Janie Sheppard in August 2002.*
*Photograph by Cindy Weigand*

teaching, she was an elementary school principal for six years. She joined the inactive marine reserves in 1947 and active reserves in 1958. In 1982, she retired with the rank of MSgt E8 after thirty-seven years of service, twenty-four of which were considered good service for retirement benefits.

Active in the American Legion, she has been an officer in many positions, including commander and adjutant commander of Post 569 in Fort Worth.

# 20

# VERA "DEE" DIETEL CRAWFORD

*Marine Corps Women's Reserve, Quantico,*
*Virginia, El Toro, California*

"You can't believe our fear after Pearl Harbor was bombed."

Dee lay on the bed, exhausted from the marching and activities of the day.

"Hey Dee," her bunk mate called out, "throw me a candy bar, will you? I'm too tired to get undressed."

"Well, I'm too tired to get up and get you one," Dee said.

"That's okay," the girl replied. "I'm too tired to eat it anyway."

"We used so much energy during the day," Dee says, "that we bought *sacks* of candy bars at the PX for energy, but sometimes we were too tired to eat them. They about wore us out, but we lost weight and trimmed down. The muscles in our legs tightened. We really looked good, you know?"

Dee Dietel (pronounced Dee-tell) Crawford and her husband, H. S., also a marine veteran, welcomed me into their home filled with memorabilia of H. S.'s travels throughout the Pacific Theater of Operations. A pleasant, insightful person with deep faith, Dee looks years younger than her age. She said that no one had really asked her about her service to our country although she served in the branch of service with the most stringent requirements.

The fifth of seven children, Dee was born in Nebish, Minnesota, on May 19, 1918. At the time the war started, her three older brothers were too old to enlist, so she decided to join the military. "I had this strong urge that someone from my family had to represent the Dietels," she says. "I was going to start with the branch with the highest qualifications. If I didn't pass, I would keep applying until one of them accepted me."

*Marine Vera "Dee" Dietel.*
*Photograph courtesy of Vera "Dee" Crawford*

Dee traveled to Minneapolis for an interview and to take the test for the marines. "I'm not bragging or anything, but I did excellently on my test. There was something on the math part I just didn't get because I had taken no more math in high school than algebra." Once she passed the test, she raised her hand and took the oath. "I took the oath right then. I didn't think any more about it."

At the time, Dee was working at a civil service job some miles away from her home. After enlisting, she went to her hometown to tell her mother that she had joined the marines. Later, her mother wrote Dee a letter. "I still have it," she says. "It just breaks your heart because she thought I was just going to Purgatory. I don't know what people thought we girls were going to do, but they were afraid something was going to happen to their little girls." Her father didn't say much at the time. "Down in his heart, though, I think he was proud of me."

Dee had to wait three months for a troop train to go to boot camp. She traveled two days and two nights to get to Camp Lejeune, North Carolina. Once there, she had to pass another physical. "I was tired from traveling and my eyes didn't make it. I'd worn glasses since high school and they were just tired. After I begged them, they let me take the eye exam the next morning and I passed with no problem."

Reveille was at 5:00 a.m. "Before we did anything, we were doing calisthenics, then we went to mess about six o'clock," she says. "After that, we had drill for about four hours of the day. I mean, we were on our feet constantly, taking commands and learning how to take orders. After lunch, we had courses in the history of the marines, some English and grammar. They gave us three college credit hours for our coursework. It was really quite involved." By the end of the day, the girls were ready to retire. "When we hit the bunk at nine or so, we were off to sleep," she laughs.

The recruits were allowed to specify what they wanted to do after basic training. Dee indicated she wanted to attend Parachute Rigging School. "I was selected and was thrilled to death," she says. However, the school didn't start for a month, so she was put on mess duty at Cherry Point in the meantime.

"Lord have mercy," she says. "That was an experience because we got up at 4:00 a.m. and had to fix stuff to serve to the other marines, then we had to clean up. We got so tired, we just lay down on the wooden floor and slept. Now, these weren't pretty, smooth planks. They had constructed our barracks so rapidly that they were uneven boards and rough as a cob. We got slivers in our backs, but we did it anyway. We'd sleep until time to fix the next meal. That lasted for a month."

Dee then went to Lakehurst, New Jersey, for Parachute Rigging School. "This was very interesting learning to pack parachutes," she says. "From there, we were assigned to various bases where we could actually be on duty. Seven of us were sent to Quantico, Virginia, where we actually worked in the parachute loft. There were civilian employees there, also." Dee laughs when asked if she ever tested one that she had packed. "Oh no, they were afraid that something would happen to those little girls."

At Quantico, Dee met her future husband on a training flight. "Every night they had training flights out of Turner Field nearby," she says. "They always sent two parachute riggers to make sure everyone had his parachute on correctly and knew how to operate it, and to assist in case we needed to jump. One time when it was my turn, I passed out the chutes, then a good-looking marine on the crew came back and talked to me. He was the radio operator who had just returned from overseas. Afterward, he asked me if he could walk me home, which he did. I was very much smitten with him."

They dated for a couple of months, and then he was shipped overseas for the second time. "That first night, he told me he was going to marry me," Dee says. "I thought he was just pulling my leg. When he left to go overseas,

I thought I'd never see him again because he'd either get killed or he'd forget about me." However, they corresponded by letter.

Dee's mother finally was resigned to the fact that she was in the military. Dee's going home on leave reassured her mother that nothing was going to happen to her little girl. One time on a trip home, Dee and her family gathered at the home of an aunt. Also present was a cousin on leave from the navy. "Everybody was so impressed with my uniform and how I looked," she says. "I'll never forget how proud my father was. He just beamed."

One day, there was a notice on the bulletin board that parachute riggers were needed in El Toro, California. "I thought that sounded like fun," Dee says, "so my friend and I, Edith Berkowitz, a darling little Jewish girl from New Jersey, signed up for transfer to California. We went on a train similar to a troop train, but it was all women marines being sent out there."

The men had an interesting custom before they tested the parachutes. Dee explains, "We wore a red scarf under our uniforms. When the men went up to test a parachute, he wore a girl's red scarf. I didn't have a boyfriend, so no one took mine up. Somebody tested my parachute, but I never found out who.

"When we packed a parachute," she continues, "you signed every time. It takes two people to pack a parachute and both have to sign the form. Once on a training flight, H. S.'s plane ran into trouble. For a while, it seemed they might have to abandon the plane and parachute out. However, the pilot was able to land the ailing plane on a small airstrip and everyone was okay. He was wearing a parachute I'd packed. That was interesting."

Dee stayed in the marines until the end of the war. After the Japanese surrendered, our troops started coming home. Dee's mood turns somber suddenly when she remembers one trip to the administration office. "There was a squad of marines that had been prisoners of war. They were the saddest looking, skinniest, oh. . . ." Dee has to pause before she can continue. "They had lost their hair and they looked sick and like they were in a daze. They were treated so badly.

"Honestly, the Japanese were the cruelest people in the whole world, I do believe," she continues. "I'm sorry to say this, but when you've been through the war, you can't help but feel that way. We were on the west coast, on the Pacific, and we were all marines and that's who was going over there. The war with the Japanese was very close."

Being a Christian, Dee wrestles with her feelings and what she believes the Bible says she should do, but reconciling her emotions is difficult. "I would never in this world buy a Mitsubishi because they made arms, you know, for their defense and they used nothing but prisoners of war for labor. They didn't feed them; they just worked them until they dropped. It's hard to forgive them." Dee sighs and collects her thoughts before she can continue.

"Let me say something about interning the Japanese here," she says. "You can't imagine how frightened, how shocked we were to have Pearl Harbor bombed and then, you see, they landed on the Oregon coast or somewhere. They had balloon bombs that floated to shore hoping to set

*Vera "Dee" Crawford holding her uniform, August 2002.*
*Photograph by Cindy Weigand*

fires. One of my brother's jobs was to walk up and down the coast and look for bombs. That's what he did for our country. They say it's possible there are still some out there. The Japanese occupied one of the Aleutian Islands but were driven out.

"It's over and we should be big enough and Christian enough to forgive them." Moments of silence pass before she speaks again. "So where do we go from here? I hope I can find it in my heart to forgive the Japanese before I die."

Dee was discharged from the marines on December 7, 1945, as a buck sergeant and was in Minnesota in time for Christmas. As required by law, her job was waiting for her. In fact, someone had called her parents asking when she could return to work. "I was a clerk typist then, but I eventually got my degree and was an environmental information specialist."

H. S. had been sent to occupied China and was on the first American aircraft to land there. Since he was a marine regular, H. S. had to serve four years before being discharged in 1946. After being the best man at a buddy's wedding in Alabama, he rode a bus all night to Minneapolis to see Dee. Together, they traveled by bus to Bemidji where her parents lived at the time.

In 1947, they married and eventually had two sons. After living in Oklahoma City, Oklahoma, and Dallas, Texas, they moved to Carrollton in 1998. Their two sons live nearby. "They claim they are the only brothers in Texas raised by *two* marine sergeants," Dee laughs. "They're real proud of that."

Of her time in the service, Dee says, "It was such wonderful interlude in my life. One that I will never forget." And nothing bad ever happened to her mother's little girl while Dee was in the military.

"This is not a time when women should be patient. We are in a war and we need to fight it with all our ability and every weapon possible. Women pilots, in this particular case, are a weapon waiting to be used."

—Eleanor Roosevelt, 1942

# 21

# FLORENE MILLER WATSON

*Women's Auxiliary Ferrying Squadron, Women Airforce*
*Service Pilots, Air Transport Command, Ferrying Division,*
*5th Ferrying Group, Dallas, Texas*

"My father told me he thought that I would probably be a better pilot than the boys."

Florene Miller finished the preflight check on her plane. After looking at her map one last time, she climbed into the cockpit of the Stearman PT-17. The fleece-lined, leather flight suit, helmet, and heavy boots required for winter flying made movement awkward. She adjusted the chamois over her face to keep it from freezing. Heavy mittens made grasping her map difficult. Chosen to lead the group of six women sent to deliver planes from the manufacturer, Florene took off first, using only a map, compass, and wrist watch as navigational tools.

Once aloft, Florene looked out over the countryside. Identifying landmarks was difficult in the wintry Montana landscape. Towns were few and far between; there were just snow-covered railroad tracks, obscured lakes, and minimized hills. About an hour into the flight, a gust of wind swirled through the cockpit. The map flew out of the airplane. *What'll I do! I can't lead without a map!*

"Cool it!" she scolded herself. "You've got five girls out there. You'll be okay."

Florene gestured for another pilot to take the lead, but no one would volunteer. She slowed down to force them ahead, but each time, they slowed down so as to not be the leader. The six circling yellow biplanes looked like geese following a mother goose over the snow-covered landscape.

*Florene Miller, WAFS 1942.*
*Photograph courtesy of Florene Miller Watson*

I've got to take care of myself, she decided. Before the map flew out, Florene remembered seeing an airstrip on the map used in cross-country training. Veering off course, she located the field and flew low to assess the conditions. Snow was piled high to the sides, and patches of ice glistened on the runway.

*I can't land there. I have to land there.* Florene landed cautiously, rolling to a stop. She looked around. All the airplanes, still following her, were safely on the ground. Each made a safe landing. One of the other pilots finally conceded to Florene's predicament and indicated she would take the lead. Florene nodded. Soon they were on their journey once more.

"Later, the girls each admitted that they knew without a doubt what my problem was," Florene says, "but each refused to take the responsibility.

"We were all experienced pilots, or we wouldn't have all landed safely," she continues. "We made women pilots look decent. Had we been just out of a training school, I'm afraid we wouldn't have. Fortunately, this group didn't make a bunch of errors." The women took off from the icy airstrip and continued to their destination without incident.

Charismatic and energetic, Florene tells her story in a voice that belies her age. Told with wit and wisdom, the story of her life is one of confidence and achievements made possible by her upbringing. One hears of parents giving their daughter life and technical skills that she would need to succeed and a daughter learning those lessons well.

One of four children, Florene Miller was a sophomore at Baylor University in 1939 when her father, T. L. Miller, bought a metal, single-engine Luscombe airplane. Florene, her father, and two brothers learned to fly in that plane. Their younger sister, Garnette, was considered too young to fly. For an article on "The Flying Millers," a reporter asked her father why he had bought the plane. His reply surprised Florene and her brothers. "He said he wanted his children to have a skill to contribute to the war effort.

"My father was a real thinker, always miles ahead of the next guy," Florene continues. "Whenever he made a prediction in the past, he was always right. This is what frightened us kids when he made that statement. He had not said that to us. We read it for the first time in the newspaper. I think he knew the United States would enter the war."

Mr. Miller was not placating his daughter because she had a unique hobby; he truly believed Florene could serve her country in wartime as a pilot. "In the beginning," she says, "my father told me, 'You know, I bet you'll be a better pilot than the boys.' He did not minimize what he thought girls could do nor did he fear for me. He thought I could come up with the same skill my brothers had.

"I grew up on my father's lap until the day he died," Florene says. Her father once told her, "I will help you get anything you want, whatever it is, but I'm going to help direct your efforts in reasonable ways." Mr. Miller didn't want her to desire something "way out of sight" but would help her achieve anything decent, reasonable, and realizable.

There were only three thousand licensed women pilots in the United States at the time and the entry of the United States into the war was two years away. What seemed possible and reasonable to Mr. Miller was not shared by the general public and certainly not the military. Yet, three years later, her father's prediction came true. Florene Miller, daughter of T. L. and Flora Miller, became the twelfth woman in American history chosen to fly military airplanes. The group was known as the Women's Auxiliary Ferrying Squadron, WAFS.

Florene remembers watching amazed at age eight as barnstormers in open cockpit planes flew into her hometown of San Angelo. After her father bought her rides as a passenger, Florene knew she wanted to fly. By twenty years of age, she had earned private, commercial, instructor, and ground school licenses.

Upon earning her instructor's license, Florene trained men to fly in the War Training Program in Odessa and later Lubbock. The WTP was a special government program enacted to encourage civilians who weren't of draft age to learn to fly. By then her older brother, LaMonte, had been drafted into the army.

On July 4, 1941, tragedy struck the Miller family. Mr. Miller and LaMonte, who was home on leave from the army, were killed when their Luscombe crashed into a mountainside en route to Ruidoso, New Mexico. Florene and Chris Watson—friend, flight student, and her future husband—came upon the wreckage while driving to meet them in town.

"It was difficult at the time coming upon the accident like that," she recalls, "but looking back, I'm glad it happened that way. My brother was killed instantly, but I got to spend nearly two hours with my father in the hospital before he died."

Knowing the hazards of flying and being a sensible family, they had held family meetings to discuss what they would do if one of them got killed. "In many discussions," Florene says, "we came to the conclusion that we thought we knew enough about scripture to know that God deals with us separately and not corporately. What would happen to one of us would not necessarily increase the chances of that same thing happening to another one of us."

After two of them were killed, that left the rest of the family to react to it. The two remaining pilots, Florene and her younger brother, Dolph, a commercial pilot, looked at each other and said, "Do we believe that or don't we? You put up or shut up," Florene says. Within a week's time, both she and her brother were flying, but "scared out of our wits." Florene and her brother got over that correlation between the deaths of their father and brother and their own, "but it took awhile," she says.

Florene was in Odessa instructing male pilots when the Japanese bombed Pearl Harbor. After the United States entered the war, the demand for experienced male pilots overseas created a shortage stateside. Airplanes needed ferrying from army base to army base and to points of embarkation. Professional pilot Nancy Harkness Love convinced the army air force brass that she could recruit enough other professional women pilots to fly them.

Her plan was put into action in September 1942. Based in Wilmington, Delaware, the pilots would fly for the Air Transport Command (ATC).

The requirements for the WAFS were that they had to be high school graduates between the ages of twenty-one and thirty-five, have a commercial license with a two-hundred-hp rating, and have five hundred hours flying time with fifty hours in the previous six months. Male pilots entering the ATC were required to have only two hundred hours flying time, while the original twenty-eight WAFS averaged eleven hundred hours each when entering.

While she was vacationing in Florida in October 1942, friend and former instructor Don Teel told Florene about the WAFS, the first she had heard about the group. He told her qualified women pilots were being notified. "I called home and had received a telegram," Florene says, "but what he told me is really what got me motivated." She called Wilmington and got the details. "I thought, 'I'll do that,' and got the go-ahead from my mother." At her own expense, she boarded a train in West Palm Beach, Florida, bound for Wilmington.

Before they were permitted to ferry airplanes, the pilots had to complete six weeks of training to learn the military way of doing things and how properly to do the paperwork. Nancy Love told the women that they might only ever get to fly light aircraft, but she would try to get permission for them to fly larger planes. In fact, their first ferrying mission was to fly Piper Cubs, but they soon graduated to larger aircraft.

One mission was to fly the open-cockpit Stearman PT-17s from Great Falls, Montana, when her map flew out of the cockpit. The ATC had sent about seventeen men and six women to ferry the planes. "We had been weathered in for about a week," she says, "waiting for it to *warm up* to ten degrees below zero so the oil could be heated enough to start the engines."

Florene attributes their safe landings not only to the fact that they were experienced pilots but also to the limited flight training they did receive during their brief orientation. "In Wilmington, men got to use the big airport runways," Florene says, "but they had us girls go several miles out of town and use a tiny grass airstrip with trees on all four sides. From the air, it looked like a postage stamp. There was a cemetery on the south side of the trees.

"This is where we practiced our takeoffs and landings," Florene continues. "We joked that we'd end up in the cemetery one way or another. When we landed, it was a real chore to get the thing stopped before we hit the trees. We flew the Fairchild PT-19. A bigger, faster plane wouldn't have made it no matter how good we were. As it was, we had to use a special maneuver called 'the slip' to land the plane."

In mid-1943, the WAFS joined with another group of women pilots trained to fly "the army way" at Sweetwater and who became known as the Women Airforce Service Pilots, the WASP. Florene was sent to Love Army Air Field, Dallas, to be the WASP commanding officer. The assignment required that she have instrument training in the LINK Trainer, which she received from a special instructor—her mother.

"My mother was a gutsy woman," Florene says. "After she lost a husband and a son, then had a daughter and son go off to the military, she didn't go around scared out of her wits, whining. She and my younger sister moved to Dallas and enrolled in SMU." When Florene was assigned to Love Field, Mrs. Miller decided to learn to instruct in the LINK Trainer.

"I probably got better training than anybody as I look back on that," Florene laughs, "because she would dream up every hard problem she could think of to mess me up on a flight doing this or that, making me correct for it. Just as I got out of one problem, she'd dream up another one. I was put through the paces. I said to myself, 'She's just trying to crash and burn me, and I'm not going to allow it.' She was honing my skills." Her mother was insuring her daughter had the skills necessary to do her job well to keep her safe.

Flying military airplanes wasn't without its hazards, however. Thirty-eight WASPs died in service to their country during the two years the program was active. After the deaths of two of the original WAFS, Florene remembered that family meeting after her father and brother were killed. "When someone in our particular flying group of women got killed," Florene says, "you could think that if it happened to them, it could happen to you. It was up to you to calm yourself and depend on the Lord to do what you determined He would have you do. You go right along, but you really did kind of bite your fingernails in times of crisis," she laughs.

During her time of service, Florene flew bombers, and fighter, training, and cargo airplanes, every type that the Army Air Corps used. She attended Pursuit School in Palm Springs, California, and Officer Training School in Orlando, Florida. Florene also served as a test pilot and tested radar equipment before it was shipped overseas for use.

Florene and WAF Barbara London were chosen by the military to determine whether women could be airline pilots. They successfully proved the experiment by flying military men from Detroit to Chicago in a DC-3 airliner for a specified time. There were no female civilian airline pilots at that time. The military was satisfied with their performance.

At the time they were flying, the WAFS and WASP were civil servants, not military, as women in other branches of service were. The war went better than anticipated, and men returned from overseas. Pilots wanted to fly rather than become eligible for draft into the ground forces. They wanted the WASP's jobs. As a result, the program was deactivated in December 1944. The WASP didn't officially receive military status until 1979, but Florene harbors no ill will. "When the war was going on, it's all hands on deck," she says. "It could have gone on a few more months, but with the war ending, I don't know what they would have done with us. I don't know of anything left undone."

After the war, Florene married Chris Watson and they had two daughters, Gail and Jean. When the girls were of school age, Florene returned to college at Lamar Tech University and received a B.A. degree. She earned a master's degree in business with honors from the University of Houston and taught business and secretarial classes there for several years. She also taught at Howard County College in Big Spring and at Frank Phillips College in Borger for a total of thirty years of teaching.

*Florene Miller Watson, May 2002.*
*Photograph courtesy of Florene Miller Watson*

Married for fifty-seven years, Florene and Chris reside in Borger. She serves as chaplain of the postwar WASP organization and states, "It's a position that humbles me and honors me." She's also active in civic, aviation, community, and church organizations. A superb public speaker, Florene is invited to speak throughout the United States and abroad.

Florene Miller Watson: skilled pilot, commanding officer, caring mother, college instructor, chaplain, leader. One of only four recipients, she was awarded the Daughters of the American Revolution Medal of Honor in 2001. In June 2001, and again in June 2002, Florene was honored as an Eagle in the prestigious "Gathering of Eagles" celebration at Maxwell Air Force Base in Montgomery, Alabama. Male honorees include fifteen heroes from WWII, the Korean War, Vietnam War, and the space program.

Florene's story and accomplishments have been recorded in several books, and she's been the subject of numerous articles. An honored guest at veterans' events and an inductee into several aviation halls of fame, she accepts her place in history with grace and dignity. Florene indeed heeded her parents' instruction and learned her lessons well.

# 22

# MARIE MUCCIE GENARO

*Women Airforce Service Pilots, 43–2, Air Transport*
*Command, Ferrying Division, 2nd Ferrying Group,*
*Wilmington, Delaware; 5th Ferrying Group, Dallas, Texas;*
*33rd Ferrying Group, Kansas City, Kansas*

"I risked my life flying that airplane. It was a piece of junk."

In the dim light of the hangar at Houston Municipal Airport, Marie Muccie checked out the BT-13 assigned to her, then climbed into the cockpit
for a night of practicing touch-and-go landings. After takeoff, she rose to
eight hundred feet, circled the field, and touched down, immediately throt-
tling forward to make another pass. As she climbed the third time, the aircraft started vibrating. Nicknamed the "Vultee Vibrator," the single-engine
monoplane was known to vibrate at times, but this was more violent than
she'd ever experienced. So fierce was the motion, Marie thought she would
be thrown from the plane. As if things weren't bad enough, Marie noticed
that her engine was on fire. She called the tower and explained her emergency.

"You could climb to two thousand feet and bail out," the man in the
tower told her.

"Oh," Marie said weakly. She climbed to two thousand feet, opened
the hatch, and looked down into the darkness. "I'm not bailing out," she
said to herself and closed the hatch.

"I'm not bailing out," she informed the tower. "I'm bringing it in.
Will you clear the field?"

"You're what?" the man asked.

"I'm not bailing out. I'm bringing it in," Marie repeated.

"Okay," he said. "You're cleared to land. Bring it in, but get out of
that thing as soon as you can in case it explodes."

*WASP Marie Muccie.*
*Photograph courtesy of Marie Muccie Genaro*

Marie descended as quickly as possible. The vibration of the airplane bounced her back and forth in the cockpit as she circled and landed, scrambling out of the airplane before it came to a complete stop. Fire trucks, red lights flashing, roared out to the plane to extinguish the fire. When the smoke cleared, a mechanic examined the engine. The flight instructor stood nearby. "You know what," the mechanic said to Marie, "there's only one bolt holding that engine in. If that bolt had come out, you'd been a goner. You wouldn't have been able to bail out."

The instructor turned to Marie. "Go back to the flight line and get another plane to finish your night training."

"Oh, I don't feel like flying anymore tonight," Marie said. "I've had a rough night, really."

"Look," the instructor said, "if you don't fly now, you won't fly tomorrow or the next day. You'll never fly again. You've just got to go right back up. Go get in one of those planes and finish your night training."

"Will you have the mechanic check the engine to make sure the bolts are all in?" Marie asked.

"Of course we can't do that," he said.

Marie slowly walked to the flight line and checked out another plane.

"Naturally, I went back up," Marie says, "because that's the best thing I could do. I didn't feel like it after that bad episode, but I probably wouldn't have flown again if he hadn't made me do it." Marie Muccie Genaro ferried airplanes for the Army's Ferrying Command during World War II with the Women Airforce Service Pilots, WASP.

A graduate of the second graduating class of 1943, designated 43–2, Marie's flight training started in Houston with the Women's Flying Training Detachment, or WFTD. When she finished training, Marie and her class-mates flew the advanced trainers, North American's AT-6, to Sweetwater for graduation. In 1943, the WFTD and WAFS joined to form the Women Airforce Service Pilots, WASP.

As a teenager, Marie, her two sisters, and a few friends became inter-ested in Amelia Earhart and her activities. They formed the Earhart-Noonan club. The group met at the local airport near Trenton, New Jersey, where Marie was born, to watch the planes and dream of flying. Marie also built model airplanes and flew them in air meets. "One time," Marie says, "I built a big gas-powered model and entered a contest. The object was to see how many minutes the planes stayed in the air. I was the only girl who entered this air meet, and I came in third. I thought that was pretty good."

After a while, Marie got bored with model airplanes. She wondered what it was like to fly a real airplane, but flight instruction cost $8.00 an hour. "That doesn't sound like a lot," she says, "but it's expensive when you don't have any money. I asked the owner of the airport if he had any jobs for me. I told him I'd wash airplanes, direct them to hangars, anything that needed to be done for flying lessons. He was so amazed that a woman would want to take flying lessons, that he gave me a job. He thought more people might come out to see a woman fly."

At age nineteen, Marie had her private license. She quickly accumu-lated three hundred hours and was working toward her instructor's rating when the United States entered the war. For security reasons, the govern-ment forbade flying within fifty miles of the coast, so the airport Marie flew out of was closed.

"I was out of a job," Marie says, "and didn't know what I was going to do. I had all this flying time and didn't know what I was going to do with it." She went to inland airports looking for a job but found nothing. Then she read in the paper about a training program to teach women to fly the "army way" in Houston with Jacqueline Cochran as director. She applied and met Cochran in New York City to learn more about the pro-gram. With three hundred hours of flying time, Cochran told Marie the group could use her. However, Marie wasn't twenty-one, which was the minimum age to enter the program, so she needed her father's written permission.

When she asked her father to do this, his response was not what she wanted to hear. He said, "You want me to give you permission to go fly army airplanes and kill yourself?"

Marie followed with an argument he couldn't counter. "I told him I would apply for the Royal Air Force because they didn't have an age requirement." Prior to the United States' entry into the war, Cochran had recruited a group of professional women pilots to ferry airplanes in England because of that country's desperate need for pilots. Twenty-five women qualified and went to Great Britain to fly airplanes for the British Air Transport Auxiliary. WASPs weren't allowed to fly across the Atlantic. "The little thing he didn't know," Marie confesses, "is that they had a height requirement of five feet, four inches. I'm five-two." As it turned out, she didn't get called for several months and turned twenty-one years old in the meantime.

Marie reported to Houston Municipal Airport. There she was told if all went well with the training program, another location would be chosen. Cochran chose Sweetwater, Texas, as the location for the only all-woman flight training program in American history. "The first three classes started in Houston," Marie says. "The school in Sweetwater was ready when I finished my six months of training, including night flying, so we flew the advanced trainers, AT-6s, to Avenger Field at Sweetwater on graduation day." Of sixty women accepted for training, forty-three graduated.

"I understand they had barracks which weren't that great," Marie says of the classes that entered the program after the first three. "They rented cheap motels for us, and we had two girls to a room. I guess we were privileged. A bus picked us up for training and brought us back afterward. My only connection with Sweetwater is that I graduated there."

After graduation, Marie had the choice of going to California, Delaware, or staying in Texas. "Well, I'd trained in Texas, so I didn't desire to stay there," she says. "I thought it would be nice to be closer to home so I could see my family, so I chose Delaware, but I was so busy that I never got to see my family."

At Wilmington, Marie ferried a variety of aircraft including the Piper L4-H, Fairchild PT-19, BT-13, Cessna AT-17 and UC-78, Beechcraft AT-10, North American AT-6, and the Boeing C-73. "Most of the time we flew new planes," Marie says, "but once I delivered an AT-6 to a junkyard at Fort Dix, New Jersey. I'd told them that they should just take it apart and send it there in pieces, but they insisted that I fly it instead.

"I want you to know that plane was not flyable," she says. "It kept losing pressure while I was in the air, so I'd have to land to let the mechanics fix it up enough for me to get it a little farther. What should have been a four- to five-hour flight took me twelve hours over a period of eleven days. I risked my life flying that airplane. It was really a piece of junk. I tried to tell them it wasn't flyable. I really loved flying the new planes, though."

*Marie on wing of AT-6. Photograph courtesy of Marie Muccie Genaro*

Marie flew out of Wilmington for a year or so when she was given the choice of ferrying pursuits (now called fighters) or bombers. Despite her height, Marie chose bombers. "I liked the idea of having two or more engines out there instead of one in case one of the engines failed," Marie says. "I was amazed that they accepted me. I had to have the seat all the way forward plus two cushions behind me to reach the rudder pedals." She reported to Kansas City, Kansas, location of North American, the manufacturer of the B-25 bombers.

At this time, Marie also began training for her instrument rating. First, she had flight simulation training in a LINK trainer, then instruction with a qualified pilot, followed by a flight with a check pilot. This pilot had the

*Marie in winter flying suit.*
*Photograph courtesy of Marie Muccie Genaro*

final word on whether or not she had earned an instrument rating. Marie's check pilot was Capt. Michael Genaro, her future husband. "He took me up," Marie says, "and didn't pass me. I thought I had done everything I was supposed to do." This happened three times. Each time, he offered no specific reasons why he hadn't passed her. Finally, Marie told him she would report him if he didn't sign the papers stating that she had passed instrument training. Reluctantly, Captain Genaro signed the papers.

"After I got my instrument rating," Marie says, "I wished I didn't have it because I never liked flying instruments. I liked to see out of the airplane to see where I was going. Looking back, I understand Captain Genaro's caution about exposing me to the possible dangers associated with flying instruments." Indeed, almost immediately, Marie was confronted with a situation in which she had to fly instruments on a stormy day.

"On June 10, 1944, I was assigned to copilot with Capt. Webster Brown to ferry a B-25 bomber from Kansas City to Lubbock, Texas," Marie says. "What would have been an easy run for this flight became a terrifying nightmare when we encountered a Texas panhandle summer storm.

"As we approached our destination, low on fuel," Marie continues, "I called the tower for landing instructions. This is when the nightmare began. The tower told us, 'We are ceiling and visibility zero—the field is closed.'" The man then referred Marie and Captain Brown to another field.

"I said to the man in the tower, 'We're too low on fuel, please give us instructions for landing *now!*'"

The tower gave Marie and Captain Brown instructions to land and promised to help guide them in. "As we made our approach to land," Marie says, "the man in the tower shouted, 'Pull up! Pull up! You're headed for some trees at the end of the runway! Go around and try again.' We were glad he told us because we couldn't see a thing."

They circled the field to make another attempt to land. "The second try was even grimmer," Marie says, "and I decided we needed a miracle for us to make it. We got our miracle on the third try as we landed without damage or injury. After we landed, the gas tank was completely empty. When I look back at that incident, I truly believe God was sitting in my copilot seat during the entire flight."

Few people knew women were flying airplanes after the United States entered the war, even at air bases. "My copilot and I would land these big bombers and get out," Marie says. "The men directing the planes would ask if we were nurses and ask where the pilots were. We loved to see their mouths drop when we said, 'You're looking at them!' "

Marie also experienced adverse reactions to women flying. The government's motto, "Free a Man for Combat," for recruiting women to all services, was not popular with some men. "A lot of the men at the bases resented us because they didn't want to go to combat. And I didn't blame them, but that's the way it was."

By the summer of 1944, the loss of pilots in the European Theater of Operations was less than expected, and they started returning home. They wanted stateside jobs as pilots rather than be drafted into the army to fight in the Pacific theater. Rumors circulated that the WASP program would be deactivated.

"I'd flown for a year and a half with few breaks, and I was worn out," Marie says. Since the program was to disband soon, Marie resigned, then

*Marie Muccie Genaro by an AT-6 at the Pima Air and Space Museum,*
*Tucson, Arizona, October 5, 2002.*
*Photograph courtesy of Sue Legacy and Laura Holland*

married Captain Genaro and settled in Dallas after the war. They had four children, three daughters and one son. She also has two grandchildren living in Oregon.

Marie has been an entrepreneur in the health food industry and in headwear design. A resident of Austin for twenty years, Marie is an avid seamstress, designs jewelry, and enjoys short-term trading in the stock market.

*Author's note: Following a short illness, Marie Muccie Genaro folded her wings on January 11, 2003. She was a great lady. I'm honored to have known her and to have her story included in this book. Thanks to her wonderful family for their continued support.*

# 23

# LOIS BROOKS HAILEY

*Women Airforce Service Pilots, 43–3, Camp Davis,*
*North Carolina; Liberty Field, Hinesville, Georgia;*
*Biggs Field, El Paso, Texas*

"They had to chop up the plane to get me out."

Lois Brooks banked the Douglas RA-24B SBD dive bomber into the last turn into final approach at Biggs Field, El Paso, Texas. She pulled the lever to lower her landing gear. Based on the instrument panel, the left wheel didn't go down. Pulling up, she apprised the tower of her situation. "Brooks to tower, my landing gear won't come down, please advise." The man in the tower told her to try again, then called out, "Somebody get Captain McDonald!"

As Capt. Claud McDonald rushed to the tower, Lois tried two more times to lower the landing gear, but to no avail. When the captain arrived, he went through the emergency procedure with her twice, but the left wheel still would not go down.

"Okay, Brooks, you're going to have to land with wheels retracted," he said.

"I landed that plane on its belly," Lois says. "In some ways, it was easier than landing on wheels. The only damage was a bent prop tip. They fixed the stuck locking pin and put on a new prop. It was flying the next day."

Officials and mechanics inspecting the plane determined that the locking pin was immovable. For her skillful landing of the plane, Lois was awarded a commendation from Captain McDonald that read: "This operation was performed in a skillful manner causing minimum damage to aircraft and no injury to the pilot. It is a pleasure to forward this commendation of calmly executed and well performed emergency procedure."

*WASP Lois Brooks.*
*Photograph courtesy of Andy Hailey*

Lois and I talked at the sixtieth reunion of the formation of the Women Airforce Service Pilots in Tucson, Arizona. The group, started by Jacqueline Cochran, was originally called the Women's Flying Training Detachment and trained at the municipal airport in Houston, Texas. At the age of eighty-seven, Lois needed a walker to get around, but her mind was still sharp and she had no trouble navigating through her experiences as a pilot during WWII.

Lois Brooks was born the fifth child of a family of six on January 18, 1915, in Reno, Nevada. "Except for my four sisters, there were only boys in the area for me to play with," she says. "I loved it and was unhappy when a girl moved into my area. When I turned twelve, my mother put her foot down and wouldn't let me go out and play anymore. I didn't like that."

Not being able to go out and play didn't stop Lois from becoming a pilot as an adult. She had graduated from Reno High School and the University of Nevada, Reno, and was teaching in an elementary school in Minden, Nevada, when her friend and stepbrother got her into flying. "The stepbrother wanted to be an airline pilot," she says, "and needed a couple of partners to help buy a new 1939 Taylorcraft airplane. It cost $1,995, had a 65 hp engine, single ignition, and no brakes, just a tail skid.

"Instructors and planes were few in the area," she continues. "I flew out of Vista Airport, a cow pasture strip east of Reno. We landed close to the hangar, cut the switch, and dragged quickly to a stop. To turn around, you had to pick up the tail and push it around. Taxiing had to be fast with the tail up with only rudder control."

By teaching, Lois was saving money with hopes of being accepted to the Juilliard Music School in New York City to study violin. "Within the year, my two partners had their instructor rating and sold out to me for $333 each." As the new owner, she then moved the plane to Minden. After the United States entered the war, Lois had to move the airplane to a secure airport in Carson City, then eventually sold it. However, she rented other planes such as an Aeronca, a Waco, Travelaire, and Kinner-Fleet. By January 1943, she had five hundred hours flying time and her commercial license. It's believed that Lois was the first woman pilot to get her commercial license in Nevada.

At that time, she received a telegram from Nancy Love asking her to apply for the Women's Auxiliary Ferrying Squadron. "I was afraid to travel cross-country to Delaware and maybe not pass the flight test," Lois says. "Then I got a telegram from Jackie Cochran. I went to San Francisco, Cali-

*Lois Brooks in 1943.*
*Photograph courtesy of Andy Hailey*

fornia, to meet Cochran, but met a representative instead. I told the woman that I had no intention of joining, but I had wanted to meet Jackie Cochran who I knew as a famous acrobatic pilot. The representative told me to report to Mather Field for a physical if I changed my mind.

"One reason I had no intention of joining," Lois continues, "was that I didn't think I could pass the air force physical because I wore glasses. I became curious because the men talked about how hard the physical was and I wanted to find out for myself, so I went down there. I passed the physical and they accepted me."

In January 1943, Lois joined the Women's Flying Training Detachment, WFTD, pilot training program at the municipal airport near Houston, Texas. Later, on August 21, 1943, the WFTD joined the Women's Auxiliary Ferrying Squadron and became known as the WASP. "Training was uneventful," she says "except one girl was killed in Houston in a PT-19 with her instructor. They came back and told us it was pilot error. I wondered why it was pilot error when an instructor was in the cockpit. As time went along, I learned that pilot error could mean that a girl froze at the controls or sometimes the instructor was showing off."

(The trainee who was killed was Margaret Oldenburg. Killed on March 3, 1943, she would have been in the next class to graduate, 43–4. According to the Army Airforce Accident report, the cause of the accident was reported as "undetermined." Norris O. Morgan was the instructor.)

After completing flight training, Lois and her classmates flew BT-13s and BT-15s to Sweetwater for graduation ceremonies. Her first assignment was at Romulus Army Air Base, Romulus, Michigan, with the Third Ferrying Command. "We had been there only a short time when Jackie Cochran called twenty-five graduates from the class of 43–3 to Washington, D.C., for a top-secret meeting with Gen. Henry 'Hap' Arnold, head of the army air forces, in his Pentagon office. He explained that we were to be a secret trial in tow-target work at Camp Davis, North Carolina," she says. "This flying involved towing a target for antiaircraft artillery practice with live ammunition. Altitudes varied, depending on the weapon, from as low as five hundred feet to as high as eighteen thousand feet. We were loaded on a DC-3 and we were off to Camp Davis." Laughing, Lois says, "The pilot couldn't find the spot, so he landed in Wilmington, North Carolina, to get directions, then we flew *back* to Camp Davis.

"The first thing we heard when we arrived at Camp Davis," she continues, "was that two men in an O-47 had gone down in the swamps but walked out. That was telltale that the planes we would have were worn-out navy. They had been worn out in Pacific action early on. From there, they were sent to us. We flew the Douglas 'Dauntless' A-24s and Curtiss 'Helldiver' A-25s."

At Camp Davis, another WASP was killed. "Mabel Rawlinson and an instructor were training at night," Lois says. "They were having engine trouble and were only at about two hundred feet when they flew over our barracks, so they couldn't make a good approach and landing. They made it to the field, but the plane broke in two. The instructor in the rear cockpit was bruised, but okay. Mabel was in the front cockpit. This plane had a reputation for having a hatch that would stick and couldn't be opened. Mabel was trapped inside and the plane caught fire. Fire got her."

Lois flew tracking missions at Camp Davis for about three months when a friend, Lois Hollingsworth Ziler, became interested in flying radio-controlled targets. Lois and fourteen WASP were transferred to Liberty Field, Hinesville, Georgia, for this training. "We were trained to fly radio-controlled target planes from a mother ship," Lois says. "This was the earliest start in drone target or drone flying."

After radio-control training, five WASP were assigned to Biggs Field, El Paso, Texas. To get there, Lois and Betty Deuser Budde had to hitch rides in a B-25 and a B-34. "The only place for us in the B-25 was to stand in a small space behind the cockpit," Lois says. "We had to stand the whole time. If we had to go to the bathroom in the B-34, there was a bucket in the back to go in. If I had to go, Betty held my top coat around me and vice versa."

En route to March Field, California, the plane encountered a cold front. "The pilot tried to fly over it. He got to eighteen thousand feet, and he was the only one who had oxygen," Lois continues. "Then he tried to go around it. We were nearly out of gas when we got through the clouds. We landed in Albuquerque and rode the train to El Paso."

The reception at Biggs was normal, with one exception. "The leader of our flight wasn't happy about getting five women for his pilots," Lois says, "so he didn't let us fly out all week and sent us out on Sunday when no one was flying. We had to go to an auxiliary field alone."

On their first Sunday, Kay Menges Brick piloted a C-78, with Betty Deuser Budde as copilot, to Condron Field north of El Paso to practice. Lois flew as safety pilot in a PQ-8A. Betty successfully flew and landed the PQ-8A on the dirt landing field at Condron while Lois sat in the cockpit

*Lois beside airplane in 1939. Photograph courtesy of Andy Hailey*

ready to take over if needed. Upon landing, Kay remained in the pilot seat of the C-78. Betty, still in the copilot seat, took hold of the beeper box that controlled the PQ-8A, and they prepared for takeoff.

"We lined up for takeoff," Lois says, "and Betty gave the drone power. The drone's rudder jammed and it ran in front of the mother ship. I thought I could overpower it, lift off, and proceed. Well, some men had graded the field and left about a six-inch ridge of dirt on the field. I thought if I got up to 60 mph or so, I could lift off before hitting it. Instead, the nose wheel broke as it hit the ridge and the plane flipped over. Betty and Kay tried to get me out, but couldn't lift the plane."

Kay flew back to Biggs Field, calling the distress signal "Mayday" all the way to get someone's attention. Upon arrival, Kay picked up three men

*Lois Brooks Hailey in October 2002.*
*Photograph by Cindy Weigand*

and flew back to the auxiliary field. "I think they had to hack up the PQ-8A quite a bit to get me out," Lois says. "I broke my two front teeth in the crash." In the meantime, for about an hour, Lois was hanging upside down. Luckily, the PQ-8A did not catch fire as others had.

At Biggs Field, Lois towed targets for ground to aerial gunnery practice both at high altitude, eighteen to twenty thousand feet, and low altitudes, five hundred feet minimum. "We were assigned to tow target squadrons. The target was like a windsock, we called it a sleeve. For the high altitude target-towing," she says, "they fired live 90 mm shells at the target which was a few thousand feet behind us. At low altitude, the target was about a thousand feet behind the airplane and was well controlled. They could only shoot at us in a certain range. Any farther, the target and airplane would be too much in line with each other."

Tow-target flying wasn't the only mission the WASP performed at Biggs. "We also flew for search light training at night," Lois says, "and sprayed tear gas on the troops in El Paso's desert for the men's training in gas warfare. We also flew in formation and singly for radar tracking."

Other missions at Biggs that the WASPs flew include simulated strafing missions with the sun at the pilot's back and buzzing troops and gunnery positions. Airplanes they flew include the Lockheed B-34 bomber, A-25, Twin Beech AT-11, AT-7 (C-45), AT-17, BT-13, PQ-8A, and PQ-14.

Biggs Field was Lois's last assignment before the WASP were disbanded in December 1944. Lois remained in El Paso and taught flying for three years with the GI Flight Training Program and was a flight examiner. One of her civilian students was her father, whom she taught to fly when he was sixty-five years of age. She also taught Andrew Samuel Hailey, her future husband. After they married, Lois earned her M.A. degree at the University of Texas at El Paso and taught band and orchestra in El Paso's public schools for thirty years. She has a son, Charles Andrew, who is an engineer/analyst in Houston.

In her retirement, Lois spends her time writing letters to the editor, volunteering at the local War Eagles Museum, attending WASP and similar gatherings of women in aviation and the military, visiting family in Houston and Reno and, most importantly, taking lots of naps.

# 24

## MADGE LEON MOORE

*Women Airforce Service Pilots, 44–4,*
*Perrin Field, Sherman, Texas*

"I was always adventurous."

Madge Leon banked the plane and started on the last leg of her night solo flight. She couldn't wait to land and crawl into bed. Peering into the darkness, she squinted until she caught a glimpse of the runway lights. *Finally.* Into the microphone of her radio she said, "Tower, this is Leon requesting permission to land." Receiving no response, she tried again. Still no answer. *Drat! The radio must be out.*

After buzzing the tower as she had been taught, she turned her AT-6 back to look for the green light giving her permission to land. At the flash of the light, she made her final approach. Her plane touched down softly and rolled down the runway. Suddenly, a huge mound of dirt and asphalt loomed in front of her. Madge slammed on the brakes.

"When I saw that pile of dirt," Madge says, "I thought, 'uh-oh, I've had it now,' and just stood on the brakes. It's a wonder I didn't go clear over but managed to get stopped before anything happened."

Madge Leon Moore flew military airplanes during World War II. An affable person who is fun to be around, she tells her story in a rich, mellow voice with traces of a west Texas accent where she spent her childhood.

Born in the tiny town of Rule in Haskell County, on January 22, 1922, Madge was always adventurous. "As a child, I always wanted to go down a 'new' road, only there were no new roads in west Texas. We didn't have seasons either. There were only two, hot and cold, and both were windy."

Madge's father owned several movie theaters in small towns in the

WASP Madge Leon.
*Photograph courtesy of Madge Leon Moore*

area. When he discovered a novel way to advertise them, Madge finally got the opportunity to exercise her adventurous spirit. The family lived in Haskell at the time. In nearby Stamford, there was an airfield and the instructor there needed to finance a new airplane, so he sold ten hours of flying for fifty dollars. "Daddy gave him fifty dollars and went up with the guy," Madge says. "Then Dad threw out circulars over the towns where he had theaters." Mr. Leon landed without having used all ten hours.

He returned home that evening and told his daughter what he'd done. "When he told me about it, I got so excited," Madge recalls. "I said, 'Let me have the rest of the time!' " The next Sunday, Madge's parents and some friends took her to Stamford. "I had my first airplane ride and pretty soon, I was driving to Stamford three or four times a week to take lessons. That was the summer I finished high school."

There were also some young businessmen in Haskell taking flying lessons at the same time. "They were so fascinated with the fact that a woman, a girl, was flying," Madge says. "They wanted to ride with me and the instructor let me take them up. You were supposed to have a private license to take up passengers, but the instructor was lenient. I guess he was the only official on the field. Later, I took my boyfriend for a ride."

On her way to college that fall, Madge took another special passenger for a ride. "Mother drove me to college and we stopped at Stamford. I took her on her first airplane ride ever."

Madge attended college at Texas State College for Women, now Texas Woman's University, and became involved with a dance troop that performed throughout the country. "I was just too busy dancing to fly," she says. Then she transferred to Southern Methodist University in Dallas.

"I heard about the WASP program when I was a senior at SMU," she says, "so I immediately wrote Jacqueline Cochran. Then I drove to Fort Worth for an interview. I had to take a physical just as the men had to. I was accepted into the program with the class of 44–4. I reported to Avenger Field on November 1, 1943.

"I rode the train overnight to Sweetwater," she continues. "When I arrived, I went to the Bluebonnet Hotel. It was just abuzz with all these women talking. I saw a blonde woman wearing a gabardine suit. When she turned around, I was surprised because she must've been thirty-five, which was the age limit to get into the program. She was the wife of the famous author Damon Runyon. We had to wear turbans when we flew to keep our hair in place, but she wore little hats she fashioned. Later, she withdrew from primary because her husband got sick."

As Madge knew, the weather in west Texas could be unpredictable in November and December. "During the week, the weather would be bad, then turn good on weekends, and that's when we had to fly. I remember one Sunday I thought I just had to get off base so I checked out," she laughs. "When I checked back in, I'd been gone fifty-eight minutes. It felt good to get away, though."

Each class had a different experience in their flight training. The primary trainer for the class of 44–4 was changed from the Fairchild PT-19 to the Stearman PT-17. "We changed to the PT-17 because we were going to skip the basic phase of training and go directly to advanced training in the AT-6. The PT-17s had a more narrow landing gear and were harder to fly," Madge says. "A girl that had soloed in a Fairchild PT-19 washed out in the PT-17, but the AT-6 was a honey to fly. Everybody liked it."

Madge graduated from flight training May 23, 1944. Her father, a World War I veteran, and mother attended the graduation ceremony. "My daddy pinned my wings on me," she says proudly.

She was assigned to Perrin Field, a basic flying school, near Sherman, Texas. "We reported June 6, which was D-Day in Europe," she says. "My classmate and I were the first two WASP to report to that field and they

*Madge with her parents in April 1944. Photograph courtesy of Madge Leon Moore*

didn't know where to house us. We ended up in a building behind the officer's club. It was a low building that had four rooms with outside doors. They weren't connected, and the latrine was in a separate building.

"We had two cots and some vertical shelves," she laughs, "but no mirrors or anything like that. We'd get up in the mornings with our hair all

*Madge in front of AT-6. Photograph courtesy of Madge Leon Moore*

tousled and sleep in our eyes. To go to the latrine, we'd zip on our zoot suits over our pajamas."

On the way to the latrine, Madge and her friend had to pass the officers' mess hall. Busboys were on the back porch pretending to clean the garbage cans or engaged in some other activity. "When we appeared, they whistled and that was the sign for every pilot at breakfast to look out at us," Madge laughs. "Oh, it was embarrassing. Soon, we found a room in town to live in until they renovated the building and put in bathrooms. They made it real nice."

The afternoon of the first day they reported, they and three officers had to deliver some planes to Oklahoma. "We knew how to fly, of course, but we weren't taught formation flying," she says. "I looked out and there was a plane on each wing. I didn't know what to do, so I just flew on. When we got to our destination I started to land as I had been taught, which was to fly downwind, parallel the runway, make a right angle turn to come in to land. Well, those instructors flew like fighter pilots," she laughs. "They flew over the field, peeled off, and landed while I was still doing my nice turns. Oh, it was real fun."

The war was winding down while Madge was at Perrin Field. Bases were closing throughout the nation. She flew many planes, usually from bases that were closing to Kelly Field in San Antonio for storage. "Some of my classmates flew all kinds of planes, but I just flew training planes like BT-13s and AT-6s," she says. "We had to wait in San Antonio for the instructors at Perrin Field to finish for the day and come get us. Most of the time, we got home very late."

Madge also worked in the engineering department. After planes had been repaired, the WASP took them up for "slow time" to make sure they were operating correctly. "That was just drudgery," Madge says. "All we could do was fly straight, level, and slow for an hour."

From Perrin Field, Madge and fellow WASP Alice Stevens (Rohrer) returned to Avenger Field for advanced instrument instruction. Upon returning to Perrin, they taught instruments to the pilots there.

Madge met her future husband at Perrin Field. "He was the only pilot who offered to carry my parachute," she laughs. After the WASPs were deactivated in December 1945, she married Stanley Moore and concentrated on being an air force wife and mother to their two sons. They were stationed at bases in Illinois, Kansas, California, Alabama, South Carolina, and San Antonio, Texas, as well as in the Philippines and Japan. They eventually retired in San Antonio, and Madge became involved in various activities such as the Boy Scouts and the PTA.

Of her time as a WASP, Madge says, "I wouldn't take anything for my experience. I was an only child and fortunate my parents were always supportive."

When we talked, Madge mentioned that her mother was still alive at 106 years old. My curiosity piqued, I asked to meet her. Although Madge told me not to expect much in the way of a response, she took me to the nursing facility where her mother lived. Mrs. Leon was not able to say much, but when I asked her what she thought about her little girl wanting to go fly military planes, she responded clearly, "Well, if that's what she

*Madge Leon Moore in June 2002.*
*Photograph by Cindy Weigand*

wanted to do, I would support her." Unable to speak much more, we looked at photographs from Madge's album. Occasionally, Mrs. Leon would point at Madge in a photo and ask, "Who's that? Me?" At another place, in another time, this supportive mother might have flown military airplanes for her country, too.

# 25

## ELIZABETH "BETTY" WILLIAMSON SHIPLEY

*Women Airforce Service Pilots, 44–4, Independence Army Air Field, Independence, Kansas; Perrin Field, Sherman, Texas; Foster Field, Victoria, Texas*

"There was the challenge of flying that I liked."

Betty Williamson leveled off the open-cockpit PT-17 and checked the instruments. After glancing out over the countryside, she secured her leather flight suit around her neck against the cold January wind and settled in for the long flight to Alabama. She had been in the air less than an hour when she felt the urge to go to the bathroom. *Now what am I going to do?*

Frantically, she looked around for a place to land but didn't see a level strip of land anywhere. Finding no place she could use as a runway, she trimmed up her engine and unbuckled her seat belt. She struggled to unzip the jacket of her flight suit and pull the pants down in the cramped confines of the cockpit.

"After all that effort," Betty laughs, "I couldn't go, so I pulled my pants up and zipped my jacket. There was no place I could do a forced landing, and I still had to go, so I trimmed up my engine, unzipped my jacket, and got my pants down. Then I got the envelope of my flight map. You know, I used that and threw it out. When I landed in Alabama, the sergeant asked, 'Williamson, what happened to your map envelope?' I told him it just flew out. I'll never forget it."

At that time, military airplanes had relief tubes for men, but there were no adaptations for WASP faced with this predicament. I've heard several WASP relate various experiences, but Betty is the only one who has dared

WASP Betty Williamson.
Photograph courtesy of Betty Williamson Shipley

share how they dealt with these situations, although almost everyone is curious to know.

Betty was born on October 4, 1916, in Zamboanga, Philippine Islands, where her father was in private business. After her father concluded his business dealings in the Philippines, the family eventually settled in Fontana, California, a community populated by people who had lived all over the world as they had.

While attending college at Santa Barbara State University, Betty considered becoming an airline stewardess. "They wouldn't take you unless you were a nurse," she says. Then she saw a pilot and his wife perform a daring stunt. "He flew under a bridge near Riverside while his wife stood on top of the bridge," she says. "I was so impressed, I decided I wanted to fly. Also, my brother became a navy pilot. That inspired me to go into aviation to keep up with him."

After she saw that aviator fly under the bridge, Betty never considered any other branch of the military. "I knew that's what I wanted to do," she says. "There was the challenge of it that I liked. I thought maybe if he could do it, I could do it."

*Betty in her dress uniform, 1944.*
*Photograph courtesy of Betty Williamson Shipley*

She had just graduated from college and was teaching in Burbank, California, when she heard about the WASP program through a family friend, Ethel Sheehy, executive assistant to the director of the WASP program. At that time, entry into the program required that students have thirty-five hours of flying time.

"I went to Blythe for flight instruction," Betty says. "If you've ever been to Blythe, California, you know it's hotter than Hades. It can get up to 128 degrees in the summer. I was sopping wet most of the time. When I went to bed at night, after flying all morning, my legs would just jump. I was most interested with what was happening to my body while taking flying lessons."

Before long, Betty earned the required hours. "I got a good instructor and got my hours fast," she continues. "When he told me I could solo that J-2 Cub, I was thrilled to death. Then I applied to the WASP program. Knowing Ethel Sheehy helped me get in sooner because I didn't have to have all the background checks. I had to take all the other tests the army air force required, though."

When she arrived in Texas, Betty was taken aback by her surroundings. "I wondered what the heck I was doing there," she says. "It was so barren and horrible looking coming from California where it was so beautiful. Also, in a forty-minute drive [in California], I could go swimming in the ocean or be climbing a mountain." However, Betty discovered that only the countryside was barren. "I soon learned that the warmth of the Texans made up for all that. I came to love the Texas people."

Primary flight training was started in the Fairchild PT-19, an airplane with a 175 hp engine. After only a few hours, she changed to the Stearman PT-17, a plane with a 220 hp engine. When she advanced directly to North American's AT-6, the advanced trainer, Betty also got a new instructor. "I had three rides with this instructor who swore at me every time I took off," she says. "I'd never heard such words in my life. They were so bad I couldn't even think straight or do anything right. He put me up for an elimination ride, which just broke my heart because my father believed I could do anything. I was put up for a pink slip." Such a slip indicated unsatisfactory performance and listed the problems.

For the elimination flight, Betty had an instructor who was a military officer. "We went up and did everything—spins, stalls, whatever—then we landed," she says. "The instructor looked at me and said, 'You know, Williamson, there's nothing the matter with you.'" However, Betty had to go up with one more instructor. "He traded me to Mr. Eckley who I'll love until the day I die, because I got along fine with him and we did very well." Betty passed this phase of her flight training.

Looking back, Betty has an interesting perspective on this incident. "You see, we had a personality clash. This wasn't sexual harassment, we just didn't get along," she says. "There was nothing wrong with my flying, and he didn't hate women. We just didn't get along. I was a college graduate and he wasn't."

To earn her wings, Betty had to make night solo flights in the AT-6. "I can't remember what city it was, but I can remember flying over oil fields and seeing flames come up from the rigs," she says. "Another night, I took off for Dallas and the ceiling dropped five hundred feet. I can still hear my instructor saying 'Williamson's up there and scared to death,' and I was. Fortunately, I landed fine. I was the first one in my class to complete night training."

Following graduation in May 1944, Betty was assigned to Independence, Kansas. "They had some students there, and we helped with the instruction flying BT-14s. My classmate and I did a good job, but more instructors weren't really needed there." From Independence, Betty went to Perrin Field, Sherman, Texas. In engineering, she flew "slow time" on planes, ferried aircraft from closed bases, and transported various personnel to different bases. "I even flew a doctor and his dog down to Randolph Army Air Base in San Antonio," she laughs.

"The colonel at Perrin thought I should be somewhere so I could fly bigger airplanes," she says, "so he transferred me and my classmate, Ina Barkley, to Foster Field near Victoria, Texas. They said if you ever want a rich man, there are a lot of them down there, but I wasn't interested." At Foster, WASPs towed targets for aerial gunnery practice. "I didn't want to do that because they shoot live bullets at you, and some of those lieutenants

*Betty Williamson ready for takeoff.*
*Photograph courtesy of Betty Williamson Shipley*

weren't very good shots. Fortunately, I didn't have to. I would've if they'd told me to, though."

Instead of towing targets, Betty trained Mexican fighter pilots in instrument flying. "I knew a little Spanish from living in the Philippines," she says, "but they didn't know much English. They had more flying time than I ever thought about having as far as flying straight and level was concerned, but they'd get under the hood, and we'd practice instrument flying, then we'd land. When they came out from under the hood," she laughs, "they'd say, 'you are so beautiful.' What do you say then?"

After three months instructing pilots, Betty became anxious to get back to Perrin Field. "I was engaged to Lieutenant Shipley, so I pulled some strings of some sort to get back there," she laughs, "and then I was doing the same thing, slow-timing and checking things." It was at this stint at Perrin Field that she flew the airplane to Alabama.

Betty married and resigned from the WASP a couple of weeks before they disbanded. She was offered, as were all WASPs, a commission in the U.S. Air Force Reserves. Betty declined because her husband was a regular army air force pilot and was gone a lot and didn't want her to accept. "I wanted to take that commission. Sometimes I wish I had," she says.

While her husband, Frances, was in the air force, they lived on air bases in Japan, the Philippines, Georgia, and Arizona. Betty returned to teaching and taught in all these places. In 1969, when her husband retired, Betty accepted a teaching assignment at Randolph Air Force Base, where she

*Betty Williamson Shipley in June 2002.*
*Photograph by Cindy Weigand*

taught for fifteen years. "I feel fortunate to have been a WASP, to do all those things. It was a wonderful opportunity for women, but my time as a teacher was very important to me, too," she says. She has two sons, David and Charles, who live in Arizona. Betty stays busy with the post-WASP organization, which holds a reunion every two years.

# 26

# DOROTHY A. LUCAS

*Women Airforce Service Pilots, 44–7, Gunnery Squadron,*
*Moore Field, Mission, Texas*

"I would have gone into combat if I'd been ordered to."

Dorothy concentrated on her flight pattern, counting the planes as they zoomed past. "One, two, three, four, five, six," she sighed with relief, and maneuvered the AT-6 into the next turn. The cadets, also flying AT-6s, pulled up, circled, and came back for another pass at the target Dorothy pulled behind her plane, guns blazing. She was glad she couldn't hear the shells.

"I never was afraid they'd shoot me," Dorothy says, "but I was afraid they might fly into the cable that held the target. They were practicing aerial gunnery and really came in fast. The whole thing was about a forty- to fifty-minute mission for me to fly. The boys didn't want to tow targets because they thought it was too boring, but we WASP were glad to do it."

Dorothy is fun loving and has a sweet spirit. When we started talking about the war years, however, the tone in her voice instantly became serious as she related her experiences. Albeit brief, her time with the WASP was memorable. Entering the program in February 1944, she earned her wings and graduated with the seventh class to graduate in 1944, designated 44–7. She flew until the group was deactivated in December of that year.

Born in Norfolk, Virginia, Dorothy worked in the War Department in Washington, D.C., and attended George Washington University at night when she heard about the WASP program. "A girlfriend told me about an organization in which they taught girls to fly," she says. "We wanted to join something, but we didn't want to be a WAVE or WAC or marine, so we looked into the program."

*WASP Dorothy Smith, 1944.*
*Photograph courtesy of Helen L. Hall*

With the age limit in the program of twenty-one to thirty-five, the girls were too young, so they decided to get the required thirty-five hours of flying time in the meantime. They went to Frederick, Maryland, for flying lessons. "We flew in Aeronca Chiefs and Piper Cubs to earn our private licenses. My mom was very supportive. In fact, she loaned me two hundred dollars so I could get my flight time. It cost nine dollars an hour, which was a heck of a lot of money back then. Incidentally, I paid her back later," she laughs, "when I got rich."

In the meantime, the age limit for admission to the flight program had been lowered to eighteen. "We applied and went to Bolling Field for our physicals," Dorothy says. "Both of us were accepted, but when we got ready to go, my friend told me her parents didn't want her to fly airplanes and wouldn't let her go. I said to her, 'You mean you're going to make me go to Sweetwater, Texas, by myself?' I didn't even know where it was." Her friend responded that, yes, Dorothy would have to go by herself. "Ironic thing is, she became an airline stewardess and was killed in an airline crash."

Dorothy found out where Sweetwater was and had just started flight instruction when she received bad news. "I had only flown about five or six hours," she says, "when my brother, who was a lieutenant in the air force, was killed. He was a navigator in a B-17 bomber in England. It nearly killed me and my mother. I didn't know if I could go on," Dorothy says pensively. "Mama thought I should come home, but I had been at Sweetwater such a short time. I said, 'Mama, I just can't.'"

Fortunately, Dorothy had an understanding instructor. "He really persevered with me," she says. "I was afraid to fly for about two weeks, then all of a sudden, I gave him a really good flight, and he said, 'You did great. You're going to be okay.' And I *was* after that. He allowed me to solo at nine hours. I think you're supposed to do it at eight."

According to Dorothy, her class had some formation flying and had to make a two-thousand-mile cross-country flight. "I was assigned to go west," she says, "which tickled me because I could go somewhere new. One leg of the flight was with a check pilot, the rest we flew alone. I flew to Tucson, down to El Paso, then back to Avenger Field. Just before I got there, smoke started coming into the cockpit. I thought, 'I'm about to grad-

*Dorothy with other WASP in front of AT-6. Dorothy is second from right, back row.*
*Photograph courtesy of Dorothy Lucas*

*Dorothy A. Lucas in June 2002.*
*Photograph by Cindy Weigand*

uate and my plane is going to crash and explode.'" Dorothy called the tower and was told to fly straight in. "On final approach, I looked down and there was the meat wagon. That's the ambulance. I was so scared. Smoke was coming out. I tell you, I think that AT-6 was still rolling when I jumped out. It was really frightening at the time, but the plane didn't explode."

After she earned her wings, Dorothy reported to Moore Field, an advanced flying school for fighter pilots near Mission, Texas. "I had to look that one up," she laughs. She was assigned to the gunnery squadron. "This was okay with me. I towed targets for the cadets so they could practice aerial gunnery," she explains. "An enlisted man in the back unwound a cable that had a flag-like cloth attached to it. This is what they fired at.

"My job," she continues, "was to fly straight and level at a certain altitude. I never took chances. I flew a set pattern up and out so many minutes and came back so many minutes, et cetera. Six cadets, flying with an instructor, made passes at the target. When we finished, I flew low over an auxiliary field, and the fellow in back released the target. The cadets had cameras on their guns and filmed the passes so they could see how well they had done."

Dorothy also did some administrative flying. "Once, I flew a captain, who was a doctor, up to Randolph Field," she laughs. "You know, I could tell he was nervous flying with a girl, but it didn't bother me. I was a qualified pilot. When we got there late in the afternoon, he jumped right out. I

*Dorothy gives thumbs-up before her flight in AT-6, summer 2002.*
*Photograph courtesy of Steve Sehnert, West Houston Squadron,*
*Commemorative Air Force, © Commemorative Air Force*

guess he was so happy we didn't crash. He asked me out to dinner, but I told him I had a date later that night." She had met an instructor who trained the cadets. Dorothy even knew the number of the young man's plane.

"One time after a training run," she laughs, "I dropped the target and was landing on the auxiliary field when he was watching. I wanted to impress him with a really good landing. Well, I leveled off too high. The plane dropped and bounced all the way down the runway. It was the worst landing I'd ever made. I didn't think he would ever ask me out again."

Dorothy remembers another flight in an open cockpit Stearman PT-17 to Dodge City, Kansas. "I had never flown one," she says, "and didn't know you had to use full flaps and all that. They just put me in it and said go. It was December and very cold. When I got there, I was frozen, just frozen even though I had on a lined leather suit." She also remembers taking planes to Oklahoma City several times. Each time she ferried a plane, she returned to Moore Field by train.

The young man she dated did ask her out again, and after the WASP program was deactivated, Dorothy and Al Lucas married and had five children—Helen, Jana, Melanie, Marnie, and Tom. They were married for fifty-six years when he passed away in 2001.

Of her time as a pilot during World War II, Dorothy says, "I wasn't afraid, and I would have flown in combat if they had ordered me to. It'd been okay with me because when I was in the cockpit, I was just as good as any male. We had the same training."

As a special treat for her eightieth birthday, Dorothy's daughter, Helen L. Hall of Austin, arranged for her to have a ride in an AT-6. During the flight, Dorothy took the controls, made a pass over the hangar, and waggled the wings to members of the family watching the flight from the ground.

# 27

# LINDEN N. ANDERSON

*American Red Cross, 91st General Hospital,
Oxford, England*

"We had to stay up so they could afford to be down."

Linden walked into the noisy, crowded mess hall of the hospital. Utensils scraped, cooking pans clanked. Despite the hubbub, there was a loud hum of people trying to carry on conversations. She carried her tray to a place beside a doctor and sat down. Although Linden had just witnessed something that should have upset her, she started enjoying herself.

"Here I am in this mess hall eating like a pig, carrying on, and laughing," Linden recalls. "I said to the doctor next to me, 'Don't I have any heart? Don't I have feelings?'" The doctor's response surprised Linden. He said, "Oh, yes you do. *We* have to keep detached because there's nothing that a patient wants less than to have someone taking care of him that might be sicker than he is. So, we have to keep a smile on our faces, a positive attitude, or we can't take care of these people." She then adopted her motto: *You have to stay up so they can afford to be down.*

In WWII, our servicemen faced enemies other than those on the battlefield. In combat, the men faced a tangible enemy, an enemy with a face; one that fired guns and rifles, stabbed with bayonets, threw grenades, and set land mines. If injured, soldiers faced the foes of boredom and low morale. As a recreation worker with the American Red Cross, Linden's job was to ensure that patients stayed busy and entertained until they could go home or return to duty.

Linden N. Anderson was born the eighth child of a large family in Manor, Texas, on January 14, 1908. Her family moved to Round Rock where she attended public schools through eighth grade, then graduated

*Linden N. Anderson, American Red Cross.*
*Photograph courtesy of Linden N. Anderson*

from a private Swedish academy. After one year of college, she taught school in Pflugerville. "That was so long ago," she laughs, "that you didn't have to have a permanent teacher's certificate to teach school."

Linden taught in Pflugerville and New Braunfels for ten years while she finished her degree. Then she started questioning her career choice. "I was looking for a way to get away from teaching. I liked it. I loved it and I liked the kids, but I asked myself if I wanted to be a teacher the rest of my life." After the attack on Pearl Harbor, she also wanted to do her part in the war effort, so she applied to the civil service. "I was glad I finished my degree because I was hired as a file clerk right away."

She commuted from New Braunfels to Randolph Field, San Antonio, to her new job. One day in New Braunfels, she happened to meet a friend downtown wearing a spiffy seersucker uniform. That chance meeting changed Linden's life. "I asked her what kind of uniform it was, and she told me it was a Red Cross uniform." Her friend told Linden that she was working at Brook Army Hospital in San Antonio as a social worker and encouraged Linden to apply. Again, she was glad she had earned her degree. "A single girl with a college degree was easy pickins. They called me for an interview right away," she says. The Red Cross offered something else that interested Linden—the possibility of adventure.

Linden traveled to Red Cross headquarters in St. Louis, Missouri, for an interview and physical. "I had to fill out reams of paperwork," she recalls. Red Cross officials told her she had the qualifications to be a recreation worker in military hospitals. "They liked me because I could sing and accompany singing on the piano; and I was used to doing athletics with the kids like baseball." Linden was more than twenty-three years of age, which meant she could go overseas.

The Red Cross training center for recreation and social work was at American University in Washington, D.C. "A lot of us girls are in our thirties by this time," Linden laughs, "and here I am outside kicking soccer balls. We had to learn the rules of Ping-Pong and pool and those sorts of things. Well, that was right up my alley." She remembers seeing Jimmy Stewart's sister, Ann, who was also at American University.

There was another aspect of ARC training Linden particularly enjoyed. "We had to learn how to do parties," she says. "Troops came in from a nearby military battery. Those guys were glad to come over to our big gymnasium. We'd put on parties and dances for them." On a limited budget, the girls made do with what they had. "We just did it with crepe paper, good will, a lot of ambition, and spunk," she says. "We had a lot of fun, but we were pretty tired at the end of the day 'cause the training program didn't give us much rest."

In addition to training for recreation work, she was required to take the same basic training as army nurses. "We had to do everything they did except nursing duty," she says. "We had to learn to march and scrub latrines. We learned how to climb up a ladder to get on and off a ship and go through the gas chamber and did everything they did." Linden not only trained with nurses, while on assignment, she lived with them. "I found nurses just absolutely wonderful people," she says. "Some of the best friends I've ever had are the nurses I met as a Red Cross worker."

The Red Cross staged Linden at Camp Kilmer in New Jersey until she received her assignment. "I knew I wasn't going to the Far East because we only received winter uniforms," she says. The group finally boarded the British ship *Aquitania* and set sail across the Atlantic. In the hold of the ship were stored one regulation-sized suitcase, a footlocker, and a bedroll that they didn't see until they moved into the hospital. "All of us folks were from the country. I had never been on a ship before. I'd heard about being seasick, but didn't think anything about it," Linden laughs. "I think we were still in view of the Statue of Liberty when I felt light-headed. Then I got sick. Everybody got sick."

The ship carried so many passengers that they ate only two meals a day in shifts with snacks available between meals. Four to five people shared a cabin. Often, they congregated in a large lounge where Linden remembers sitting on the floor because there weren't enough chairs for everyone. "We wore our 'Mae Wests' [life preservers] at all times. In the mornings, they'd tell us to go up on deck so the English stewards could clean the ship. We'd take our helmets with us in case we got sick, and we always had a towel over our shoulder." Gradually, the seasickness subsided.

She estimates there were thousands on the ship and that it took eight or nine days to reach their first stop, Glasgow, Scotland. "There were life boats, but not enough," she says. "I don't suppose three hundred people could have got in those. No, we'd have just gone down."

From Glasgow, they journeyed to Wales where they stayed for six weeks before going to the 91st General Hospital established by Harvard University near Oxford, England. Linden describes the hospital. "The buildings were in a line and you walked along a ramp from one ward to another. We had a large recreation hall with a piano, and Ping-Pong and pool tables. We also had a library. The Red Cross offices were in a house on the compound. There was a Quonset hut where we showed movies. It was about a two thousand bed hospital, but we averaged seventeen hundred with a staff of about five hundred."

Linden enjoyed entertaining the ambulatory patients. "These patients were restless. They were waiting to go home or waiting to go back to duty, so we took them on trips," she says. "We got free tickets for symphony concerts, special movies, and the theater. We accompanied the patients to these." Anxious to keep the men occupied, the commanding officer of the hospital kept a bus at their disposal for these trips. "We also took patients on picnics and boat trips on the Thames River," she says. "It was fun."

The nonambulatory patients were more of a challenge to keep busy. "There weren't as many blinded patients as you might think. Most patients were orthopedic," she says. "If you're shot, your arms or your legs are gonna get hit. We had guys with arms in slings; some were on crutches. Others had their teeth wired up or half their faces blown off. Many couldn't leave the hospital. They needed some recreation."

Among the activities was doing crafts. "We took a craft cart around loaded with all kinds of stuff to give them and teach them how to do it. Things like how to punch holes and lace wallets. We did jigsaw puzzles with them and wrote letters for them. Working with bed patients was the hardest program for me. It was so tedious going from bed to bed, teaching them to do things."

Working with injured patients, Linden often repeated her motto, but sometimes that wasn't enough. "One Christmas there was a young soldier who had lost his eyesight. I'd been paying a little more attention to him because he looked so young," she says. "One day I went to see him, and his father was there. His father was a colonel, and he'd been brought in from France by special favor to visit his son. I could hardly stand to see that man sitting by the bed and his dear son couldn't see him. Someone had sent me a little artificial Christmas tree, so I took it down there and gave it to him. He said, 'Let me feel it,' and I gave it to him and he held it. That's the only time I cried over a patient."

Upon occasion, especially holidays, Linden would arrange to entertain a whole ward at once. "We took bingo games in there, or I'd take the piano and play the piano for them and they'd sing," she says. "Our piano was on rollers and could be moved from ward to ward."

She arranged for Daphne Miles, a local dance instructor who once had a dance studio in London, to bring students to entertain the patients. Linden wanted to make it special for the guys, so she asked Miss Miles to bring children. People questioned her decision to bring children to a hospital. Linden explains why she thought this was important. "These guys had babies back home. They'd left all that," she says. "They were so hungry to see a child or a toddler. It was apparent when they saw these little kids. They just hooted and hollered. Some of the kids could hardly dance and would stand up there and just suck their thumbs. The boys loved anything we could arrange with kids." Linden exchanged Christmas cards with Daphne until Daphne's death two years ago.

Other volunteers from Oxford assisted Red Cross workers with the patients. Young women came in groups to be hostesses at the Saturday night parties in the recreation hall. Others helped the hospital-bound patients with their crafts. English children would pick flowers, and the volunteers put them in vases to place at bedsides. "You know, to add a touch of home," Linden says.

At Christmas, Linden arranged for Christmas trees, and the Oxford volunteers helped decorate them with ornaments and lights provided by

Red Cross. The RC also provided a gift box for every patient. It held stationery, a pen, a package of cigarettes, and toiletries. "We made stuff, too," Linden says. "The guys saved the shiny wrappings off the cigarette packages and we made decorations. Somehow, we got the trees decorated. Every tree had lights, not very many, but we got 'em." Linden remembers the people of Oxford fondly. "I can't say enough good about those volunteers."

ARC workers and volunteers were not the only ones to entertain patients at the 91st. "We had quite a few celebrities that came like Joe Lewis and movie stars like Bebe Daniels and Ben Lyon," Linden remembers. "Even the Queen of England visited. We were not expected to curtsy. She came into the recreations hall where I was stationed and I had a private, five-minute talk with her. Very sweet, sweet woman. Shy, sort of."

Linden enjoyed her work but put in long hours. The ARC was responsible for ordering and keeping inventory for all the crafts and other activities. "We had to keep a list of who had every tool or whatever to make sure we got it back. Events had to be scheduled way ahead of time and we wrote many, many thank-you notes. We trained volunteers and tracked their hours. There were lots of things to do."

When possible, Linden accepted invitations to visit volunteers in their homes but never went empty-handed. "These people were rationed to the teeth," Linden says. "They had plenty of vegetables and bread, but there were things they didn't have, so I'd go to the mess hall and get butter, or a half a pound of sugar, or a can of salmon to take with me." She would have liked to take them clothing. "They were even crocheting and knitting their underwear. Soap was a luxury. I would take them a bar of soap from my own supply. They'd save it until it was a sliver then put it on a rag so it wouldn't melt away."

Linden remembers that the days before D-Day were strangely quiet. "We knew something was going to happen, because we cleared out as many patients as we could," she says, "but we didn't know what." The morning of the invasion of Normandy, France, Linden heard an unfamiliar noise, "There was this droning, droning, droning. We looked up and the planes were like a group of migrating birds. Every plane was pulling a glider. They all had black and white stripes painted on the wings."

Soon, we started getting patients. "We got seven hundred in the first group. They brought them over by ship and ambulance buses to our hospital." While they were busy after D-Day, Linden recalls an even busier time. "We were the busiest after the Battle of the Bulge. They were just coming in by the hundreds." The hospital reached capacity. "We didn't have enough wards," she says, "so they put up tents. A lot of the walking patients had to live in tents."

Following V-E Day, the hospital received POWs from the concentration camps. "We got in hundreds, but most of them were walking by that time," she says. "They already had some treatment, but they were sent to our hospital to recuperate. All that summer after the war we got POWs. Oh, they wanted to sing. There was that song, 'Don't Fence Me In.' We sang and sang."

The hospital also took in German POWs and put them to work. "We had some assigned to our building to clean or whatever we wanted them to do. While I was packing up music to come back to the states, this young POW came over with a songbook. He wanted me to play 'The Blue Danube' for him. They let us give them jigsaw puzzles that were missing pieces and guitars and ukuleles. No, these POWs weren't mistreated a bit, but they were kept in a locked compound when not working."

After the war, Linden packed up and returned home on the *Queen Mary*. She briefly tried teaching again but was discontented. "The kids were bad," she says. "Their fathers had been away and their mothers working." She joined her sister in California and found a civil service job. "I hadn't been there six weeks when I got a letter from the Red Cross. They still needed people and asked if I could come back. I just left my job and got re-uniformed." Overseas ssignments were in Japan, Korea, Libya, and Germany. Stateside assignments were in military hospitals at Fort Sill, Oklahoma; Sheppard Air Force Base, Wichita Falls, Texas; and Corpus Christi Naval Air Station. Linden retired in 1973 and settled in New Braunfels.

Ninety-four years old when interviewed, Linden stays busy with volunteer work at church and various organizations. "I don't feel I had a wasted life. I was useful in the way that I am," she says. "I'm not one of these who's going to go pray over a patient or hum to them or anything. I just want to be natural. The main thing is to ignore their illness. I didn't let patients know I felt sorry for them. I've had fun; more fun than most people have. I don't have any regrets. I liked serving my country, but it's a lark because it was adventure."

Linden's work has always included taking care of details, and she does so now. "I know my days are not numbered any more than anybody's," she says, "but I think my years are. I told my niece I want no testimonials at my funeral. I'm donating my body to the medical center and told her if she had

*Linden N. Anderson in May 2002.*
*Photograph by Cindy Weigand*

any testimonials, I'll rise up out of that tank. I don't want a reception, either. All I want is for them to play a tape of my sister singing 'The Lord's Prayer.'" This she wants for her sister more than herself because her sister had a beautiful singing voice.

In closing, Linden offers some advice that we all should take to heart. "Just enjoy people and earn your space on earth."

"Let the generations know that women in uniform also guaranteed their freedom. That our resolve was just as great as the men who stood among us. With victory our hearts were just as full and beat just as fast—that the tears fell just as hard for those we left behind."

—Army nurse in World War II

# *Appendix 1*

## A BRIEF TIMELINE OF WORLD WAR II IN EUROPE

| | |
|---|---|
| December 7, 1941 | Japanese bomb Pearl Harbor. |
| December 8, 1941 | United States and Britain declare war on Japan. |
| December 11, 1941 | Germany declares war on the United States. |
| January 13, 1942 | Declaration of the United Nations signed by 26 Allied nations. |
| January 26, 1942 | Germans begin U-boat offensive along the United States' east coast. |
| January 26, 1942 | First American forces arrive in Great Britain. |
| April 1942 | Japanese Americans sent to relocation centers. |
| May 14, 1942 | WAAC established by U.S. Congress. Texan Oveta Culp Hobby appointed director. |
| May 30, 1942 | First British air raid on Cologne; 1,000 bombers participated. |
| June 19, 1942 | Mass murder of Jews by gassing in Auschwitz. |
| June 25, 1942 | Eisenhower arrives in London. |
| July 30, 1942 | WAVES, Women Accepted for Voluntary Emergency Services, authorized by U.S. Congress. Mildred H. McAfee, director. |
| August 17, 1942 | First American air attack in Europe. |

| | |
|---|---|
| September 19, 1942 | WAFS and WFTD (later WASP) established by U.S. Congress. Nancy Love and Jacquelyn Cochran, directors respectively. |
| October 18, 1942 | Hitler orders execution of all captured British commandos. |
| November 23, 1942 | SPARs, Women's Reserve of the U.S. Coast Guard Reserve, established by U.S. Congress. Dorothy C. Stratton, director. |
| December 2, 1942 | Professor Enrico Fermi sets up atomic reactor in Chicago. |
| December 31, 1942 | Battle of the Barents Sea between German and British ships. |
| January 14–24, 1943 | Conference between Churchill and Roosevelt in Casablanca. Roosevelt announces the war can only end with unconditional German surrender. |
| January 27, 1943 | First bombing raid by Americans on Germany at Wilhelmshaven. |
| February 2, 1943 | First big defeat of Hitler's armies in Stalingrad. |
| February 13, 1943 | Marine Corps Women's Reserves established by U.S. Congress. Ruth Cheney Streeter, director. |
| March 16–20, 1943 | Battle of Atlantic reaches peak with 27 merchant ships sunk by German U-boats. |
| July 16, 1943 | 1st Separate WAAC Battalion arrives in England commanded by Cpt. Mary Hallaran. |
| July 24, 1943 | British bombing raid on Hamburg. |
| July 27–28, 1943 | Firestorm in Hamburg caused by Allied air raid. |
| August 17, 1943 | American daylight air raids on Regensburg and Schweinfurt, Germany. |
| November 18, 1943 | Large British air raid on Berlin. |
| March 18, 1944 | British drop 2,500 tons of bombs during an air raid on Hamburg, Germany. |
| June 6, 1944 | D-Day landings. Allied invasion of Europe. |

|  | Largest invasion force in history: 175,000 troops, 4,000 invasion ships, 600 warships, 10,000 planes. |
|---|---|
| June 12–13, 1944 | Germans start attacking Britain with V-1 bombs. Improved V-2 rockets target London as well as Antwerp. Kill and maim thousands. |
| July 3, 1944 | "Battle of Hedgerows" in Normandy. |
| July 14, 1944 | Large contingent of WACs arrive in Normandy, 38 days after D-Day. |
| July 20, 1944 | Germans attempt assassination of Hitler but fail. |
| August 4, 1944 | Anne Frank and family arrested. |
| August 15, 1944 | Allied invasion of Southern France begins. |
| August 20, 1944 | Allies encircle Germans in the Falais Pocket. |
| August 25, 1944 | Paris liberated by Allied French troops after four years of German occupation. |
| August 31, 1944 | WAC advance party arrives in Paris. |
| September 13, 1944 | U.S. troops reach the Siegfried Line. |
| October 21, 1944 | Massive German surrender at Aachen. |
| November 7, 1944 | Franklin D. Roosevelt elected to a fourth term as U.S. president. Harry S. Truman, vice president. |
| December 16–27, 1944 | Battle of the Bulge in the Ardennes. Last major German counteroffensive. |
| December 17, 1944 | Waffen SS murder 81 U.S. POWs at Malmedy. |
| January 1–17, 1945 | Germans withdraw from the Ardennes. |
| February 3, 1945 | The all-black 6888th Central Postal Battalion, 30 officers and 800 enlisted women, depart U.S. for overseas. |
| February 13–14, 1945 | Dresden destroyed by firestorm after Allied bombing raids. |
| March 6, 1945 | Last German offensive of war in Hungary. Defend oil fields. |
| April 1945 | Stolen Nazi art and wealth discovered in salt mines. |

| | |
|---|---|
| April 11–15, 1945 | Allies liberate Buchenwald and Bergen-Belsen concentration camps. |
| April 12, 1945 | President Roosevelt dies after suffering massive cerebral hemorrhage. Vice President Truman sworn in as president. |
| April 30, 1945 | Hitler commits suicide. |
| May 7, 1945 | Germany surrenders unconditionally to General Eisenhower. |
| May 8, 1945 | V-E (Victory in Europe) Day. |
| June 5, 1945 | Allies divide Germany and Berlin and take over government. |
| July 1, 1945 | U.S., British, and French troops move into Berlin. |
| July 12, 1945 | Col. Oveta Culp Hobby resigns due to poor health. |
| July 16, 1945 | First atomic bomb test. |
| July 17, 1945 | U.S. air attacks on Tokyo continue. Planes drop leaflets threatening destruction from the air if the Japanese don't agree to unconditional surrender. |
| July 30, 1945 | Torpedoes sink USS *Indianapolis* in Indian Ocean. |
| August 6, 1945 | U.S. drops first atomic bomb on industrial city of Hiroshima, Japan. |
| August 9, 1945 | U.S. drops second atomic bomb on Nagasaki, Japan. |
| August 14, 1945 | Japanese agree to unconditional surrender. V-J, Victory in Japan, Day. |
| September 2, 1945 | Japanese sign surrender agreement. |
| October 24, 1945 | UN becomes official. |

*Sources:*
http://history.acusd.edu/gen/WW2Timeline/Prelude23.html
http://historyplace.com/worldwar2/timeline/ww2time.htm
http://www.awm.lee.army.mil/NCO_History_WAC/index.htm
http://www.stg.brown.edu/projects/WWII_Women/NewTimeline.html#1941

# *Appendix 2*

## CHRONOLOGY OF EVENTS AT PHILIPPINE ISLANDS AND SANTO TOMAS INTERNMENT CAMP

| | |
|---|---|
| March 1941 | Air raids drills and war maneuvers start. |
| Summer 1941 | Gen. Douglas MacArthur assumes command of U.S. forces in the Far East. Military dependents and some civilians leave for United States. |
| November 1941 | Last army transport leaves Manila for U.S. 87 army nurses on duty; 12 navy nurses at Canacao Naval Hospital, outside Manila. |
| December 7–8, 1941 | Pearl Harbor, Hawaii, bombed. Wake Island, Guam, and Midway attacked. Camp John Hay in Baguio and Clark Field at Fort Stotsenberg on Philippines bombed. Five army nurses from Sternberg Hospital, Manila, go to Stotsenberg Hospital to help. |
| | Roosevelt declares war. |
| December 10, 1941 | Canacao Naval Hospital in Cavite shelled. |
| December 11, 1941 | Canacao Naval Hospital evacuated. Twelve navy nurses move to Sternberg Hospital in Manila. |
| December 13, 1941 | Fort McKinley, seven miles from Manila, evacuated. Twenty army nurses moved to Sternberg Hospital and reassigned. |

| | |
|---|---|
| December 22, 1941 | Camp John Hay, two hundred miles from Manila, evacuated. Two ANC leave with other medical personnel; walk to Bataan to join the allied forces. Major portion of General Homma's army lands at Lingayen Gulf, north of Manila. |
| December 24, 1941 | Stotsenberg Hospital Clark Field evacuated. Twenty nurses arrive at Sternberg Hospital. ANC evacuate Sternberg. 25 American (24 ANC, one NNC) and 25 Filipino nurses ordered to Bataan via trucks. General MacArthur leaves Manila for Corregidor; declares Manila an open city. |
| December 25–26, 1941 | ANC to evacuate all personnel still in Manila. 20 ANC leave the city by ship; 1 to Bataan Hospital to set up Hospital #1 at Limay, Bataan; 19 to Bataan to set up Hospital #2. Seven other ANC arrive on another boat at Limay. |
| December 25–28, 1941 | Ten ANC and one physiotherapist evacuate from Sternberg Hospital for Corregidor. Twelve ANC and one dietician remain behind in Manila. |
| December 28, 1941 | Ruby Bradley and Beatrice Chambers, ANC, return to Baguio and surrender. Interned at Camp John Hay, now a POW camp. Physicians and other medical personnel remain in the mountains, try to reach Bataan. |
| December 29, 1941 | 12 ANC and one dietitian evacuated from Sternberg Hospital to Corregidor. Corregidor bombed for the first time. Military personnel move underground into Malinta Tunnel. |
| December 31, 1941 | Last ANC leaves Manila on a provisional hospital ship, arrives in Australia. Last army military personnel leave Sternberg Hospital. 11 navy nurses with other naval medical personnel interned at Saint Scholastica Girls School in Manila. First patients admitted to Hospital #2, Bataan. |
| January 1, 1942 | Four wards functioning at Hospital #2, Bataan. |

|  | Josie Nesbit arrives from Corregidor to become chief nurse at #2. |
|---|---|
| January 2, 1942 | Japanese enter Manila. 11 navy nurses surrender and held at Saint Scholastica Girls School with patients and other medical personnel. |
| January 4, 1942 | First group arrives at Santo Tomas for internment. |
| January 9, 1942 | Seven wards functioning at Bataan Hospital #2. |
| January 16, 1942 | 182 major operations performed at Hospital #1, Limay, Bataan. |
| January 23, 1942 | Medical personnel travel into the Bataan jungle to Little Baguio to set up a new site for Hospital #1. |
| January 25, 1942 | 18 nurses leave Limay. Hospital #1 relocated to Little Baguio to avoid enemy bombings. |
| January 31, 1942 | Central kitchen opens. Prior to this, internees were on their own with food they brought into camp or got by any means such as thrown over the fence by Filipino servants, etc. |
| February 6, 1942 | 48 ANC and 23 Filipino nurses working at #2; seventeen wards functioning. Japanese reinforcements land on Luzon. |
| February 10, 1942 | Edith Shacklette named chief nurse at Hospital #1. |
| February 15, 1942 | Three men shot for escaping. |
| February 20, 1942 | Lull in the Bataan fighting. Nurses hold first of two dances at Hospital #1. |
| February 21, 1942 | 113 China refugees arrive from Sulphur Springs. |
| March 1, 1942 | Quinine on Bataan exhausted. |
| March 8, 1942 | 11 navy nurses taken to Santo Tomas Internment Camp, Manila. |
| March 11, 1942 | General MacArthur leaves Corregidor for Australia. General Wainwright assumes command of Bataan and Corregidor forces. |

| | |
|---|---|
| March 30, 1942 | Bataan Hospital #1 bombed. Final Japanese assault on Bataan begins. |
| April 3, 1942 | Capt. Maude Davison visits Bataan from Corregidor. More nurses ordered from Corregidor to Bataan to help with increasing casualties. |
| April 5, 1942 | Japanese increase attacks on Bataan. Easter. |
| April 8–9, 1942 | 72 ANC and one NNC ordered from Bataan to Corregidor accompanied by 26 Filipino nurses, one dietician, one physiotherapist, one Red Cross field director and five civilians. Hospital #1 group leaves Mariveles dock about 11:30 p.m. and arrives about 3:00 a.m. at Corregidor. Hospital #2 group caught behind exploding ordnance. Reach Mariveles around sunrise. |
| April 8, 1942 | Earthquake. |
| April 9, 1942 | Allies on Bataan surrender to the Japanese. Last boat with Hospital #2 nurses leaves Bataan about 8:00 a.m. All American and Filipino women safely on Corregidor by 1:00 p.m. |
| April 15, 1942 | Last wheat bread distributed in STIC. |
| April 29, 1942 | Two PBY planes leave Corregidor with 23 nurses and other passengers. One hits rock on takeoff after refueling, unable to take off, leaving ten ANC stranded and later captured. Other PBY plane arrives safely in Australia. |
| May 1, 1942 | Continuous bombing and shelling of Corregidor. Nurses care for patients in Malinta Tunnel Hospital. |
| May 3, 1942 | 11 army and one navy nurse leave Corregidor on a submarine. Arrive safely in Freemantle, Australia. |
| May 6, 1942 | General Wainwright surrenders Corregidor to Japanese. 54 ANC among the American forces on Corregidor. Nurses ordered to remain inside Malinta Tunnel. |

| | |
|---|---|
| May 10, 1942 | Ten nurses stranded on Mindanao surrender. |
| June 17, 1942 | 43 Consular repatriates depart. |
| June 25, 1942 | 54 army nurses, staff and patients ordered out of Malinta Tunnel. Hike 2.5 miles to Middleside Hospital on Corregidor. |
| July 1, 1942 | Japanese take over financing of Santo Tomas Internment Camp from Philippine Red Cross at 40 centavos per person per day. |
| July 2, 1942 | 54 ANC removed from Corregidor about 5:00 a.m. and arrive Manila 11:00 a.m. Transported by truck to Santo Tomas Internment Camp (STIC). Taken to Santa Catalina Convent, outside the main campgrounds. |
| July 27, 1942 | Second executive committee takes over. |
| August 24, 1942 | Santa Catalina Hospital starts. |
| August 25, 1942 | 54 army nurses move into main internment camp (STIC). |
| September 9, 1942 | Ten army nurses stranded on Mindanao arrive in Manila. Total of 64 army nurses now at STIC. Army nurse Maude Davison in charge of Santa Catalina prison hospital. 11 navy nurses work under her command. |
| September 12, 1942 | 153 internees leave for Shanghai. |
| October 31, 1942 | 11 of high commissioner's staff arrive. |
| December 17, 1942 | South African relief supplies arrive. |
| December 19, 1942 | Internees arrive from Cebu. |
| December 23, 1942 | First movie shown. |
| December 25, 1942 | First POW Christmas. 64 army nurses share presents and special meal outside Santa Catalina Hospital. |
| January 6, 1943 | Canadian relief supplies arrive. |
| January 12, 1943 | 28 men taken to military camps. |
| January 16, 1943 | Tacloban, Leyte internees arrive. |

| | |
|---|---|
| March 10, 1943 | Bacolod, Negros internees arrive. |
| May 12, 1943 | First major contingent, 526 enlisted women and 114 WAC officers, arrive in Sydney, Australia, for duty in SWPTO. |
| May 14, 1943 | 11 navy nurses move to the newly established internment camp at Los Baños and set up a hospital with Laura Cobb in charge. |
| May 17, 1943 | Reinternment of aged, sick, and children previously living outside camp. |
| June 21, 1943 | Iloio, Panay internees arrive. |
| Summer 1943 | Army nurse Ruby Bradley arrives at STIC from John Hay Internment Camp in Baguio. Army nurse Beatrice Chambers decides to stay at John Hay. |
| September 26, 1943 | 127 civilians from STIC and Los Baños leave on a repatriation ship. 65 ANC in STIC; 11 NNC at Los Baños. |
| November 15, 1943 | Flood. |
| December 10, 1943 | Second Los Baños transfer, including first group of women. |
| December 15, 1943 | American relief supplies arrive. |
| December 25, 1943 | Second POW Christmas. Food less plentiful. Nurses share Red Cross relief supplies. |
| January 1944 | Japanese War Prisoners Division takes over management of Philippine POW camps from civilian command. Issues series of restrictive orders. |
| January 2, 1944 | Davao, Mindanao internees arrive. |
| February 1, 1944 | Army nurse Josie Nesbit notes signs of weight loss and malnutrition in the nurses. |
| February 1, 1944 | Military Administration takes over Camp. Filipino doctors and nurses, also market vendors barred. Daily cereal ration 400 grams per person per day. |

| February 7, 1944 | Package line closes. |
|---|---|
| February 18, 1944 | Second Executive Committee abolished and 3-man Internee Committee appointed by Japanese. |
| February 20, 1944 | Military take over Bodega and food supplies. |
| February 21, 1944 | Sulphur Spring Camp Closed. American mail arrives. |
| February 22, 1944 | Local newspaper prohibited. |
| March 1944 | Nurses allowed to send home censored twenty-five-word postcards. |
| March 1, 1944 | Three U.S. Army doctors arrive. |
| May 12, 1944 | Last ricebread distributed in STIC. |
| June 6, 1944 | Central kitchen starts cooking permanently in outside kitchen. |
| July 20, 1944 | STIC internees photographed with numbers on their chests in groups of five. |
| August 1, 1944 | All money, except 50 Japanese pesos, to be turned in for deposit with Bank of Taiwan. |
| September 13, 1944 | Daily cereal ration 300 grams per person in STIC. |
| September 15, 1944 | Daily cereal ration 250 grams per person in STIC. |
| September 20, 1944 | Daily cereal ration 300 grams per person in STIC. |
| September 21, 1944 | Death rate from malnutrition in STIC and Los Baños increasing. American pilots bomb Manila for the first time. |
| September 26, 1944 | Complete census of Los Baños, Baguio, ordered assembled, copied, and delivered in 48 hours. |
| October 9, 1944 | Front part of STIC taken over by Japanese military for storage of supplies including arms and ammunition. |
| October 14, 1944 | Chairman of Internee Agents banished to Los Baños. |
| October 20, 1944 | General MacArthur and allied troops land on southern Philippine island of Leyte. |

| | |
|---|---|
| November 17, 1944 | Net daily cereal 255 grams per person in STIC. |
| December 5, 1944 | Last Los Baños transfer. |
| December 12, 1944 | Net daily cereal ration 210 grams per person in STIC. |
| December 20, 1944 | Net daily cereal ration 187 grams per person in STIC. |
| December 23, 1944 | Chairman of Internee Committee and three others arrested and subsequently taken out of camp by military police. |
| December 25, 1944 | Third POW Christmas. Food scarce; no gifts or parties allowed; 3,785 internees in STIC. Leaflets dropped: "The Commander in Chief, the Officers and the men of the American forces of Liberation in the Pacific wish their gallant allies, the People of the Philippines, all the blessings of Christmas and the realization of their fervent hopes for the New Year–Christmas 1944." |
| December 26, 1944 | Complete census of POW camps ordered. |
| January 2, 1945 | Allies land on Luzon, Philippines. |
| January 6, 1945 | Japanese staff, ordered to leave, spend all night packing and burning papers. |
| January 7, 1945 | Committee members held as hostages all day pending planned departure of the commandant's staff. |
| January 9, 1945 | Commandant issues statement that he and his staff aren't leaving and expresses concern over food situation. |
| January 10, 1945 | Leaflet dropped: "The Battle of the Philippines is in its final phase." |
| January 11, 1945 | American airplanes fly over camp. Internees see stars on wings. |
| January 14, 1945 | War Prisoner's Bureau moves from Far Eastern University into Educational Building. |
| January 17, 1945 | One man escapes from gym. |

| | |
|---|---|
| January 31, 1945 | Chairman of Camp Medical Staff jailed by Japanese for refusal to exclude the words *malnutrition* and *starvation* from death certificates. For month of January, average daily calories issued by Japanese Army are 723.7. |
| February 3, 1945 | Ten U.S. planes fly over STIC and drop goggles with message of good tidings. |
| | About 6:00 p.m. continuous machine gun fire heard to the north. Fires break out all around, especially to the north. |
| | 9:00 p.m. **THE TANK ARRIVES**. 1st Cavalry liberates STIC. All 65 ANC in STIC alive after almost three years as POWs. |
| February 4, 1945 | Third anniversary of the Inauguration of STIC, plus one month, 37 months long. |
| February 5, 1945 | Army nurse Mabel Robinson arrives with nearly one hundred ANC. (Dorothy Davis Thompson is in this group.) Relieve STIC army nurses (including H. R. Brantley) from duty. Army nurse Beatrice Chambers, from Baguio, reunited with other army nurses. |
| February, 12–19, 1945 | 66 ANC nurses, two dietitians, one physiotherapist, one Red Cross field director, and civilian nurses flown to Leyte. Medical tests performed. Nurses given uniforms and promoted one grade and presented with medals. Pat Hutchinson was on Leyte at this time. |
| February 19–23, 1945 | ANC nurses island hopping across the Pacific to the United States. |
| February 22, 1945 | 11th airborne division liberates Los Baños Internment Camp. 11 navy nurses freed. |
| February 23, 1945 | 66 ANC nurses arrive in San Francisco. Reunited with friends and families, then taken to Letterman Hospital for evaluation. |

| | |
|---|---|
| March 1945 | All nurses released from hospitals and travel to their hometowns. |
| March 10, 1945 | 11 navy nurses arrive in San Francisco. Taken to Oak Knoll Hospital for evaluation. |
| May 8, 1945 | Germany surrenders. |
| July 5, 1945 | General MacArthur announces fighting in the Philippine Islands is over. Complete Allied victory. |
| August 6, 1945 | Atomic bomb dropped on Hiroshima. |
| August 15, 1945 | Japan surrenders. |

*Sources:*
Elizabeth M. Norman, Ph.D. *We Band of Angels: The Untold Story of American Nurses Trapped on Bataan by the Japanese.* New York: Pocket Books, a division of Simon and Schuster Inc., 1999.
Chronology of events compiled by STIC internee Peter Richards and given to Dorothy Davis Thompson.
http://www.awm.lee.army.mil/NCO_History_WAC/index.htm

# FURTHER READING AND
# OTHER RESOURCES

Ashabranner, Brent. *A Date With Destiny: The Women in Military Service For America Memorial*. Brookfield, Connecticut: Twenty-First Century Books, a Division of Millbrook Press, Inc., 2000.

Brokaw, Tom. *The Greatest Generation*. New York: Random House, 1998.

———. *The Greatest Generation Speaks*. New York: Random House, 1999.

Danner, Dorothy Still. *What a Way to Spend a War: Navy Nurse POWs in the Philippines*. Annapolis, Maryland: Naval Institute Press, 1995.

Granger, Byrd Howell. *On Final Approach: W.A.S.P. WWII*. Scottsdale, Arizona: Falconer Publishing Company, 1991.

Gruhzit-Hoyt, Olga. *They Also Served: American Women in World War II*. New York: Carol Publishing Group, 1995.

Holm, Jeanne, Major General, USAF (Ret.), ed. *In Defense of a Nation: Servicewomen in World War II*. Washington, D.C.: Military Women's Press, 1998.

Jopling, Lucy Wilson. *Warrior in White*. San Antonio: Watercress Books, Everett and Associates, 1990.

Keil, Sally VanWagenen. *Those Wonderful Women in Their Flying Machines: The Unknown Heroines of World War II*. New York: Four Directions Press, 1979.

Norman, Elizabeth M., Ph.D. *We Band of Angels: The Untold Story of American Nurses Trapped on Bataan by the Japanese*. New York: Pocket Books, a division of Simon and Schuster Inc., 1999.

Treadwell, Mattie E. *The Women's Army Corps: The U.S. Army in World War II*. Washington, D.C.: Office of the Chief of Military History, 1954.

Turner, Betty Stagg. *Out of the Blue and into History*. Arlington Heights, Illinois: Aviatrix Publishing Inc., 2001.

Sarnecky, Mary T., DNSc, RN, CS, FNP, Col. (Ret.). *A History of the U.S. Army Nurse Corps*. Philadelphia: University of Pennsylvania Press, 1999.

Williams, Denny. *To the Angels*. San Francisco: Denson Press, 1985.

Williams, Vera S. *WACs: Women's Army Corps*. Osceola, Wisconsin: Motorbooks International Publishers and Wholesalers, 1997.

http://history.navy.mil/

http://home.swbell.net/cahailey/

http://www.awm.lee.army.mil/

http://www.history.navy.mil/

http://www.uscg.mil/hq/g-cp/history/collect.html

http://www.usmc.mil/history.nsf/

http://www.womensmemorial.org/

www.rice.edu/fondren/woodson/exhibits/wac/

www.twu.edu/wasp

www.wasp-wwii.org/

# INDEX

# ABOUT THE AUTHOR

**Cindy Weigand** has a degree in biology, but women in history is her passion. This book was born when her personal interest in women in aviation history led her to begin research into the contributions of the Women Airforce Service Pilots in World War II. Astonished that she had not read about these women growing up, she widened her research to include women in all branches of the military. Noticing a dearth of information on the subject, she decided to chronicle the lives of American servicewomen.

Her articles have appeared in *Pennsylvania Magazine*, *Texas Co-op Power*, and the *Friends Journal* published quarterly by the Air Force Museum Foundation, Inc. In June 2003, her article in *Texas Co-op Power*, "Yankee Doodle Pilots of World War II," received an Award of Merit in the Dalton Pen Writing Contest sponsored by Warwick Publishing. She works as an instructional aide at a middle school in Georgetown, Texas, where she lives with her husband, Willis, and daughter, Candace. *Texas Women in WWII* is her first book.